IF YOU LOVE MYSTERIES
AND YOU KNOW IN YOUR HEART
YOU CAN WRITE ONE . . .
DON'T WAIT ANY LONGER.
BECOME PARTNERS IN CRIME
WITH THE PROFESSIONALS
AND START WRITING *THIS WEEKEND*!

Discover:

- Tips on creating a killer, victim, sleuth, and sidekick
- The writing secret that made Agatha Christie famous
- One of the biggest decisions you must make—to shift, or not to shift, point of view
- Three essential guidelines for imagining your sleuth
- How to avoid "hitting the wall" around page 50 and getting stalled
- How monologues can bond your sleuth and your reader

. . . and so much more

THE WEEKEND NOVELIST WRITES A MYSTERY

Also by Robert J. Ray

THE WEEKEND NOVELIST

THE WEEKEND NOVELIST WRITES A MYSTERY

Robert J. Ray and Jack Remick

A DELL TRADE PAPERBACK

A DELL TRADE PAPERBACK

Published by
Dell Publishing
a division of
Bantam Doubleday Dell Publishing Group, Inc.
1540 Broadway
New York, New York 10036

Permissions follow on page v.

Library of Congress Cataloging in Publication Data

Ray, Robert J. (Robert Joseph), 1935–
    The weekend novelist writes a mystery / by Robert J. Ray & Jack Remick.
        p.   cm.
    Includes bibliographical references.
    ISBN 0-440-50658-1
    1. Detective and mystery stories—Authorship.   I. Remick, Jack.   II. Title.
    PN3377.5.D4R39   1997
    808.3'872—dc20   96-42991
                                                                               CIP

Printed in the United States of America

Published simultaneously in Canada

May 1998

10   9   8   7   6   5   4   3   2

BVG

For Margot and Helen

Acknowledgments

We would like to thank Jean Femling and Roland Stephan for reading the manuscript in progress. Special thanks to fiction writers in our workshops who helped us to refine our techniques for teaching writing. Thanks to editors Jacob Hoye and Eric Wybenga for their help in shaping the manuscript. Thanks to Attorney Linda Steinman for guiding us through the shoals of copyright and permissions.

Contents

Introduction

The world of mystery writing is a vibrant and exciting place. The vibrancy comes from the thrill of the hunt, the chase, the sacred quest. Like the knight on horseback questing for the Dragon or the Holy Grail, the modern-day sleuth takes on the challenge, and the strict moral burden, to root out evil, to assign guilt, and to impose good.

In simplest terms, the object of the quest is payment. The quester who brings home the Grail *(treasure, secret, amulet, sacred child,* et cetera) is rewarded by money or love, by a flagon of ale, or perhaps by a royal pardon. On the other side of the equation, the evil dragon who steals the child or who devastates the peaceful village must pay for the crime in dragon's blood. And if you replace the evil dragon with a more modern monster—the killer fish of *Jaws,* for example, who disrupts the tourist trade in the peaceful seaside hamlet of Amity, Long Island—the payment is still made in blood. In a classic clash of Good versus Evil, the fish who eats people dies to make the town safe. And whether the evil force is a dragon, a fish named "Jaws," or a serial killer called "The Beast," payment happens at the climax of the story.

In mystery fiction, the killer is the ancient dragon who pays for taking the victim's life. By killing, the evil killer rips a jagged hole in the fabric of society. The jagged hole makes everyone edgy. Edgy people respond with panic: What if the fabric rips some more? What if the next rip is closer to home? What if it rips up my street? My neighbor? My family? Me? Where is the end to this awful ripping and tearing? How do we stop it? Who is responsible here?

To repair the hole, to restore order to society, someone calls for help. That call for help, whether note or phone call or a client's visit to a rundown office in San Francisco of the 1930s, is the kickoff for your mystery tale. The quester who answers the call is your sleuth.

As the instrument of society, the sleuth's job is to set things right. The process for setting things right, for knitting up the fabric, is ritual sacrifice. Ritual sacrifice, making the killer pay, makes everyone feel better, especially when the blood is offstage: "I feel quite pleased," says Miss Jane Marple (the sleuth in *The Body in the Library*), "to think of [the killer] hanging."

Miss Marple feels pleased because the killer who pays by hanging tried to frame a "fall guy," someone to take the killer's place on the gallows tree. As we'll see later in this book, the police in *The Body in the Library* are so hungry for a scapegoat to pay for this killing that they build a killer profile to fit the wrong man. While the police track the trail of the designated fall guy, Miss Marple cracks the case. Miss Marple has to hurry to the rescue (the action in *Body* takes only a couple of days) because she understands society's urgent need for payment.

Knowing the importance of making the killer pay is the writer's secret weapon. Knowing this secret early on, before you begin writing, gives you control over your story. From that first weekend when you start writing, the killer, who may not enter the book until you're halfway through, is your focus. Killers leave footprints, clues to follow, objects in their wake. Tracking down the clues gives you the plot for your tale.

· · ·

The Weekend Novelist Writes a Mystery guides you through the process of writing a mystery in fifty-two weekends. Each weekend has a specific task. On Weekend 1, for example, you'll create your killer, the villain who takes a life, the one who must pay. A big part of creating a character is probing for motive: Why does the killer kill? What drives this monster to take a human life? Because motive lurks in the past, your quest will lead you into "back story," a traumatic event in the early life of your killer, a dramatic turnstile between innocence and experience. Using your writing as discovery, a kind of brainstorming on paper, will help you find answers. Was your killer born to kill? Or was your killer driven to kill by circumstance? What was the circumstance? How old was your killer? When did your killer become a monster?

Probing a character's past in a paragraph or two is important preparation for writing the story. It's also fun to dig up secrets. Depending on the book you write, the way you structure your tale, you might share these secrets with the reader very early. Or you might wait, holding off until the end. Probing the past gives the writer access to knowledge not available to the reader. This knowledge is power. Because you know the secrets, you maintain control of the story elements. Because you maintain control, you have the power to decide when and where and whether or not to use this information. If your story calls for it, you can plug this secret information into a dossier, a police file in a manila folder: "Killer M," the file says, "lost her mother when she was eight. Her father died when she was sixteen.

"She made her first kill when she was thirty-five. The victim was an innocent teenager. The motive was greed. The killer had a plan. She wanted the house on the beach, the big bank account, the big man in town."

Writing your way into a character's past unearths motive not only for the killer, but for the other main characters as well. Probing motive tells you why the victim dies. It tells you why the sleuth detects. It tells you why the sleuth's helper helps. Digging into motive sharpens your powers of analysis and observation. Since writing a mystery is a rational act, you'll be exercising your analytical muscles when you write, when you create, when you plot, and when you read other writers.

Having Fun with Writing

Creating characters for your mystery is fun. You build a body, a shape with height and weight and substance, mind and memory. You add a face, ears and eyes and teeth. You add secrets unearthed from the character's past. To cover the secrets, cloaking them from the reader, you dress the character. To make use of the wardrobe you just created, you bring the character into a scene in your story. One way to bring a character into a scene is wardrobe items: the femme fatale enters dressed like a shabby Cinderella; the killer enters naked, wearing a towel over one shoulder. Another way to bring characters onstage is through action that reveals character: the sleuth hides behind a cloud of cigarette smoke. If you write action before you know what it means, then the action pushes you to ask a question: Why is the sleuth hiding?

A scene in fiction is like a scene on the screen or stage: a single action or a series of linked actions played out in a single setting in a finite period of time. King Lear howling on the heath is a scene from Shakespeare. Hannibal Lecter killing Pembry and Boyle inside the makeshift cage in Memphis is a scene from *Silence of the Lambs*. Scarlett O'Hara proclaiming, "I'll never go hungry again," at the midpoint of *Gone with the Wind* is a scene.

Scenes help the writer envision the page as a stage. In this book, we use the term *onstage* to bring a character into the story. Scenes help you organize your material into units of dramatic action. Getting organized makes plotting a breeze.

In mystery writing, the scene that starts the quest for the killer is the "Crime Scene," that grim place of death and blood that is cordoned off by yellow police ribbons. One trick to scene writing is to analyze what's going on as you write.

Inside the circle is sacred turf. Access to the sacred turf is limited. To understand the power of the sacred turf inside the closed circle, the importance it holds for your writing, try playing various character roles. Dive inside the head of a character. Put yourself into the scene.

In Role One, for example, you become the Head Cop. You flash your badge. A uniformed officer raises the yellow ribbon. You pass under the barrier, a threshold-crossing into the place of death.

There's no immediate conflict here, no drama rising like steam from the page, so you try another role. In Role Two, for contrast, you become the eager Crime Reporter. You replace the Head Cop's shiny police shield, symbol of power and authority, with a press pass. Practicing your writer's craft, you move in for a close-up of the press pass. It's creased and worn. The upper right-hand corner is torn away. There is a black rectangle where a photo used to be glued on. You shove your press pass into the face of the uniformed cop. The cop smirks, shakes his head, and waves you back. No entry allowed.

To lock on to drama, you write things down as you analyze your Crime Reporter's emotions. If you were that Crime Reporter, how would you feel? Would you feel frustrated? Thwarted? Left out? Angry? You want a story and you have paid your dues in the profession and now you deserve a shot. The time is 4:00 A.M. on a cold, wet night and you're here at the crime scene because everyone else is sick or covering other stories. You've spent five years writing obituaries. They're cutting staff at the paper, downsizing, and you need this break. To survive, you need this story, right here, right now, tonight. And that cop waving you away makes you mad.

Trying out for Role Number Three, you leap from the head of the Crime Reporter into the shoes of a relative of the deceased. What do you say to this uniformed functionary to get inside the closed circle? What amulet of authority do you flash? Do you really want inside? How do you feel about death? Does it scare you? Does it excite you? Are you the killer? Do you know the killer? Did you see the killing?

In Role Number Four, you go for it, leaping from sobbing relative to the cooling corpse. Playing the dead victim gets you the top spot inside the closed circle. Playing dead in a mystery puts you at dead center. It's cold here. Wet and chilly and dank. Why are you here? How long have you been here? How are you dressed? How did you die? What is the last thing you remember before dropping off the edge? Would you like to be cremated? How well do you know the killer?

When you write a mystery, you write to entertain. The key to entertainment is drama. Drama, whether on the stage or the screen or the printed page, is produced by conflict. Role playing at the crime scene helps you define dramatic conflict. A simple definition of *conflict* is two agendas clashing. In real life, conflict arises when your agenda (you want your teenager home by eleven P.M.) clashes with the agenda of someone who is not you (your teenager bops through the door at 2:30 A.M.).

In the world of fiction, conflict arises when the agenda of Character A clashes with the agenda of Character B. In the role-playing crime-scene scenario above, the Crime Reporter's agenda is to get a story. To get a story, the reporter must cross the yellow police barrier and snuggle up to death. The agenda of the uniformed policeman is to stop unauthorized entry to the closed circle. To the reporter, the uniform is an obstacle to be overcome, a wall between herself and the story. To the uniform, the reporter is a nuisance, a nonentity. No badge means no authority at the crime scene. A simple action, if impeded, brings conflict into your story. The first conflict you write about in your mystery is about control: who controls the crime scene and who does not. Analyzing the roots of this conflict allows you to explore the elements of fiction: dialogue, action, and setting.

Dialogue is your shortcut to dramatic conflict. If the Crime Reporter says "Coming through," and if the uniform answers "Back off, babe," the sparks of conflict are already flying. If you write the scene and then step back, what do you see? What are the shapes? What are the patterns?

Stepping back from the crime scene, you see a closed circle of sacred or sacrosanct space defined by a threshold, the yellow ribbon or yellow rope. The threshold is controlled by a threshold guardian, in this case the uniformed cop. The drama in your scene is created by an outsider who wants inside who gets stopped by an insider whose job it is to guard the sacred space.

Because it evokes the power of myth and legend, sacred space is an important concept for the mystery writer. If you are inside and X wants in, you write about what it means to be inside the closed circle. If X barges in, you lose control of the turf. *Gorky Park*, by Martin Cruz Smith, opens this way, with the sleuth losing control of the crime scene to an officer of the KGB: "A squad of KGB agents in plainclothes were led from the cars by a squat, vigorous major called Pribluda." When Character X invades the sleuth's sacred space, he sets up a conflict that helps you write faster and better.

Preparing to Write

At each step in the writing, *The Weekend Novelist Writes a Mystery* offers advice, suggestions, tips, and specific instruction. The mark of the eager beginner is to start writing willy-nilly, before the preparation is done, before the plans are drawn, before the characters are dressed to enter the story. A carpenter building a house needs plans, supplies, a foundation, models, helpers. A writer writing a mystery needs a plan, a model to follow, characters with the strength to carry the plot. The mark of the professional is to prepare before you start writing.

You have fifty-two weekends. Each weekend is writer's gold, a precious sacred time devoted to the writing. For the first few weekends, while you're trying out new writing moves, the learning curve will feel steep. Your notebook will burgeon with material, your computer will boil with the fires of creation. Teach yourself to be patient. Starting out right is important because it girds you for the long journey of writing the book. For a long journey, you need strong legs.

You'll write the book in three phases. Phase One is the first draft, where you write to discover what you know and what you need to know about this case. In your first draft you write fast and loose, flying along, the wind in your face, leaping and laughing and having fun. Phase Two, your second draft, is more thoughtful, more reflective. In your second draft, you write closer to the page, filling in gaps you left on your speedy first writing. You think a lot. You brood and analyze. Phase Three, your final draft, is a planned rewrite that pulls the book into shape.

· · ·

Getting Started

• *Warming Up.* Writing is exercise. Warm up before you write. To warm up, you can speed-write or do stretching exercises or jog around the block. Writing is rhythmic, so any rhythmic activity will help you get started.

• *Mind Mapping.* Mind mapping means you doodle on paper as you map the workings of your mind. There are two basic forms of mind mapping: 1) the branching diagram Tony Buzan describes in *Use Both Sides of Your Brain;* 2) the cluster diagram used by Gabriele Rico in *Writing the Natural Way.*

• *Jumping In.* When we create, we take the plunge without knowing everything beforehand. We dive because we must, because sitting there thinking about the writing won't get us going, won't let us sniff the ground, won't lock us on to the evil scent of the killer's trail. If you are a mystery reader, you know what you've got to do: write a rousing tale that hooks the reader early and entertains all the way to the last page. This book guides you in the process, in how to write an entertaining book on weekends.

One way to jump in is to develop a profile of your story. To develop a profile, you jot down categories that need filling: working title, type of tale, setting, time, main characters (killer, victim, sleuth, et cetera) notes on the murder (weapon, wounds, time of death, motive, et cetera), body discovered by (witnesses, suspects, scapegoats, et cetera).

A Write-Along Mystery

To help you write your first mystery, we'll be writing along with you. When you interview your killer, we'll interview ours. When you create your victim, we'll create ours. The working title of our model mystery is *Murder on Drake Island.* By filling in the story profile, using the categories above, we can develop some helpful ideas.

Here's our sample profile.

Working title: Murder on Drake Island.

Type of tale: Serial killer mystery; amateur sleuth.

Setting: Drake Island, off the coast of South Carolina. Access by ferry, helicopter, cruise ship, speedboat, small aircraft. On Drake Island, the power is often interrupted and the phone lines are often not working.

Time: Contemporary.

Main characters: The killer is Myra Jane Severance, a gourmet chef, who runs the best restaurant in town. The victim is Lacey

Anne Baxter, sixteen, the illegitimate granddaughter of Major Philip Baxter, a rich old man. The sleuth is Helene F. Steinbeck, a published mystery writer with a bad case of writer's block.

Notes on the murder: The murder takes place after midnight on a deserted beach road. The victim is a passenger. Someone else—not the killer—is driving. Rain is falling, medium heavy, enough to produce mud. The killer creates confusion by shining a bright light into the eyes of the driver. The vehicle slams into a beach boulder, knocking the driver unconscious. The killer kills the victim—leaving her serial killer signature. The murder weapon is a sharp knife, perhaps a scalpel. The killer strips off the victim's clothes, then adds a wardrobe item that connects her to the previous victims. At this point, we'll probably need two prior victims to create our serial killer.

Body discovered by: The grandfather and his butler.

Witnesses: Walk-on characters who saw the victim leaving with the van driver.

Suspects: Outcasts or outsiders who look good for the crime. A skinhead, perhaps. Or a weekend tourist from the mainland.

Scapegoat: The driver of the van, chosen by the killer in the back story.

Exercise

Story Profile.

Using the following categories—working title, type of tale, setting, time, main characters *(killer, victim, sleuth)*, notes on the murder *(weapon, wounds, time of death, motive, et cetera)*, body discovered by, witnesses, suspects, scapegoats, et cetera—develop a profile for your mystery tale.

Work quickly, filling in the categories. If you don't know, write "Don't Know" and keep moving. Categories you leave empty now will get filled in later, as your creative powers glow.

Books for Your Bookshelf.

We'll be using short examples from the following mysteries: *The Body in the Library,* by Agatha Christie; *The Big Sleep,* by Raymond Chandler; *All That Remains,* by Patricia Cornwell; *"F" Is for Fugitive,* by Sue Grafton; *The Maltese Falcon,* by Dashiell Hammett; *Gorky Park,* by Martin Cruz Smith; and *The Silence of the Lambs,* by Thomas Harris.

Because Agatha Christie is so important to mystery fiction in the twentieth century, and because she lasts and lasts, her writing methods deserve close study. Christie's novels make swift reading. Read several. Her *Autobiography,* available in paperback, provides a moral center for mystery writers. Follow the *Autobiography* with Janet Morgan's biography of Christie. For an insight into Christie's writing strategies, read Gillian Gill's critical biography, *Agatha Christie: The Woman and Her Mysteries.*

An excellent book that explores the historical roots of mystery is *Adventure, Mystery, and Romance,* by John Cawelti. Some sharp insights on evil (insights on evil are helpful for creating believable killers) are contained in *Escape from Evil* by Ernest Becker. For a deep look at violence—its behavior, its animal links, its ritual symbolism—try Elias Canetti, the Nobel Prize–winning author of *Crowds and Power.* For a handy reference to specific books and author biographies, see *The Encyclopedia of Mystery and Detection* by Chris Steinbrunner and Otto Penzler.

Timetables of History is a helpful writer's tool. Each of your characters has a past. With *Timetables,* you can select details (popular music, films, world events) that stabilize the past of your character. Details bring us close. Details make the setting feel real.

If your writing feels rusty, warm up with "writing practice," a ritual of timed writing developed by Natalie Goldberg in *Writing Down the Bones.* For insights on plot and structure, study Syd Field's books *Screenplay* and *The Screenwriter's Workbook.*

Other helpful books are listed in the bibliography at the back of this book.

Weekends 1–4
Character Work

Starting Out with Character

To start your mystery, you need a cast of characters—actors who take roles in your crime drama.

You need a sleuth, a character who detects, who sniffs the air for evil, who tracks evil to its lair, who stares evil in the face.

To get the mystery rolling, your sleuth needs work, something to detect, so you conjure up a crime. In this complex age of multimedia and information overload, crime is easy to find. Look at the nightly news. Glance at the morning newspaper. An alleged killer, on trial for a bloody double murder, is found not guilty by a jury of his peers. A high-school teen is killed in a drive-by shooting ten blocks from your home. A child, missing for five days, is found dead. The police are lost; they have no clues, no leads, nothing. When the police are stumped, your sleuth smells opportunity.

Because you don't know much about police work and because you're tired of reading about private eyes, you make your sleuth an amateur. She's educated, employed, reflective, curious, with a strong sense of right and wrong. Because this is your first book, and because you want the reader to know the sleuth, you start Chapter One in the morning when your sleuth wakes up. She stretches, she yawns, she showers, she reads the paper over morning coffee.

The crime for your book rises up like a phantom from the

sleuth's front page. Perhaps a child is missing. Or a pretty teenager. Because she is alone, your sleuth reads the first few lines of the paper to herself, a device for sharing important information with the reader. The newspaper piece might go something like this: "Police are still investigating the murder of an island teenager. The identity of the teen, discovered on South Beach Road sometime early Friday morning, is being withheld at this time. . . ."

This story feels promising. There is mystery as the police withhold the name and identity of the victim. There is a Christie-like setting, the enclosed world of an island. If you are eager to get started with your book, you might open with the sleuth at home, reading the newspaper. Or you might go for action, starting the book with the sleuth at the crime scene.

After you write the crime scene, you might have your sleuth checking with the police, the medical examiner, a witness who knew the victim. Because the island is an enclosed space, a known world, the sleuth networks her friends and acquaintances. Over coffee and croissants at the local pâtisserie, she gathers information and recreates the crime, sharing her recreation with the reader.

Humming with the heat of discovery, you write a couple of witness interviews. Because you have a deep interest in people, you develop the sleuth's personal life. If she's married, with children, perhaps the sleuth has a dialogue with a child about safety, the importance of not talking to strangers. If she's divorced, perhaps the sleuth gets a phone call from her ex, advising her to stay indoors, quit her job, come back to the marriage, be normal.

· · ·

After half a dozen witness interviews and several weekends of writing, you have written forty or fifty pages. The manuscript, along with your notes on the case, fills a manila folder. Your pages are organized into orderly chapters of ten pages each. You're cooking along on the story when something happens to stop you—a crisis at work, a family emergency, houseguests for the holidays—and you shelve the writing. You plan to pick it up again soon. You really want to write this book. You've invested time and energy; your sleuth is right on the edge of discovery. But when you free up some writing time, a couple of months have passed and you can't get started again. You've lost the thread. The momentum you felt when you started has faded.

. . .

If you reach this point in your writing, you're not alone. Writers stall out all the time. Like you, these writers are smart. They're well educated. They hold down steady jobs and they know how to write, how to use the language. From years of reading, they know the mystery field. Like you, they have their favorite authors, their favorite sleuth in a series.

Since most mysteries open with the sleuth, that's the way most beginning writers open their mysteries. On the surface, it might seem logical to open this way. The sleuth is the main character, the voice of the book, the character that creates the series. Killers die and victims die but the sleuth lives on. In most mysteries, the killer enters the story after the sleuth. In *The Body in the Library*, for example, the sleuth enters in Chapter 1 and the killer enters several chapters later. In *The Silence of the Lambs*, the sleuth enters in Chapter 1 and the killer in Chapter 3. In *Gorky Park*, the sleuth enters at page one, Chapter 1, and the killer enters a hundred pages later, in Chapter 7.

This is the deception of mystery writing: the sleuth enters the story because the killer, unseen by both sleuth and reader, has already been there.

Getting to Know Your Killer

What the mystery reader sees on the surface is controlled by a writer's plan. The smart writer prepares a plan before the writing starts. The plan for writing a mystery includes the killing, the main event in mystery writing. In most mysteries, the character who pays for ripping up the fabric of society is the killer who kills. The act of killing is a ritual of transformation. Understanding the raw power of this transformation—one human being turns another human being into dead meat—gives the writer an understanding of the character of the killer.

Death is commonplace, everyday. Murder is extraordinary. Death is expected, inevitable. Murder breaks the routine of life, snapping the green twig before it becomes a tree. The killer kills the victim to create a corpse to create a crime scene that brings the sleuth into the story seeking revenge. The killer is an axman, a bloody butcher who guts an innocent child.

Before you can write your story all the way to the end, you must understand what makes your killer tick. What makes this monster snatch away life? Does your killer kill for money? For a money substitute? For revenge? For control over other humans? For control over a juicy resource base? Does your killer kill for escape, for a brand-new life in a brand-new town?

Knowing why the killer kills takes you inside the killer's head and heart. Inside the heart of darkness, thinking the way a killer thinks, you discover the secrets you need to create a first-rate killer. Because of the laws of competition, a first-rate killer demands a first-rate sleuth. If your sleuth enters the story at page one, Chapter One, feeling not only second rate but also reluctant to take on the case, then your killer provides your sleuth an opportunity for character growth, character change, character transformation.

Character work—the preparation you do on characters before you start writing—solves problems that surface later in the book. If you do character work now, your characters will help you push on through, past that troublesome stopping point. For most beginning novel writers, the stopping point is somewhere around page 50.

The sleuth's quest for the killer structures your mystery tale. Once you know your killer, once you look deep into the heart of evil, once you feel the thrill of killing, once you taste blood with your killer's taste for death, you won't stop writing until you have finished the book with a payment that balances the scales of justice in a familiar biblical sense: an eye for an eye and a tooth for a tooth.

A life to pay for a life.

Character Roster

You need three characters to get started with the writing: *killer, victim,* and *sleuth.* Each character has a fixed role in your mystery.

The killer kills; the victim dies; the sleuth detects. Once you get started, more characters—helpers, witnesses, suspects, cops, hoods, small-time crooks, a rich old man, a femme fatale—enter the story.

On *Weekend 1* you create your killer, the murderer who takes a life. On *Weekend 2* you create the victim, the character who dies to create the crime scene. On *Weekend 3* you create the sleuth, the character who enters the story to analyze the crime scene for clues left by the killer. On *Weekend 4,* with your writing well under way, you'll have enough material to create a catalyst character, a mover and shaker who makes things happen as the sleuth tracks the killer. Time for that hot date with a killer.

· WEEKEND 1 ·
KILLER

Motive and Resource Base

The house on the hill in the opening of Raymond Chandler's *The Big Sleep* is the visible resource base for the novel. Equipped with a butler who patrols the opulent foyer and a chauffeur who polishes an expensive Packard, the house on the hill—its name is Sternwood Manor—exudes the heady scent of money and power.

Lured by the house on the hill, the Irish adventurer Rusty Regan marries the older daughter. When Rusty does not respond properly to the advances of the little sister, she executes him. To get some quick help with body disposal, the older sister calls in a local crime boss. When a blackmailer tries to extort money from the little sister, the sleuth is called in by General Sternwood, the lord of the manor. The story begins as the sleuth crosses the threshold into the foyer to describe the resource base.

The construction of a mystery novel starts with motive, why the killer kills. In mystery writing, you simplify the problem of motive by creating a visible resource base. If it's not the house on the hill as in *The Big Sleep,* it's money or a money substitute.

To learn more about the central importance of the resource base in the world of mystery writing, let's look at some other writers:

• *The Maltese Falcon.* The resource base in Hammett's tale of the Grail is the jeweled bird, a statue of a falcon designed for the Knights of Malta for the Emperor Charles V, the king of Spain. As evidence of their loyalty, the Maltese knights sent the king a statue of a falcon cast in gold and dripping with precious gems. The bejeweled falcon left Malta; it never reached Spain; being lost gave it mystery. Dragging its weighty past, the legendary falcon turns up in San Francisco as a black bird disguised by a coat of paint. The killer, femme fatale Brigid O'Shaughnessy, kills to protect her access to the falcon. Her victim is the business partner of the sleuth, private detective Sam Spade. To lace his resource base with irony, author Dashiell Hammett made the painted bird a fake: the killer killed for a lead bird painted black.

• *"F" Is for Fugitive.* The resource base in Sue Grafton's *Fugitive* is a treasure of common stocks the killer plans to use to fuel her dream of escape. The killer hates her stifling life, running the family motel in Floral Beach, California. When the time is ripe, with her lover by her side, she will escape this suffocating cage. When her secret lover impregnates a local teen, the killer kills the pregnant teen before she delivers. Because she kills the girl, the killer gains access to money, a cache of $42,000 (earned by her brother in small-time local holdups) that she invests in the stock market. Following the money trail leads the sleuth out of the back story to the killer's secret lover, the secret father who denied help to the teen he got pregnant. The killer in *Fugitive,* who is not a mother herself, murders three mothers to protect access to her dream.

• *The Body in the Library.* The resource base in Christie's second Miss Marple tale is money, £50,000, controlled by the rich old man, Conway Jefferson. Like General Sternwood from Raymond Chandler's *The Big Sleep,* Conway Jefferson is a cripple locked to a wheelchair. The killer in *Body* kills to gain access to that £50,000.

• *Gorky Park.* The resource base in Martin Cruz Smith's book is an empire of fur. The fur comes from Barguzinsky sables. Sable pelts, along with gold, are the backbone of the Soviet economy. The killer, who's smuggling sables out of Mother Russia to a breeding facility in rural New Jersey, kills three victims to protect his empire.

Two of the victims in *Gorky Park* are Siberians who work at the Fur Center in Irkutsk, a vital resource base representing the belly of Mother Russia. The third victim is an American university student who dies to prevent him from exposing the killer's empire of fur.

• *The Silence of the Lambs.* The resource base for Dr. Hannibal Lecter is human flesh. When he eats flesh, he devours a portion of his victim. A connoisseur, he elevates eating and digesting his victims to the level of art. When the sleuth asks him why he served up sweetbreads (thymus and pancreas), Lecter makes a death-god joke: "Haven't you ever had people coming over and no time to shop? You have to make do with what's in the fridge. . . ."

The leftovers in Lecter's fridge are sweetbreads lifted from Raspail: the victim is the resource base.

With your motive established by the resource base, you can move on to developing your killer.

Guidelines for Creating a Killer

1. *Create a Murder Checklist.*

The killer kills to get at the resource base. The kind of crime—weapons and planning and getting to the killing place and disposal of the corpse—helps to define your killer. To focus on the crime that defines the killer, use a murder checklist. A checklist helps you gather details you'll use later as you write the book. A murder checklist contains the familiar categories of *time* and *place, weapons* and *wounds, wardrobe, planning,* and *corpse disposal.* The sample murder checklist below covers the triple murder that opens *Gorky Park:*

• *Place.* The place is Moscow's Gorky Park, a strip of land south of Red Square on the east bank of the Moskva River. The killer chose this public place to dispatch the victims. There is snow, useful for burying the dead. The killer kills the victims on the frozen lake. They die wearing ice skates.

• *Lighting.* The light source is a fading Moscow sunset. The killer can see because he knows what he's doing. He has planned this murder to protect his resource base. The killer sees with the eyes of a god.

• *Time.* The killer killed at twilight. The month was February. The lighting was dim, the heavy gray of a long Russian winter. Two months pass before the corpses are discovered by a militiaman who leaves the trail to relieve himself in the snow.

• *Weapon.* The weapon is a Mannlicher 7.65mm automatic, made in Argentina. It carries eight rounds. It hits with a wallop. The killer fired five shots, two for each of the males, one for the female. The Mannlicher is not left at the scene because the killer tosses it into the Moskva River.

The other weapon used on the victims is a skinning knife.

• *Wounds.* The killer shot both men in the chest and also in the mouth. The killer shot the female in the chest only. Using his skinning knife, the killer skinned the faces to create death masks difficult to identify. For the same reason, he cut off the fingertips to remove fingerprints. Because the killer did not shoot the female in the mouth, there was enough of the head for reconstruction.

• *Weather, Season, Temperature.* The month of the killings is February. It's cold, with two feet of snow. The lake is frozen. Because of the weather, the bodies will stay buried for two months.

• *Wardrobe.* The killer, a fur trader, wore a fur coat and a fur hat and ice skates. He carried a leather bag. Inside the leather bag he concealed the Mannlicher. The victims wore overcoats and ice skates. The female wore a dress.

• *Planning.* The killer fired through the leather bag. Traces of leather cling to the bullet that killed the American, identified in the police files as "GP2," Gorky Park Victim Number Two. The gun was loaded, ready to kill. The killer chose the skating rink to lull the victims into a party atmosphere: the sables were on their way to America, time for the victims to celebrate their own passage, following those sables. The killer plans the killing to silence GP2, the American student, before he exposes the killer's resource base, the vast empire of fur. When he confesses to the sleuth near the end of the book, the killer will explain his killings as necessary.

2. *Get Organized with a Character Sketch.*

Whether in dialogue, monologue, back-story narration, profile, or checklist, the information you develop about your characters needs to be explored, pored over, looked at, analyzed, organized. The simplest device to organize information is the Character Sketch. Start with these categories—Personal *(age, sex, family,* et cetera); Objects *(weapons, tools, clothing, cars,* et cetera); Character Links (connections to other main characters); Resource Base (nearness to money or power)—and then try plotting with scene cards to drive the character deeper into the book.

Example: Character Sketch of the Killer in our Write-Along Mystery.

Personal. Myra Jane Severance, 35, is a native of Macon, Georgia. The mother ran off when Myra Jane was eight. The father died when she was fifteen. Impregnated by Uncle Ralph, her womb was taken by an abortion that also took the unwanted fetus. At university, curious about medicine and human anatomy, she double-majored in Physiology and Psychology. Excited by dissection, cutting up things in the lab. Worked her way through school as a thousand-dollar-a-night call girl.

Myra Jane is five ten. Her weight holds steady at 130 pounds. Blond hair, fair skin, a hard-edged look in her hard blue eyes. When triggered, she flips into a murderous rage.

Objects. A university diploma hangs on her office wall at the Marina Café, the best little tourist restaurant in South Carolina. In her desk drawer is the murder weapon, a surgical scalpel she stole from the university lab. In the kitchen is a meat mallet. In a box in the office closet is an empty box from Tamara's Boutique Erotique, a supplier of adult erotica located in Atlanta. Myra Jane, married to money, drives a sporty BMW. The Marina Café owns panel trucks and a Jeep Cherokee four-by-four. Her office at the café is messy. The kitchen and eating area are spotless, to draw the trade.

Character Links.

• *Victims.* Myra Jane envies Lacey Anne Baxter, who blocks her way to the Major's empire of money and power. Victims One and Two die because they are Lacey Anne look-alikes—blond, thin, sixteen—and therefore part of the plot to frame the scapegoat. Myra Jane connects to Armand DuPre, the crime writer, because she wants the world to hear her story. Myra Jane eggs husband, Edward, into suicide to clear the way to the Major.

• *Sleuth.* Myra Jane desires the sleuth. Wants to seduce her, get her under control. The sleuth says no way.

• *Catalyst.* Myra Jane wants the Major's money and power. Brings him her body and pecan pies, two of his favorites.

Resource Base. The resource base for the story is the Major's empire: finance, real estate, old family money, connections, power, Baxter's Bungalow. On her first visit as a college call girl, Myra Jane wants to be Mistress of the Bungalow. When Edward refuses to finance the Marina Café, Myra Jane barters her body to the Major, who becomes a silent partner.

Plotting with Scene Cards.

• *Crime Scene* (Act One). Three hours before the story opens, Myra Jane kills Lacey Anne, dressing her in the leather thong to continue the serial-killer pattern started with Victims One and Two.

• *Killer Onstage* (Act One). The morning after Lacey's murder, Myra Jane intrudes on the sleuth and Armand DuPre to announce the Major is organizing a manhunt for the fugitive, Julius Bugliosi.

• *Interview with a Killer* (Act Two). It's after midnight in her office as Myra Jane plays mind games with Armand, leading him into her wicked soul, leading him to death with the meat mallet.

• *Killer Mask Slips* (Act Three). In a cozy tête-à-tête with the sleuth, the killer chats about Mom, Dad, Uncle Ralph, the university, the dissecting room, et cetera.

• *Killer Confrontation* (Act Three). Arriving at the Bungalow to rescue her imagined wedding to the Major, the killer finds she has been replaced by the sleuth. The two women struggle for control.

3. *Interview Your Killer Now.*

Plotting with scene cards gives you a choice of places for a killer interview. By writing a first draft of the interview now, you probe the killer with Q & A, unearthing clues to motive, resource base, method, and pain in the back story. If you don't want the sleuth to run the interview, use a cop or a nosy writer. In this first-draft Q & A with Myra Jane Severance, the killer of *Murder on Drake Island,* the interviewer is Armand DuPre, a crime writer who's been following the Teen Angel murders. Before starting the Q & A, we like to note the time and place, and add details to establish mood, setting, and atmosphere.

Setting and Situation

The interview with the killer takes place in the owner's office at the Marina Café on Drake Island, South Carolina. The office, in contrast to the spick-and-span café, is messy. Unwashed plates, dirty glasses, stained coffee cups, stacks of food magazines. The killer, wearing reading glasses, sits behind her desk studying Armand DuPre's work on the Teen Angel killer in the Sunday magazine of a big-city daily. Armand, the weary interviewer, sits across from her typing notes into his laptop. Armand can't get access to the Prime Suspect, the scapegoat Julius Bugliosi. Using her connections (her husband is the mayor), Myra Jane has promised access to the Prime Suspect if Armand will share his writer's byline on the next Teen Angel piece. The interview begins with barter—Armand guarding his precious byline, the killer trading insights into the case.

Interview with a Killer

> A byline? You're putting me on.
> They're moving young Julius, Armand.
> Moving him? When?
> As soon as the storm lifts. They'll fly him to the mainland.
> You're an informant. I'll pay you the going rate.

I can write, Armand. See these magazines? Two dozen pieces sold in the last two years.

Great topics. Chicken cacciatore. *Salade niçoise. Menudo à la Myra.*

I've been reading your stuff, Armand. You're running out of gas. You need my energy on this, my special angle.

What angle are we talking here?

I knew the victim. I know why she died. I know about the thong.

So do I. I traced the frigging thong from Tamara's, that sicko toy store for sicko adults. You volunteering to check the list? Over a thousand sold?

It's not who buys them. It's why they are used on the bimbos.

Okay. So fill me in.

I get the byline and a guest box. Myra Jane Severance, guest writer, resident of Drake Island.

Okay. You got your frigging byline. So give on the thong.

The killer strips the victims, right?

Right.

And then he puts them into this thong.

I'm taking back my byline. I'm taking my computer back to my hotel where I will write my own piece using my own insights.

They're bimbos, Armand. The thong keeps them honest.

Funny word, *honest.*

What is a bimbo? An unformed female. These bimbos are empty teeny-boppers with raisins for breasts. No hips, skinny legs, pretty hair, skin to die for. They can turn a guy on with a look. They're loaded with silly sex but they don't have a clue what it signifies. The killer kills them to keep them honest. Now that you're typing, does that mean I get my byline?

Keep going. Don't stop. This feels like good shit.

The world is a wasteland. The bimbos with the blond hair are citizens of the wasteland. Killing the bimbos is a cleansing ritual.

Cleansing ritual. I like. I like. Why doesn't he have sex with them?

Bimbos are little pigs, Armand. Pigs are for butchering.

Why does he spread-eagle them?

It's a testament.

Testament sounds religious.

A testament to their blatant sexuality.

I like that. Blatant sexuality. It resonates.

That position, the arms out, the legs spread wide, mimics the moment a woman gives birth. Are you with me, Armand? Do you understand the irony here?

Yes. Because he cuts out their wombs.

You're good, Armand. I like you. I wish you hadn't found Tamara's customer list. If you hadn't found it, I could show you some moves.

What moves?

Write what I tell you, Armand. The killer didn't mean to cut out the wombs. Not at first. He wanted to strip the bimbos down, dress them in the thong, teach them a lesson about what it means to be a sexy teen. Then the idea came to him. The bimbo was a little Mickey Mouse watch. The killer was a watchmaker digging for a twisted, crooked mainspring. The cutting felt holy, Armand. The killer felt like God. Tell me, have you ever felt like God?

• • •

The killer interview shows the human side of Myra Jane Severance. She wants a byline, her name in print. While not ready to confess to the crime, she still wants her side of the story to be told. The victims are bimbos, sexual creatures unaware of their sexuality. They deserve to die; the killer is merely the instrument. To display their "blatant" sexuality, the killer dresses them in a leather thong. This kind of plot detail is handy when you plot (Weekends 5–9) and also when you write your first draft (Weekends 14–26). The tone of the interview (Myra Jane characterizes the killer as "a watchmaker after a twisted, crooked mainspring") suggests a killing scene of detached mechanical efficiency. The killer feels righteous. There is no guilt, only the pain of a wound from the past. In this Weekend 1 interview, the killer of Drake Island is assumed to be a male.

4. *Rip Off the Mask; Reveal Your Killer.*

At some point in the story, your killer is revealed. At the moment of revelation, the reader not only sees the killer's face, but also learns more about motive and method and planning. By rehearsing this moment of revelation on Weekend 1, you explore character traits like confidence, cruelty, isolation, selfishness, cannibalism, and the will to be divine.

• Hannibal Lecter, the killer of *The Silence of the Lambs,* reveals himself as a man of confidence and taste when he explains to the sleuth why he killed a victim named Raspail: "Frankly," Lecter says, "I got sick and tired of his whining. Best thing for him, really. Therapy wasn't going anywhere." Lecter's method of ending therapy is to kill the patient and serve up the sweetbreads (thymus and pancreas) as evidence of sacrifice. In Lecter's cannibal world, killing the victim turns something useless (a whining patient) into something useful (a tasty menu item). In the profession of psychiatry, Lecter sees himself as performing a useful social service: "I expect most psychiatrists have a patient or two they'd like to refer to me."

• Ann Fowler, the killer in *Fugitive,* reveals herself as a wounded child, isolated and selfish. The climax of the killer hunt takes place in Ann Fowler's bedroom at the motel run by her family. She's holding a shotgun on the sleuth when her father enters. Father and daughter wrestle for the shotgun. It goes off, blowing off the killer's foot. The killer weeps. Through her tears, she confesses, telling her father why she had to escape, why she killed, blaming it on him: "You were never there for me. . . . you were never there. . . ."

• Brigid O'Shaughnessy, the killer in *The Maltese Falcon,* reveals herself as a deadly femme fatale by using her sexual powers to distract the sleuth from sacrificing her to the system as his scapegoat: "Her body was flat against his from knees to chest." When Sam Spade pushes Brigid for a confession, asking her why she killed Miles Archer, the killer evades, claiming accidental death: "I didn't mean to, at first. I didn't, really."

Hiding behind her mask of the Delicate Sensitive Female, Brigid tosses the ball back to Spade: "Oh, I can't say it, Sam!" So the sleuth confesses for her, summing up motive and crime. Hoping that Miles Archer (Spade's partner) would kill her accomplice, a man named Floyd Thursby, Brigid hired Archer to tail Thursby. When they didn't kill each other, Brigid took control: "And when you found that Thursby didn't mean to tackle him you borrowed the gun and did it yourself." By confessing for the killer, the sleuth sticks to business. He brushes aside her twisted love. He gives her to the cops.

But before the cops come, Brigid, a true femme fatale, nails the sleuth with one final kiss of death: "She put her mouth to his, slowly, her arms around him, and came into his arms."

• John Osborne, the killer in *Gorky Park,* reveals himself as a wounded and innocent youth when he talks about killing the three German officers in Leningrad during World War II. Osborne's job was to feed the citizens of Leningrad. Being an innocent American, he didn't know the Russians had turned cannibal: to survive, the citizens of Leningrad were eating their neighbors. When he offered them champagne and chocolate, the Germans laughed at his naive innocence. "Did I seriously think, they asked, that it was the few rations we dropped from planes or got through on sleds that was keeping a million people alive? They roared with laughter."

Embarrassed by his own innocence, enraged by the mocking laughter, Osborne killed the Germans. When he killed, he liked the taste of death. Having tasted death in Leningrad, having killed for being ridiculed, he had no trouble killing to protect his empire of fur.

WORKING THE NOVEL

Exercises

1. *The Killer Interview.*
Warm up to your killer in an interview. Start by setting the time and place. Ask warm-up questions—name, age, profession, et cetera—and then move to questions about motive and agenda: Why kill this victim? Why in this place? How did you get there? How did you get away? Why this weapon? How long have you planned the killing? Who else was in on it? If your questions lead the interview into the past, you can discover good stuff about the killer's back story:

Use back story to locate the turning point between innocence and experience in the life of your killer. What was your first kill? How old were you? How did killing make you feel? What did you do with the victim? Bury it? Dissect it? Pin it on the wall? Burn it up in a funeral pyre?

As your interviewer, you can use the sleuth—it's good exercise to hear the sleuth speak—or a police official. Or a nosy writer hungry for a story.

2. *Character Sketch.*
Organize what you know about the killer now into a character sketch. Use these categories:

- *Personal.* Sex, age, birthplace, residence, occupation, parents, siblings, skills, weaknesses, et cetera.
- *Objects.* Home, toys, wardrobe, vehicle, tools, jewelry, et cetera.
- *Character Links.* Connections (blood, money, work, et cetera) to other characters.
- *Resource Base.* What is the Resource Base (treasure, power source, object of desire)? How does this character connect? Example: The rich old man controls the resource base. The killer kills to gain access to the resource base.

3. *Murder Checklist.*
Using the categories from the *Guidelines* (place, time, lighting, et cetera), develop a murder checklist for your killer. The murder checklist, because it triggers details about the crime, helps you develop insights about motive, method, and opportunity. Suggestions for categories:

- *Place.* Where did the murder take place? Was it indoors or out? Did the killer choose the place? How much location planning was there?
- *Time.* What time did the murder take place? Was it night or day? High noon or dim twilight? How long did the

killing take? How much time has elapsed between the murder and the opening of the book?

• *Lighting.* What was the light source? How well does the killer see to do the killing? If it's night, for example, does the killer use night-vision apparatus? If it's hot in the desert sun, does the killer wear dark glasses?

• *Weapon.* What was the murder weapon? How knowledgeable is the killer about this particular weapon? Does the weapon drag out the murder (small potions of poison administered at regular intervals) or does it deliver a quick death? Was there more than one weapon? If a firearm was used, how did the killer muffle the shots? If a knife was used, how did the killer get close enough? If an explosive device was used, how did the killer learn about explosive devices?

• *Wounds.* What kinds of wounds did the weapon leave on the victim? If a firearm was used, what did the bullets do? Is there an exit hole? Did the killer retrieve the empty shell casings?

• *Weather, Season, Temperature.* What's the month? What's the season? What's the temperature at the moment of killing? What was the weather like? Rain? Snow? Tropical storm? Hot sun overhead? Sandstorm in the desert?

• *Wardrobe.* How did the killer dress to kill? Street clothes? A business suit? A rubber apron? A parka for the snow? Ice skates? A skimpy pink teddy to distract the victim? A raincoat for the rain? Work clothes to seem normal to fellow workers before and after? Walking shoes to get back after torching the corpse?

• *Planning.* How much planning did the killer do to prepare for this murder? If the killer did not own the weapon, where did she get it? Beg? Borrow? Steal? Did the killer plan on paper, using diagrams and notes? Or did she plan inside her head?

• *Disposal.* How did your killer dispose of the body? Fire? Water? Explosive device? Burial? Food for the animal world? Chemicals?

4. *Plotting with Scene Cards.*

The scene card is an index card, either three-by-five or five-by-eight. On the scene card you jot down notes about a particular scene, one that contains your killer. To keep the scenes separate, and to have fun with this part of your writing task, you give a name to each scene. When your killer enters the story, for example, you might create a scene card called "Killer Onstage." The term *onstage* is writer's shorthand for that first moment a major character (killer, victim, sleuth, catalyst) steps into your story. On this scene card for "Killer Onstage," you jot down place of entry, time of day, wardrobe, who's already here, who's on the way, and what the killer wants.

For example, when John Osborne comes onstage in Chapter Seven of *Gorky Park*, he's naked, sporting an all-over tan. If you were writing *Gorky Park*, your note might read: "Killer is buck naked, tanned all over like a sun god, and dripping with gold. He enters to find the sleuth waiting."

A second scene card might be "First Encounter." This scene name, "First Encounter," identifies the moment in the book when the sleuth and the killer cross paths. The exact placement of this scene can come later, when you know more about your story. Coming onstage in Chapter One of *The Big Sleep*, Miss Carmen Sternwood flirts with the sleuth, falling into his arms. On your scene card, you would note the sleuth's response. Is he attracted? Is he repelled? What does he do if, later in the story, he finds the killer in his bed?

Your third scene card for the killer might be "Killer Revealed" or "Killer Confession." Study other writers to see what they do with this event in the story. Whereas Christie's killer is revealed at the climax of *Body*, John Osborne's confession in New York ("Killer Revealed") precedes by several pages the climax in the snow at the sable compound in New Jersey.

Scene cards are handy because you can shuffle them, changing their order as the story gathers momentum. If you make scene cards for each character now (Weekends 1–4), you'll have a dozen or more by the time you start plotting on Weekend 5.

· **WEEKEND 2** ·
VICTIM

The victim dies to create the crime scene that brings the sleuth into the story to make the killer pay. If the crime scene opens your book—your best writing strategy for your first venture into mystery writing—that means the victim is dead before your reader reads your opening line.

But while the reader doesn't have a clue about why the victim died, the writer must know every single detail. As the writer, you must know not only physical details—age, sex, body type, hair color, neck size, arm length, shoe size, wardrobe, and so on—but you must also know specific details about feelings, yearnings, hopes, fears. Who does the victim love? Who does she hate? What does she want? What will she risk to get it? What does she dream about? What haunts her sleep? What childhood trauma changed her life forever? What gives her immeasurable joy?

As your information develops into a character, you probe the role of your victim in your book. How is the victim connected to the killer? To the resource base? What brought the victim to the killing place? Who cares about her death? Family? Friends? A lover? Multiple lovers? How does the victim spend her time? Work? School? Prayer? Play? Cooking? Nursing? Mothering? What feat—it could be mental or physical—does she perform really well? Is she a violin virtuoso? A tennis star? A radiant actress? A great cook? A caring baby-sitter?

Before the victim shows up in your book, breaking the surface to create the crime scene, she's a person with a past. Before you can make use of this past to structure your plot, bringing the victim back in witness interviews and suspect interrogations, in photos and diaries and scrapbooks and home movies that bring tears to the eye, you have to create a character. Before she cooperates, helping your book by dying, the victim needs to get a life. She needs a childhood and parents. She needs a birthplace to establish identity and a birth date to establish age. She needs a place to live, a room in a hotel or a garage or an apartment house clinging to the side of a hill where she keeps her personal items, those physical details that become clues for your sleuth.

Guidelines for Creating the Victim

Your first step is to connect the victim to the killer. Whether it's money or blood, you can write with more depth if you understand what links the victim to the killer. Step Two is to create the Victim's Lair. Step Three is to write a monologue that takes you inside the victim. Step Four is to organize your thoughts about the victim with a character sketch. Step Five, a countdown to murder that takes you to the crime scene that opens the book, is to trace out steps to the killing place. Getting your victim to the killing place helps you build the plot on Weekends 5–9.

   1. *Make the Killer Connection.*
   With the monologue, you give the victim voice, personality, and substance. With the Victim's Lair, you provide a sanctuary, a personal space that helps to define the victim. You are now ready to make the killer connection.
   Before you can write convincingly about murder, death by gunshot or hatpin or poison dart or strangulation with a white silk sash, you need to know how the victim connected with the killer. Were they lovers? Friends? Cousins? Siblings? Family? Did they connect in pairs like Master and Slave? Doctor and Patient? Husband and Wife? Teacher and Student? Officer and Private? Warden and Prisoner? Whore and Client?
   Did the victim first meet the killer at work? At school? At church? On the street? In a hotel lobby? At the local bar? Did they swim together at the country club? Did they cell together in jail? For some options on the victim's killer connection, study other mystery authors:

   • *Blood or Family.*   Ori Fowler, one of the victims in *Fugitive*, is the killer's mom. In *The Body in the Library*, one of the victims is related to the killer.

• *Business or Money.* The three victims in *Gorky Park*, Valerya Davidova, Kostia Borodin, and James Kirwill, are in the smuggling business with the killer. Captain Jacobi, the ship's officer who smuggles in *The Maltese Falcon*, is in business with the crooks. Floyd Thursby, the accomplice of the killer, is in business with the crooks. The victims in *Body* die to protect the killer's access to the resource base.

• *Sex or Twisted Love.* Jean Timberlake, the pregnant teen from *Fugitive*, dies because she replaces the killer in the bed of Dwight Shales. Shana Timberlake, Jean's mom, dies because the killer thinks she's in Dwight's bed. Rusty Regan, the victim whose death initiates the extortion that brings the sleuth into *The Big Sleep*, dies when he rejects the sexual advances of the killer. Miles Archer, the professional detective in *The Maltese Falcon*, drops his guard because he's attracted by the sex appeal of the killer, a classic thirties femme fatale.

• *Resemblance or Looks Like Someone Else.* The two victims in *Body* look alike. The victims of Buffalo Bill in *Lambs* die because they are large enough to have skins to make Mama Suits to fit the killer, a large man. The female victims in David Lindsey's *Mercy* are all attractive and educated, with affluent lifestyles and exotic tastes for the erotic.

• *Proximity to the Death God.* Raspail, Lecter's victim in the *Lambs* back story, is a patient-client of Dr. Lecter. Pembry and Boyle, two prison guards with lots of experience, died because they got too close to Lecter. The three German officers in the *Gorky Park* back story died because they laughed at the young John Osborne. By irritating Osborne with their Teutonic scorn, these three unarmed victims gave him the taste of blood that made him a death god. At the end of *Gorky Park*, when Osborne executes seven men in the snow—a good morning's work, presided over by Irina Asanova—the killer's power over his victims is awesome. If a death god wants you dead, you die.

• • •

In our write-along mystery, *Murder on Drake Island*, Lacey Anne Baxter dies because she blocks the killer's access to the resource base, the massive fortune of her grandfather, Major Philip Baxter. The victim has known the killer since childhood. As we pointed out on Weekend 1, the killer wants to marry Major Phil and get control of his wealth.

• • •

2. *Victim's Lair.*
Once you have explored the killer connection, you build a word picture of the Victim's Lair, a bedroom, den, study, or other retreat that represents the victim's personal space.

Example—Victim's Lair. Lacey Anne Baxter's room faces the sea. The seawall is glass from floor to ceiling, a sliding door that opens to sea breezes and sea birds crying. As you face the sea, the wall to your right is devoted to an entertainment center: a big-screen TV; a videocassette player; a tape duplicator; a stereo unit with a special tape deck for voice dubbing and recording; two rows of books on classical composers, Bach, Mozart, Beethoven, Brahms. Ten rows of CDs ranging from Vivaldi and Bach to Patsy Cline and Jimi Hendrix. Racks for sheet music.

The third wall has a dresser, a dressing table, a mirror, and a cabinet containing jars of makeup, tubes of lipstick, vials of perfume. The fourth wall is packed with posters—rock stars, jockeys, tennis players—and photographs.

The photographs show the victim alone and with friends. A cluster of photos shows the victim on a hunting trip with Major Phil. He's in a special wheelchair. She stands beside the chair, one hand on his shoulder. She looks tanned and fit and perhaps thirteen years old.

An old photograph shows Major Phil before he lost his legs. He wears hunter's khaki. His right boot rests on the snout of a dead rhinoceros. Under the photo is a slip of white paper. On the paper are the words: *Kenya, under Kilimanjaro.*

In the closet, taped to the back of the closet door, the sleuth finds a photograph showing Lacey Anne dancing with Edward Severance, the mayor of Drake Island Village. Edward, a known flirt, is staring hard at Lacey Anne. Her face in profile, Lacey Anne looks at someone not in the frame of the photo. She wears a waist-length tunic of pale lace over a silk sheath with spaghetti straps. Her hair gleams. She looks young, innocent, lovely. Studying the photo, the sleuth feels a tingle of insight.

• • •

Creating a lair for your victim is an excellent strategy for imparting information to the reader. Photos take the reader back in time: Major Phil in his younger days before the accident that took his wife, his daughter, and his legs; the victim dancing with the mayor. The writer knows what the sleuth does not know: the mayor is the victim's secret dad. Could he have killed her? Would he make a good suspect?

With questions like these churning inside your head, you jot some notes before moving on to the victim's monologue.

• • •

3. *Write a Monologue for Your Victim.*

Setting and Situation. The place for the victim's monologue is the Pirate's Cove, a nightspot at the Drake Island Marina. Smoke fills the room where dancers gyrate to the music of Julius and his Reggae Nouveau Band. Lacey Anne Baxter, her voice sweet, croons to the microphone. The music is a new twist on reggae. Lacey Anne wears a tunic of pale lace over a silky sliplike dress. It's nighttime, a half-dead Thursday before the jam-packed Labor Day Weekend. In her tryout for Julius, Lacey Anne glowed: she owns the Sound that unites this motley band of musicians. Because Julius wants that Sound to keep ringing, he drives Lacey Anne home after midnight for a powwow with her grandfather. The victim's monologue gives substance to the girl child who dies to open the book:

Example—Lacey Anne's Monologue:

I'm in his room. The demo plays on tape. The voice is mine but not mine. The voice is big. I'm not big. I feel majorly weird. I hit a sweet place on the tape, filling the room with Voice, and Julius grins at me. His teeth are so great. The guys start humming along, beating the beat, hands on their knees, rapping. I stand up. I sing along with the tape. Two of me. Julius wants me for the group. I could die, go straight to heaven. Singing feels great. I say okay. Let's do it.

What will he say? What will who say? Your grandfather, Julius says. What will he say? Let's just do it. Let's split for the mainland, the cosmos, the big banana in the sky. We'll have to ask him, Julius says. Tonight. After the gig.

I'm onstage doing the gig. Sweet sounds, the boys backing me up. Julius blowing his beautiful horn. A skinhead down below, looking up. Rays from the strobes bounce off his skinhead skull. The skirt flips up and he grins. Tattoos on his shoulders. Tattoos on his brain. He reaches out for me. His fingers are white like bone. He wants my bod. Not like Julius. No way. Julius wants my voice.

Emily waves from down below. She dances really great. Looks really great also. The music grabs me. Holds me tight. Whirls me around. You're the singer, Julius says. You're the Sound. Sing your heart out, Songster Girl. Make us famous.

I'm onstage. MJ by the wall. That lady wants to be my mom. For an older person, MJ's okay. Lately, she's overdoing the eye shadow bit. Wears the black slacks tonight. The aqua blouse. Goes great with her hair. Never forget her hair all crazy catching her in bed with Phil. Like, totally blown away. Mouth open, all those teeth. Julius wants an album. Wants me on the cover. Will MJ buy an album? I wonder.

• • •

The monologue is your chance to go inside a character, probing for an emotion (hope, fear, desire, et cetera) that produces motivation that drives the character toward a goal. Paragraph one, for example, expresses the victim's joy. She's wanted for her voice. Her goal is hitting the road with the band.

The obstacle to hitting the road, the girl's grandfather, surfaces in paragraph two: "What will he say?" The time indicators ending the second paragraph—"Tonight. After the gig"—set up the victim's death trip in the death van. Singing with the band motivates her to see her grandfather. She's certain she can clear away the obstacle.

Paragraph three changes locations, from a hotel room to the gig, a live performance at the Pirate's Cove, the victim singing onstage. The leering skinhead, a perfect suspect, is destined to appear in a witness interview scene after the book opens. Emily Tallant, another witness, appears in paragraph four.

The killer, identified by the initials *MJ*, appears in paragraph five wearing black slacks and an aqua blouse. The victim's memory of conflict in the back story ("Never forget her [MJ's] hair all crazy catching her in bed with Phil. . . .") links the killer with "Phil," aka Major Philip Baxter, the victim's grandfather. The mention of the "album" jumps ahead to a future the victim will not live to see.

To organize what you discover about a character, try a character sketch.

4. *Character Sketch.*

Use the categories from Weekend 1: *personal, objects, character links, resource base, plotting with scene cards.*

Personal. Lacey Anne is sixteen, slender, boyish, with a terribly innocent sexuality. Like the other Teen Angel victims, she has blond hair and a sweet face. Her mother died in an automobile accident in Mexico. Her secret father is Edward Severance, husband of the killer. Lacey Anne lives with her grandfather, Major Phil Baxter, at Baxter's Bungalow off South Beach Road. Lacey Anne, who has the lung power of a young Barbra Streisand, wants to be a major star. Singing with the band makes this sad teen feel like she's valuable.

Objects. Lacey Anne's performance outfit—pale lace over pale silk—sets up a stripping ritual at the crime scene, where the killer dresses her in a thong to match the Teen Angel Victims One and Two. She hates her vehicle, a new Chevrolet Lumina, because it's not cool. The posters in her bedroom—Janis Joplin, Madonna, Barbra Streisand, Courtney Love, et al.—reveal her interest in pop music. Photos connecting the victim to other characters have surfaced in the victim's lair, Lacey Anne's bedroom.

Character Links.

• *Sleuth.*   As a child, Lacey Anne was coached (reading and writing) by sleuth Helene Steinbeck, who needed the money. Lacey Anne had no mother; the sleuth and the victim became close.

• *Killer.*   Myra Jane, a Cinderella girl, is jealous of Lacey Anne's access to wealth. Her jealousy turned to submerged rage when she was exiled from the Bungalow after Lacey Anne caught her in bed with the Major. Getting exiled ratchets up the killer's rage. Using pecan pies, the Major's favorite, she barters her way back inside.

• *Catalyst.*   Lacey Anne is Major Phil's only living heir. When she turns twenty-one, the trust gives her a pile of money.

• *Other Victims.*   Edward Severance, the mayor of Drake Island Village, is the victim's father and the husband of the killer.

Resource Base. Lacey Anne dies because she blocks the killer's access to the fortune of Major Phil. As we learned on Weekend 1, the killer's deeper wish is to become Mistress of the Bungalow and to control the Baxter fortune. The victim stands in the way.

Plotting with Scene Cards. Lacey Anne comes back into the story in these scenes:

• *Re-creation of the Crime*   (Act One), as Armand DuPre educates the sleuth about the Teen Angel murders;

• *Witness Interviews*   (Act One), as the sleuth interviews the skinhead and Emily Tallant;

• *Victim's Lair*   (Act Two), when the sleuth gets her first insight into secret parenthood from photos;

• *The Severance Nose*   (Act Two), where the Major accuses Edward Severance, Lacey Anne's lost father, of getting the girl killed;

• *Memory Returns*   (Act Three), where Julius Bugliosi recalls the lovely voice of Lacey Anne Baxter.

• • •

5. *Count the Steps to the Killing Place.*

On the way to the murder, does your victim dress for a party? For a date? For church? For work? For tennis or swimming or school? Dressing could be step one to the killing place. As the writer dresses the victim, the wardrobe choices reveal character. Is the victim male or female? Young or old? Rich or poor? Shrewd or starry-eyed about the rendezvous? What is step one? What is step two?

By spending time now building the steps to the killing place, you develop a feeling for your victim. When your victim dies, she's not a stick figure, not a cold corpse, not a mere statistic on the death rolls. By creating a live victim, the writer enters the back story, that part of the past that affects the book.

Because a mystery is a logical piece of work in which the reader finds out what the writer already knows, you need to organize the steps to the killing place. By building the steps with meticulous logic, you plug plot holes while you create a seamless story that flows out of the past into the present. For Lacey Anne Baxter, who dies on a muddy beach road, it all began with music lessons.

1. *Music Lessons.* To provide work for a run-down opera singer, Major Philip Baxter gives his granddaughter Lacey Anne voice lessons. The Major is surprised when she produces the voice of an angel.

2. *Naughty Naughty.* Coming home from a voice lesson, Lacey Anne discovers the Major in bed with Myra Jane Severance, the killer.

3. *The Band Connection.* As part of her plot, the killer persuades the Major to let Lacey Anne sing for Julius Bugliosi, leader of the Reggae Nouveau Band, at the Drake Island Music Festival.

4. *The Sound of Surprise.* Lacey Anne Baxter owns the Sound that unites the ragtag band led by Julius, who wants the girl to sign a contract now. The Major refuses.

5. *Dressing Ritual.* For tonight's pre–Labor Day gig at Pirate's Cove, Lacey Anne dresses in lace over skimpy white silk.

6. *Stalking.* At the Pirate's Cove performance, Lacey Anne spots Myra Jane.

7. *The Death Van.* It's raining hard as Julius helps Lacey Anne into his van. Without her voice, Julius says, the band can't get it together. She's excited about launching her career. When they reach the Baxter Bungalow, she promises to help persuade the Major.

8. *Blinded.* At a dark curve on South Beach Road, a bright light blinds Julius, who runs the van off the road to collide with a beach boulder. The light is wielded by the killer, Myra Jane Severance, who wears rain gear. Julius is stunned. Lacey Anne runs toward Myra Jane, calling for help as she stumbles into the rain.

9. *Serial Murder.* After knocking out Julius, the killer changes the victim's costume—stripping off the pale silk, replacing it with a leather thong bikini. The killer kills the victim, cuts out her womb, and leaves her spread-eagled in the mud.

10. *Scapegoat Setup.* The killer smears Julius with mud and blood. Driving him back to town, she leaves the van near his hotel. From her office at the Marina Café, she phones the Major.

• • •

Until the writer knows the back-story sequence that placed the victim's body at the crime scene—muddy road, snow in the park, pumped-out sump of an oil well—it's impossible to write an opening for your mystery that vibrates with strength and confidence. Taking the steps to the killing place is a countdown to murder. It unearths clues and develops red herrings. It helps you focus on the back story (Weekend 5) and also on the crime scene. We'll be writing a detailed crime scene on Weekends 10–13. With the victim dead, the scapegoat knocked out, and the killer triumphant, you are ready to move on to the exercises.

. . .

WORKING THE NOVEL

Exercises

1. *Monologue.*
Probe the interior of your victim by writing a monologue. A good way to break the ice when you're starting out is to begin with "I remember . . ." or "I remember that day. . . ." Using the first person pronouns—I, ME, MINE, instead of third person (SHE/HER, HE/HIM/HIS)—gives you access to the victim's interior, her hopes, fears, dreams. If you set a scene with time and place (after midnight at the Pirate's Cove, a smoky nightclub at the marina on Drake Island), you give the monologue a feeling of reality. If you let your victim see the killer, you add the thrill of dramatic irony to the piece.

If you write better under time pressure, try setting your kitchen timer. Give yourself ten to fifteen minutes for the monologue.

2. *Character Sketch.*
Using the same categories from Weekend 1—personal; objects; character links; resource base; plotting with scene cards—write a character sketch of your victim. If you have more than one victim, sketch the victim who dies to create the crime scene.

Start the sketch with name, sex, and age, and then move to physical characteristics like height and weight, body type and hair color and hairdo, wardrobe and jewelry. You use the writing here to trigger your creativity about the past, the killer connection, the murder, the killing place, and the crime scene. A wardrobe item like the ice skates worn by Valerya Davidova leads the sleuth of *Gorky Park* to the owner, Irina Asanova, the friend from Siberia who connected the killer to the victims. A wardrobe item like the thong worn by Lacey Anne Baxter can lead the writer to develop scenes for the plot.

3. *Killer Connection.*

In a passage of narrative summary, explore the connection between your victim and your killer. Are they connected by blood? By family? By friendship? Did they meet at work? In church? At school? How long after they meet does the victim die? Who else dies?

The connections you develop in a narrative summary will provide you with pieces of the plot:

Example: Rusty Regan, the victim in *The Big Sleep,* dies because he rejected the sexual advances of Carmen Sternwood, the killer with the sharp little teeth. Geiger the pornographer dies because he took nude pictures of Miss Carmen. Joe Brody, a small-time crook, dies because he shot Geiger. Brody's killer is Geiger's lover, a boy named Carol. Harry Jones, a snitch, dies to cover up a link between Rusty Regan and the gambler who owns the joint where Carmen gets drunk. Lash Canino, the gunman who kills Harry Jones to shut him up, dies because he shoots at the sleuth. Using the barter system, the sleuth trades the dead Canino to the cops to lead them away from Miss Carmen.

4. *Steps to the Murder.*

In a passage of narrative summary, explore the events leading up to the crime. Why does the victim go to the killing place? Does she go alone, like the victim in *The Maltese Falcon?* Is she with friends, like Valerya Davidova in *Gorky Park?* Is she in a vehicle, like Lacey Anne Baxter in *Murder on Drake Island?* Is the meeting with the killer planned? Is it a surprise? What is the victim wearing? Did she dress for this meeting? Is she naked when she dies?

Once the victim arrives at the killing place, how much does she suspect? Does she sense death arriving? How well does she know the killer? Is she drugged? Drunk? Happy? Sad? Laughing? Crying?

When you write this exercise, take this opportunity to practice your craft. For example, you could start out with narrative summary ("She wore her best dress. Her skin felt warm, smooth, American. She hated the shabby overcoat. A new one waited in America. A fur coat. A sable") and then shift to monologue: "On the day I died I wore Irina's ice skates. On the day I died I skated across the pond. It was the *1812* Overture that day, the twilight silver and pearl and my skates bit into the ice and . . ."

If you hear the voices of victim and killer, you could eavesdrop, then write a few lines of dialogue:

VICTIM: What a lovely day, John.

KILLER: Not as lovely as you.

VICTIM: What was that sound?

KILLER: What sound do you mean?

VICTIM: A sound. A moment ago. It sounded like cannon fire.

KILLER: Just music. The *1812* Overture.

VICTIM: Of course. Tchaikovsky. Have you seen Kostia?

KILLER: He felt the call of nature.

5. *Plotting with Scene Cards.*

Use the information gleaned from the preceding exercises to create scene cards that bring the victim back to life as you write the book.

You know, for example, that the death of your victim in the back story, before the book opens, creates the "Crime Scene." That's your first scene card. To make the writing easier on your first mystery, we suggest you begin your book with the crime scene. On this card you jot down wardrobe items and the color of the victim's hair and where the victim lies and how long the victim has been there. If you move in for a close-up—zooming in to focus on specific detail—you can exercise your senses by noting smells and kinds of wounds. A close-up is helpful in creating a card for the Crime Scene in *Murder on Drake Island:* "The sleuth bends down for a closer look at the victim. She catches a whiff of mud and perfume. The victim is nude, white, dead. Across the throat is a red slash made by the killer."

The death of your victim could generate three more scene cards: "Witness Interview," "Suspect Interrogation," and "Victim's Lair."

In a witness interview scene, the sleuth digs up the victim's past, searching for clues. Setting can be useful in witness interviews. Kinsey Millhone, the sleuth of *"F" Is for Fugitive,* conducts her interviews in a bar in Floral Beach, California. Two of the witnesses— Tap Granger and Shana Timberlake—become victims of the killer.

In a suspect interrogation scene, the sleuth (or substitute interrogator) tries to connect the suspect with the victim. Witnesses can become victims or suspects; suspects can become helpers. In *Gorky Park,* the sleuth ends his interrogation of the suspect, William Kirwill, with a plea for help. Kirwill, out for vengeance, refuses.

In a Victim's Lair scene, the sleuth or sleuth substitute searches the place where the victim lived, hunting for clues to the murder. When the sleuth visits Jean Timberlake's hillside hovel in *Fugitive,* she relives that moment of teenage excitement when the victim, a poor girl, climbed the stairways to riches and comfort to find safety in her lover's arms. In *Gorky Park,* a visit to the Victim's Lair turns up the sable connection, the link between murder and fur.

With the scene cards generated by your victim, you have created a foothold for the sleuth. On to Weekend 3.

· WEEKEND 3 ·
SLEUTH

The sleuth defines your mystery for your reader. The sleuth is your voice, your persona, the face you choose to present to the world, the major character who carries your series, the way Miss Jane Marple and Hercule Poirot carried their respective books for Christie.

Creating a good sleuth takes time, sweat, patience. It saves time if you replicate some of your own traits when you create your sleuth—same sex, same age, same build, same astrological sign, same arena of operations, perhaps an occupation you know from the inside, saving you from arduous research—while you alter certain specific details of income, education, economic class, vehicle, wardrobe, lair, closet, dresser drawer, wallet, purse, credit cards, computer, shoe size, and various sexual liaisons.

If you're serious about mystery writing, if this is not a one-book fling with the heroic hunter who tracks the killer through the book, then you'll probably write half a dozen books starring your choice for Sleuth One. If Sleuth One is a male of medium build with a gift for quirky ratiocination who wears a rumpled raincoat and who chews on an old cigar and who wears thin with your readers after half a dozen books, then you might study the market and create a new series starring Sleuth Two. Sleuth Two is a female, tall, slender, vulnerable beneath her mask of beauty, tough but sympathetic, great with computers, action oriented and athletic, with a knack for forensic medicine and a heart open to romance with Mr. Right.

If you're a mystery reader, you probably have at least one favorite sleuth. You read books by Author X because you like the sleuth, because you find her interesting, engaging, tough, smart, attractive, and sympathetic. You like the sleuth's style, the way she works a case. You admire the way she hangs in there, struggling against all odds, to bring the culprit to justice. You love the way she cares.

That's your goal this weekend: to create a sleuth that will capture the mind of your reader, the sleuth that will make you famous in your time.

• • •

How do you create a sleuth? Do you start with a character profile? A list of ingredients? Do you start with a word portrait, writing a passage of solid description that paints the sleuth's visage as reflected in one of those three-sided department-store mirrors? Do you start at home, in the morning, with the sleuth just waking up?

Some mysteries start in the office of the sleuth, a home away from home, a kind of sleuth's lair. The typical sleuth's office is Spartan, one desk, two chairs, one coatrack, one telephone, one window facing the alley or a grubby brick wall. The sleuth is dressed, ready to take on the quest. If the phone rings, it's a client. If the door opens, it's a client.

The Maltese Falcon, a book that made its author world famous, starts in Sam Spade's office. As a model for creating a sleuth that outlasts the writer, Hammett's *Falcon* deserves some study.

Like his creator, Dashiell Hammett, Spade is tall, angular, and stooped. Hammett worked for the Pinkerton detective agency. Spade is a private eye. Hammett wore business suits. In this opening scene, and in much of the book, Spade wears a business suit. Sleuths are outsiders, the hunters for society. To keep from being hunted themselves, sleuths dress mainstream. It's part of the disguise, part of the sleuth mask.

Hammett drank and fooled around. Spade drinks. He fools around with his partner's wife and also with the killer. When Spade's office door opens in Chapter 1, the killer walks in. If you were writing *The Maltese Falcon*—a scapegoat quest that uses an object of desire as a red herring—you would jot notes something like this on your scene card for "First Encounter," created on Weekend 1: "V-formation eyebrows on my sleuth. Yellow-gray eyes and a bony jaw and pale brown hair. A tall man, six feet, with rounded shoulders. He's early forties, wearing a business suit. *Action:* the secretary ushers in a visitor, Miss Wonderly, wearing blue to match her eyes. *Reaction:* the sleuth feels a ripple of sexual attraction. Miss Wonderly is the killer disguised as a client. *The job:* the killer sends Spade's partner to fetch her little sister back. The little sister is a fake and death lurks in the subtext: what the killer really wants is for the sleuth's partner, Miles Archer, to kill her accomplice, Floyd Thursby. If Archer kills her accomplice, the killer gains access to the falcon."

If you were planning a book with the range of Hammett's *Maltese Falcon*—a tough-minded sleuth who gets emotional about revenge, a deceptive killer with lots of sex appeal, an object of desire whose possession promises the possessor control of a vast resource base, a victim who dies in the dark—you would be smart to dig deeply into your sleuth's personality. Where did your sleuth come from? What prompted your sleuth to take up detecting? Is your sleuth an amateur like Miss Marple or a professional like Sam Spade or Arkady Renko? Is your sleuth on her first murder case, like Clarice Starling in *Lambs*? How does your sleuth react to violence? To pressure? To betrayal? Does your sleuth talk a lot? Listen a lot? Watch from the shadows? Is your sleuth active or passive? Is your sleuth an avenging angel?

Guidelines for Creating the Sleuth

Step one is to develop a back story for your sleuth. In the back story, you focus not only on the early years—parents, siblings, school, et cetera—but also on how the sleuth came to be a detective and her role in the community where the crime takes place. Step two is the character sketch, organizing what you wrote in the back story. Step three is to create scene cards that drive the sleuth through the book. Step four is to let the sleuth talk. The examples below develop the sleuth for our write-along mystery.

1. *Back Story*—Helene Steinbeck.

She came to the island to escape the city. Came without her books and without her man. Came with her computer even though she was a writer with writer's block and a dozen "gunless" mysteries, tales of detection set in New York City. She came to the island to escape a relationship gone sour. She wanted to go to Paris, but she was broke, so she drove south along the coast—New Jersey, Maryland, Delaware, Virginia, and the Carolinas—and when she came to the end of the road she saw a sign for Drake Island. The road ended at a ferry terminal. There was room for her vehicle, an old Chevrolet. She paid the fare and the loader waved her to the last parking slot.

That first month on Drake Island she met Myra Jane Severance—beautiful and blond, with slanted eyes like a cat's. Myra Jane owned and operated the Marina Café, where the sleuth sat at a table nursing a cup of coffee, trying to break her writer's block. The sleuth rented a cottage for September. She extended for October. On a windy day the killer introduces the sleuth to Major Philip Baxter, a rich old man in a wheelchair.

The Major was a fan. He'd read all her gunless mysteries and was eager for the next one. The sleuth still had writer's block, so she took a job tutoring the Major's granddaughter, Lacey Anne. She tutored Lacey Anne until the girl went away to school. The sleuth was out of work. The writer's block continued.

The Major was a power on the Village Council. When the town marshal's job came open, he pushed through an appointment for the sleuth. She'd grown up with crime in the house; her father was a police detective in New York City. At City College in New York, the sleuth had majored in sociology with a special emphasis on criminal behavior. To get the town marshal's job, the sleuth had to qualify with firearms. At the qualifying shooting range on the mainland, she met James T. Worthington, a sergeant in the state police. James T. was handsome. And forceful. And married. And currently unavailable.

A couple of years before the murder of Lacey Anne Baxter, and before the beginning of *Murder on Drake Island,* the sleuth began a relationship with Armand DuPre, a crime writer and stringer for two big city dailies. Armand, who proclaimed himself a proud descendant of Sir Francis Drake and an African princess stolen from her tribe by slave traders, proved to be an unfaithful lover. He was five years younger than the sleuth. When she discovered he had other women, the sleuth sent Armand away.

Along came James T. Worthington, of the state police, clutching his divorce decree. The sleuth was lonely. To replace Armand, she had a brief romance with James T. There is no man in her life as the book opens.

On the night of Lacey Anne's murder, the sleuth gets a phone call from the Major. His granddaughter is lying in the mud on South Beach Road. Get here fast, the Major says, before the sonofabitch who killed her gets away.

· · ·

2. *Character Sketch*—Helene Steinbeck.

Personal. Helene Steinbeck, thirty-nine years old, is a New Yorker. Born in the city, grew up there. Educated at CCNY (sociology, criminology, French); master's degree in creative writing at Columbia. Jobs: waitressing, bartending, copyediting at two publishing houses, police dispatcher for the NYPD, writer. When she arrives on the island, Helene has a dozen mysteries and writer's block. She stands five feet nine inches tall. Her summer weight runs between 125 and 130. In winter she puts on fifteen to twenty pounds and hates herself. Brown hair, hazel eyes, pierced ears, stylish eyebrows. Her mother is dead. Her dad, Frank Steinbeck, is a retired NYC cop.

Objects. For her job as town marshal of Drake Island Village, Helene wears pressed jeans, button-down shirts, and a khaki jacket bearing the mermaid logo of the island. On the beach in summer she goes native: shorts, tank tops, Mexican huaraches. She drives a two-door green Explorer equipped with car phone and a spring-loaded holster for her Glock 9mm automatic. The holster is bolted to the transmission housing. She writes with a silver fountain pen. Inkwells in her office and in the study at home. The sleuth's lair is a cottage on the edge of the village. Zen interior, bare and peaceful. A few books. Barbara Walker's *Woman's Encyclopedia. American Heritage Dictionary.* The complete Willa Cather.

Character Links.

• *Killer.* Meeting killer Myra Jane Severance, Helene felt kinship—a connection with a soulmate—and danger. They both love poetry. The Marina Café is Helene's second home.

• *Victims.* Helene coached the young Lacey Anne in spelling, writing, reading aloud, dressing, walking, smiling, avoiding trouble. In a weak moment, Helene allowed herself to be seduced by Armand DuPre, who dies at midpoint. Armand has information about the Teen Angel murders. Edward Severance, the mayor, is Helene's boss.

• *Catalyst.* Helene connects with the Major through her books. The Major is a lecher; he eyes Helene like a side of beef. He gets her the town marshal job; she owes him.

Resource Base. As her book income dwindles, Helene needs a job. The Major, a power broker, gets her hired as town marshal. In solving the case, she will jeopardize her position. She loves Baxter's Bungalow. Her favorite room is the Quarterdeck, a raised platform in the big living room, built to copy the quarterdeck on Captain

Ahab's *Pequod:* jawbone tiller, pewter mug rack, rigging, mainmast, Ecuadorian doubloon, et cetera.

3. *Plotting with Scene Cards.*

Scene cards are stepping-stones, footholds for the sleuth. Other characters are wounded; they die; the sleuth must reach the end; must claim the sleuth's reward. From the examples below, take a minute to glean ideas for sleuth scene cards:

Scene Card for the "Crime Scene"

Suggestion: use death detail to show sleuth emotion. For example, is your sleuth cool and detached, like Miss Marple as she inventories the corpse in *Body?* Or is she horrified, like Arkady Renko viewing the death masks in *Gorky Park?*

Detail: When you create your scene card for the crime scene, it's a good idea to record the emotion for the reader in a reaction or a line of dialogue. Miss Marple inventories the body from the top down. Her only reaction ("She's very young") uses a muted sleuth sadness to conceal a clue.

Detail: If your sleuth reacts with horror, try masking her emotions. In *Gorky Park,* Arkady Renko hides behind a veil of cigarette smoke, "his habit whenever he dealt with the dead." While the sleuth smokes, a KGB officer cracks open the frozen clothing of the victims.

Detail: If your sleuth is a passive observer, like Dr. Kay Scarpetta in the crime scene of *All That Remains,* transfer the emotion to someone close to the victim, like the victim's mom: "As I stood by and watched, I could sense hope blossoming in her mind."

Putting the ideas to work: In the crime scene card for *Murder on Drake Island,* Helene Steinbeck clashes with the Major: she wants to gather evidence, follow the book; he wants an immediate manhunt for Julius Bugliosi. The Major shows only anger at the death of his granddaughter; the sleuth, on viewing the body, vomits.

• • •

Scene Card for "Re-creation of the Crime"

Suggestion: Use a game or an analogy to show the process of detection, which shows the workings of the sleuth mind.

Detail: When he re-creates the crime at militia HQ in *Gorky Park,* Arkady Renko has his men act out the murders in a role-playing game. With himself in the killer role, the sleuth casts his big detective as "Beast," the big male victim; the smaller detective plays "Red," who had red hair. "Beauty," the female victim, is played by a wooden chair.

Detail: When she re-creates the crime in *All That Remains,* Dr. Kay Scarpetta uses an analogy to military "kill zones," where officers in training hunt each other down at night. In Scarpetta's re-creation, the killer plays death games with the victims, running down the male while the trussed-up female watches. Analogy takes Dr. Scarpetta into the past, where, for a moment, she becomes the victim: "I held my hands in front of me, as if they were bound at the wrist."

Putting the ideas to work: In the Marina Café, Armand DuPre uses white napkins to represent the victims and a knife to represent the killer.

• • •

Scene Card for "First Encounter"

Suggestion: Use wardrobe items to measure sleuth power.

Detail: In that first meeting with Hannibal Lecter in his cage, the reader gets to know student sleuth Clarice Starling as the killer dissects her like a butterfly moth. Stripping away wardrobe items (the sleuth's good bag, cheap shoes, and cheap tiger's-eye beads), the killer defines the sleuth in economic terms: "a well-scrubbed, hustling rube with a little taste . . . not more than one generation out of the mines." The killer is right—the sleuth who has come to set him free is a poor girl clawing her way up.

Detail: When he meets Osborne in the bathhouse for party bigwigs, Arkady Renko wears a towel and some purplish bruises left by Kirwill, his American assailant. To show the power and sleek confidence of the killer, another American, the writer brings Osborne into the room naked. While the killer's brazen nakedness calls attention to his deep Arab tan, verifying his sun-god power, the sleuth is pale, ghostly, a wraith with lank Russian hair. Osborne's wealth, symbolized by his gold watch and gold lighter, defines the sleuth in economic terms. The killer is rich; the sleuth is poor.

Putting the ideas to work: The sleuth's first encounter with the killer in *Murder on Drake Island* takes place in the Marina Café. Armand DuPre, the crime writer, is re-creating Teen Angel murders One and Two. The killer enters, dressed beautifully, her hair lovely, her eyes hard and mocking. The sleuth is still muddy from the crime scene. Myra Jane flirts with Armand, taking his mind off the pattern of the crimes.

· · ·

Scene Card for the "Killer Confrontation"

Suggestion: Use the symbolism of the blood sacrifice to release sleuth emotion.

Detail: At the killer confrontation in *Fugitive,* the sleuth banters with the killer (a female of her generation) about the art of love. The banter masks danger as the killer asks: "What do you know about relationships?" The sleuth answers on a note of sadness: "Hey, I've been married twice." Because she holds the shotgun (it symbolizes the power of life and death), the killer can hit back ("You're divorced") with a tough-guy tone: "You don't know dick." Sadness and sleuth sympathy flood this scene when blood flows, when the killer loses her foot to a shotgun blast: "If love is what injures us," queries the sleuth, "how can we heal?"

Putting the ideas to work: When the sleuth confronts the killer in *Murder on Drake Island,* she wears full battle dress—boots and jeans and a heavy sweatshirt. The killer's scalpel represents the horror and precision of the Teen Angel murders. In her blood lust, the killer will sacrifice young and old alike to get control of the Major's fortune.

•   •   •

Scene Card for "Sleuth's Reward"

Suggestion: When you write the end of the book, use a physical object like money to focus the sleuth on the meaning of the scapegoat quest.

Detail: In *The Big Sleep*, Philip Marlowe turns down money—a hefty $15,000 offered by Vivian Regan—because it's dirty and because he's clean: "That would be the established fee. That was what he [the victim, Rusty Regan] had in his pockets when she shot him. That would be what Mr. Canino got for disposing of the body. . . ."

Detail: In *The Maltese Falcon,* Sam Spade hands over the killer, three pistols, the falcon, and a thousand-dollar bill he took from Gutman, payment for pain and suffering, defining himself as a tough guy of the hard-boiled school.

Detail: In *Fugitive,* Kinsey Millhone figures her time down to the nearest dollar: "I'm billing Royce Fowler for $1,832 against the two grand he advanced." Over the phone, the client says keep the change.

Putting the ideas to work: The sleuth of *Murder on Drake Island* wants to resign. The Major offers her more money to stay. When she refuses, the Major offers her lots more money to live at the bungalow, be his "companion." The sleuth refuses. Unlike the killer, she won't be bought.

•   •   •

At this early stage of preparing to write your mystery, you create scene cards to pull your sleuth through the book, from Act One to Act Two to Act Three. Focusing on the end of the book this early has benefits: the quest is over; the scapegoat-killer has paid; the sleuth is weary from the hunt. A weary sleuth at the end of the story might reveal the key that enables you to unlock the heart of the sleuth.

You use scene cards to display your sleuth fading, isolated, falling in love, fearful, lost, wounded, locked in the jaws of near death, and finally triumphant. Scene cards shoot Polaroids of your sleuth in motion.

• • •

As your scene cards multiply, driving the sleuth deeper into the book, you'll have enough sense of the character to start writing scenes. The easiest way to begin is to write some dialogue. Let the sleuth speak.

4. *The Sleuth Speaks.*

Miss Marple's first word when she answers her telephone in St. Mary Mead is "Yes." Arkady Renko's first word is "Exactly." Renko uses the word like a shield; he's trying to ward off the blustery invasion of the KGB major when he spits out the sleuth's name: "Renko!" Sam Spade's first words—he calls out, "Yes, sweetheart?" to Effie Perine—suggest a note of intimacy that's buried in the back story. When the phone rings, the weary Dr. Scarpetta refuses her call to adventure: "I'm not here," she tells her maid; when the maid persists, the sleuth dives deeper into avoidance. "No one's home," she says.

As you work with your scene cards, add dialogue lines. As you add dialogue, keep asking questions about what the dialogue means. When he leaves the crime scene where Miles Archer was killed, Sam Spade makes a phone call to report the crime. What does this phone call tell the reader? What is the sleuth's mood on leaving the scene of the crime? Is he sad? Bitter? Angry? Horrified? Edgy? Guilty? Joyful? Thoughtful? Analytical? Depressed? Resigned?

In this short telephone call to his helper, Sam Spade reveals himself as a tough guy who talks tough who is also unable to face the wife of his dead partner. The language in the phone call sounds edgy. The sleuth's speech is staccato: "Precious," says Spade to Effie. "You'll have to break it to Iva. . . . No, I'm damned if I will. You've got to do it." The sleuth of *Falcon,* a tough guy, can't report the crime. Why not? What's between Spade and Iva? What's happening? What's the secret here? Is the tough guy sleuth not so tough after all?

• • •

WORKING THE NOVEL

Exercises

1. *Back Story.*

Explore your sleuth's past by writing a couple of pages of back story. "Back story" is a specific set of events connected to the story that took place in the past before the book opens.

In this back story, you seek clues to the sleuth's penchant for the art and science of detection. Probe family connections—parents, siblings, grandparents—and economic status. Did your sleuth come from wealth or poverty? How did your sleuth get educated? When did your sleuth first fall in love? How did your sleuth crack his first case? What did it feel like to solve a crime? What made your sleuth select one style of operation (avenging angel versus solicitous protector of the innocent) over another?

2. *Scene Cards.*

Create half a dozen scene cards that define the sleuth at different stages of the book. You can add insights on your sleuth to cards for the crime scene and a visit to the Victim's Lair (Weekend 2), and also for the first encounter and the killer confrontation (Weekend 1). Scenes that help to define the sleuth are "Brush with Authority" and "Re-creation of the Crime."

As your scene cards multiply, keep asking questions: Is the sleuth feeling hot or cold? Courageous or fearful? Bold or reluctant? What's the sleuth seeing? Does the sleuth know more than the reader? Does the reader know more than the sleuth? If there is blood, how does the sleuth feel about blood? If there is money, how does the sleuth feel about money?

Sleuth's Reward is a very important scene because it closes the book. What does your sleuth get for his efforts? Money? Satisfaction? A jail term? Romance? A drink in a bar? A chance to lecture fellow professionals? A chance to set things right? On your scene card for "Sleuth's Reward," jot down options for your sleuth. How does your sleuth react to the reward? In *The Big Sleep*, the sleuth refuses General Sternwood's offer of a thousand dollars to find Rusty Regan, the victim killed by Miss Carmen. Then he refuses fifteen thousand offered by Vivian Regan, Rusty's ungrieving widow. Then he has a drink: "On the way downtown I stopped at a bar and had a couple of drinks. They didn't do me any good."

3. *Character Sketch.*

Collect your insights about the sleuth in a character sketch. Work quickly, without stopping to think and consider and ponder, while you let what you know shape a picture of your lead character. Start with the sleuth's exterior, with name and sex and age and body type. Body type includes details like height and weight and build and muscle tone and where your sleuth works, works out, eats lunch, stops for the morning double *latte*. Jot notes about wardrobe and footwear. What the sleuth wears informs the reader about income and lifestyle, about taste and fashion. Sleuths dress to fit in, to create a low profile in the mystery landscape.

Jot notes about feelings and moods, wants and needs, goals and desires. Who's the sleuth in love with? Who are the sleuth's enemies? What happened in the sleuth's childhood that drove her to become a sleuth?

Jot notes about behavior. What does your sleuth read? Listen to? Watch? What does the sleuth do on Saturday night? Sunday morning? Monday morning? Where does your sleuth bank? How much money's in the checking account? Does your sleuth play the stock market? Own real estate? Where does your sleuth shop for clothes? For a new car? For groceries?

With each entry, keep an eye out for details you can use in the book.

4. *The Sleuth Speaks.*

A smart sleuth can wind up in tight situations that demand quick thinking and sharp insights. The first tight situation in *Murder on Drake Island* occurs at the crime scene, where Lacey

Anne lies murdered. Before the sleuth can get organized, she has to look the Major in the eye. Huddled in his sheepskin coat, he sits alone in his big Chevrolet Suburban. The sleuth stands outside, feeling the wind. She raps on the window. It rolls down.

SLEUTH: Major?

MAJOR: Climb in here, Marshal. I need to talk to you.

SLEUTH: I'm sorry, Major. This is a terrible thing. Are you all right?

MAJOR: Come on. It's warm in here out of the wind.

SLEUTH: All right. I'm expecting the crime-lab people any minute. [The sleuth opens the door and climbs in. The interior of the Suburban smells like cigars and good whiskey. The Major holds out his silver flask.]

MAJOR: Have a pull on this.

SLEUTH: No, thanks. Where's Ripley?

MAJOR: Answering nature's call.

SLEUTH: He needs to stay clear of the crime scene.

MAJOR: Ripley knows what he's doing. Do you?

SLEUTH: I know procedure. We keep the crime scene clean. We wait for the crime-lab people.

MAJOR: I'd like to help you on this.

SLEUTH: It's a job for professionals, Major.

MAJOR: It's a job for a hunter, Marshal.

SLEUTH: Who are we hunting?

MAJOR: Julius Bugliosi. That trumpet player.

SLEUTH: We need evidence, Major.

MAJOR: Don't give me that. She's star struck. She's sixteen years old. He came after her. She fought him. Now she's dead.

SLEUTH: Major, I haven't even seen the body yet.

MAJOR: There she is.

SLEUTH: Oh, God. Oh, no.

• • •

With your sleuth talking, you're ready for Weekend 4.

• WEEKEND 4 •
CATALYST

The killer kills, the victim dies, and the sleuth tracks down the killer.

The catalyst—the fourth character you create before you start plotting—makes things happen. The catalyst for your story might be female or male, young or old or middle aged, rich or poor, amateur or professional, dressed or undressed. Your choice for catalyst might be a criminal or a cop, a reporter or an undertaker, a sick old man in a wheelchair or a wardrobe assistant in a shabby coat and torn vinyl boots. The catalyst might enter your story flashing money or a ruby stickpin or a pair of elegant legs. The catalyst is a change agent, a motivator driven by a deep inner need that drives the plot.

Because this is Weekend 4, and because of your hard work on character, you could have two or three candidates waiting to emerge as your catalyst. The catalyst candidate might be a friend of the sleuth, like Dolly Bantry in *Body*. Dolly is important because the book opens inside her head, in a dream of flower shows and English gardens. Dolly is handy to the plot because she helps the sleuth gain access to the body by clearing the policeman out of the way. When the setting shifts to the Majestic Hotel (the actual scene of the crime), Dolly uses her money and position to whisk the sleuth off to Danemouth, site of the Majestic, to help the sleuth get closer to the major players—the killer, who wants the resource base; Conway Jefferson, who controls the resource base; the bumbling police; and Florence Small.

The catalyst candidate might be a blood relation to one of the victims. Shana Timberlake in *Fugitive* is the victim's mother; William Kirwill in *Gorky Park* is the victim's older brother. The catalyst candidate might control a resource base, like General Sternwood in *The Big Sleep;* the catalyst might be the sleuth's boss, like Jack Crawford in *The Silence of the Lambs.*

A quick look at catalysts and connections:

• *"F" Is for Fugitive.* Royce Fowler, the father of both killer and scapegoat, is the catalyst for Grafton's *Fugitive.* Royce, a sick old man, is married to Ori Fowler, the killer's mom. Ori dies in her sickbed when the killer stabs her with a hypo to clear the way for her escape from Floral Beach: Dad is dying; with Mom dead, the killer can sell the motel and split for the bright lights of Los Angeles. Royce is connected to the sleuth when he hires her, a money connection that deepens when Royce makes a Freudian slip at the dinner table, calling the sleuth "Sis," a sudden but temporary adoption by a sick old man that sucks her deeper into the Fowlers' family feud. Royce owns the Floral Beach Motel, one of the resource bases in this mystery. Because Royce saves the sleuth's life at the climax, capping off the scapegoat quest, he gets chosen as the catalyst for *Fugitive*.

• *The Big Sleep*.   The catalyst for Chandler's hard-boiled tale is Vivian Regan. Vivian is the big sister of the killer, Miss Carmen Sternwood. She is the widow of Rusty Regan, the Irish adventurer who gets killed when he rejects Carmen's sexual advances in the back story. As the eldest daughter of General Sternwood, Vivian is connected to the resource base (the old man's fabled treasure house of wealth) that attracts the blackmailer Geiger. Vivian's back-story connections—with the kid sister who killed her husband—clinch her selection as catalyst.

• *The Body in the Library*.   The catalyst for *Body* is Conway Jefferson. A rich old man with control over a resource base, Conway tried to use the victim to replace his dead daughter Rosamund.

In his first appearance in the story, rich old man Conway displays his personal power by turning the tables on the police, taking over the interrogator role: "Now I want to ask some questions in my turn, if I may." Conway is important in the plot. When the police bungle the case, Conway calls in his old friend, Sir Henry Clithering, Scotland Yard, retired. Sir Henry, acting as Conway's cat's paw, calls in Miss Marple. At the climax, Miss Marple uses Conway as bait to trap the killer.

• *The Silence of the Lambs*.   The catalyst for a complex book like *Lambs*—two deadly killers, one controlling the capture of the other before he kills again; a neophyte student sleuth who gets a lesson in detecting; and a living, breathing victim who shares with the reader her fearful descent into hell—is Buffalo Bill, aka Jame Gumb.

Jame Gumb, a serial killer, kills to obtain the skins of large young women so he can make Mama Suits to satisfy his insane urge to become his own mother. To Jame Gumb, the large young women are a precious resource.

Guidelines for Choosing a Catalyst

To choose a catalyst, you run the candidates through a litmus test: 1) connects to other characters; 2) connects to the resource base; and 3) helps with the plot.

Let's say you were writing *The Maltese Falcon.* Your two candidates for the catalyst for this treasure-hunt mystery are Effie Perine, the sleuth's helper, and Caspar Gutman, the archcriminal and archquester for the bird.

1. *Connects to Other Characters.*

The catalyst for your mystery must connect to one of the main characters—killer, victim, sleuth—in the back story and must connect to one or more characters as the plot develops. It helps to specify the connection.

Candidate A—Effie: Effie and Spade are connected by money (he's her employer) and by sex in the back story (they were lovers in the past). She knew Miles Archer, one of the victims.

Candidate B—Gutman: Gutman is connected to killer Brigid O'Shaughnessy by money: they compete for possession of the bird. Gutman and Brigid are connected by greed in the back story: their lust for the jeweled bird brought them to San Francisco, Sam Spade's turf. Gutman connects to the victims at a distance, engineering their deaths while keeping his pudgy hands clean. He connects to the sleuth only when the sleuth gets possession of the bird. Both characters (Effie and Gutman) pass the test for character connection.

2. *Connects to the Resource Base.*

The black bird is the resource base for Falcon.

Candidate A—Effie: Effie Perine guards the bird; she transports it from the post-office drop to Spade's place. Because her connection to the falcon is so recent, Effie stays in her role as sleuth's helper.

Candidate B—Gutman: The fabled black bird is Gutman's life, his passion, his reason for being. Gutman revels in the bird's history. He spends every waking moment tracking down the jeweled treasure. Because his hunger for the object of desire drives Gutman to pursue Brigid O'Shaughnessy to San Francisco—where Brigid kills Miles Archer, where Spade refuses to accept Brigid's offering of twisted love—Gutman pulls ahead of Effie in the catalyst competition.

3. *Helps with the Plot.*

At this stage of the writing, with three characters in motion and a dozen scene cards stretching from the beginning through the middle to the end, you're hunting for a catalyst to help you develop the plot.

Candidate A—Effie: Effie Perine, a tall girl with motherly instincts, opens the book by introducing the killer to the sleuth. Effie knows the victim, Miles Archer; she's his employee until the night he dies. Because she knows the victim's widow, Iva Archer, Effie gets to break the awful news of Miles Archer's death. When the sleuth leaves the office to track down killer or bird, Effie functions as message board: "Your friend Dundy was in. He wanted to look at your guns." The writer uses Effie as the voice of irony. Dundy is a cop. He is not Spade's friend. Effie's reference to the sleuth's guns marks him as a tough guy and a hard-boiled lady killer.

A secretary like Effie is handy to have around when you start writing. When the killer needs a safe house, the sleuth sends her home with Effie. When the sleuth has a headache, Effie hugs him, allowing him certain liberties that suggest intimate connections in the back story: "She . . . stroked his temple with her slender fingers. He leaned back until the back of his head over the chair top rested against her breast." When Effie exits the stage to run an errand for the sleuth, she reenters in time to help him move the dead body of Captain Jacobi, master of the *La Paloma,* who dies on the doorstep when he delivers the stolen bird. In Chapter 19, Effie delivers the bird statue to Spade's place (the sleuth needs the bird's physical presence to close his barter deal with Gutman), then makes a happy exit so she can't be used against the sleuth as a bargaining chip: "Bye-bye." At the end of the story, the writer uses Effie to isolate the sleuth from human contact ("I know you're right. You're right. But don't touch me now—not now"), because he handed the killer over to the cops.

As the sleuth's helper, Effie Perine opens and closes the book. She runs errands; she holds down the office; she helps the sleuth hide the killer or move dead bodies; she delivers the bird on time.

A character like Effie Perine (she's close to the sleuth; yet she can keep her distance from him when it suits the writer's purpose) helps you develop a note of ambiguity, one of the keynotes of good mystery writing. But she doesn't dominate scenes like Gutman.

Candidate B—Gutman: Caspar Gutman dominates the last half of the story. Gutman hires Wilmer, the boyish hitman, to kill both Floyd Thursby (the killer's accomplice who was supposed to kill Miles Archer) and Captain Jacobi (the sea captain who wanted the bird for himself). In mystery fiction, killing power translates into plot power: Gutman pushes a button and people die.

As the architect of crime and an unforgettable villain who controls resources (Gutman has money but no visible means of support), Caspar Gutman is a thirties precursor to the big-brain death-god killers like Osborne and Hannibal Lecter. With a big body that matches his big brain, Caspar Gutman overshadows the other questers, controlling the atmosphere, the mood, the topic of conversation, the air they breathe. The moment he enters in Chapter 11 of *Falcon,* Gutman's very bulk gives him presence: "The fat man was flabbily fat with bulbous pink cheeks and lips and chins and neck, with a great soft egg of a belly that was all his torso, and pendant cones for arms and legs." Whereas Effie helps the sleuth, Gutman manipulates him by withholding the secret of the bird: "I don't know for certain that I'm going to tell you [about the bird]." In Chapter 13, Gutman makes a permanent place for himself in crime fiction when he delivers his detailed lecture on the history of the jeweled bird: "All right, sir. Grand Master Villiers de l'Isle d'Adam had this foot-high jeweled bird made by Turkish slaves in the castle of St. Angelo and sent it to Charles, who was in Spain." In Chapter 18, Gutman faces off with the sleuth in a barter situation: ten thousand dollars in exchange for the bird. In Chapter 19, Gutman sweats and wheezes as he scrapes the black paint off the bird. At the climax of the tale he hisses like a snake when he discovers his desired object is a fake. Because Gutman is present at the climax, and because his discovery of fakery ends this phase of the treasure hunt, he gets the nod for the catalyst role.

Choosing Gutman for the catalyst would help you develop scene cards, the first step in generating scenes for the book.

Creating a Catalyst for Murder on Drake Island

From the writing already done on Weekends 1–3, we know that Major Philip Baxter is the catalyst for our write-along mystery. The Major controls the resource base—real estate and money—that makes him the power on the island. The visible symbol of his resource base is Baxter's Bungalow, a big house numbering twenty-five rooms, built on the rocks above South Beach. When you are confronted with a similar situation—the character appears as if born from a lotus plant sprouting from your forehead—you still need to do some character work, either a profile or a sketch, to organize what you know.

Character Profile

> *Name:* Major Philip Baxter
> *Sex:* Male
> *Age:* The Major's in his early sixties.
> *Income:* He controls vast wealth. Real Estate. Money.
> *Body/Figure:* The Major is a burly man. Powerful arms from wheeling his wheelchair.
> *Scars/Wounds:* His legs are cut off at the knee. It happened in

Mexico sixteen years ago. A car accident took his wife and his daughter and his legs.

Wardrobe Indicators: The Major's favorite wardrobe item is a hunter's vest with thirteen pockets. He wears his Teddy Roosevelt safari hat indoors and out. In bed with the killer, the Major wears a silk blindfold.

Wants/Needs/Desires: The Major wants to bring his granddaughter back to life. He wants to punish Julius Bugliosi for her death. He wants sympathy and pecan pies from the killer. He wants the sleuth to head the manhunt that nabs Julius.

Enemies: The Major's major enemy is time. The enemy out to get him is the killer. In a key scene in Act Two, the Major vanquishes an easy foe, Edward Severance, the guilt-riddled father of Lacey Anne.

Skills/Education/Training: Because Dad sent Young Phil to military school when he was six, the Major chose Harvard over Yale—Dad's alma mater. He plays chess. A good infantry officer whose deeper wish was to command armor in battle. He's good with numbers—does them in his head—so he can trip up his accountant. The Major can smell money.

Function in the Story: Like the Fisher King in the Grail Quest, the Major is a sick old man. His sickness is revealed in his manipulations of other people. The voice lessons that he forces on his granddaughter backfire when she owns the Sound that could make Julius Bugliosi famous. The Major gets the sleuth hired as town marshal so she will owe him big time. The Major, knowing how badly Myra Jane wants to preside over Baxter's Bungalow, uses her for sex. The Major is a twisted tree.

• • •

WORKING THE NOVEL

Exercises

1. *Connections.*

Develop connections between the catalyst and the characters from the first three weekends. Make sure you note the specific kind of connection: blood or family, money or business, sex or twisted love, et cetera. For example, if you have two candidates in a heated race for catalyst—like William Kirwill and Irina Asanova from *Gorky Park*—you might test them with a quick checklist.

• *The Killer and Kirwill:* Kirwill knows Osborne only by reputation. When Kirwill sees Osborne at the sable compound, he dies by the knife. They are connected by Kirwill's revenge, an unsuccessful blood-sacrifice because the detective dies before he executes the killer.

• *The Killer and Irina:* Irina sleeps with John Osborne, a sexual connection, trading her Siberian flesh for America. He's rich and she's poor. He's American and she wants to go to America. Irina introduces the killer to James Kirwill. Irina connects Osborne to Valerya, a friend from Siberia. Valerya works at the Irkutsk Fur Center.

• *The Victim and Kirwill:* Kirwill knows Jimmy Kirwill, one of the Gorky Park victims, but not the other two. The Kirwill boys are related by blood and also by guilt. When big brother Bill sends little brother Jimmy out of the country, he sends him to his death. Driven by his guilt, Kirwill seeks revenge on the killer.

• *The Victims and Irina:* Irina knew all three victims. She introduced Jimmy Kirwill—a fellow student at the university— to Osborne. She made the connection between Osborne and Valerya. When she dies, Valerya is wearing ice skates borrowed from Irina.

• *The Sleuth and Kirwill:* Kirwill connects to the sleuth with vodka when he toasts Pasha Pavlovich, Renko's friend and militia helper: "Here's to your dead detective." At Iamskoy's dacha outside Moscow, Kirwill saves the sleuth's life by killing a KGB agent. In New York, like Virgil the poet leading Dante into the Inferno, Kirwill leads the sleuth into the midnight hell of the night court and the Manhattan pens.

• *The Sleuth and Irina:* Irina is connected to the sleuth by twisted love. On their first meeting, he likes her legs. On their second meeting, she stabs a white birch with her cigarette and the sleuth feels the burn on his skin. On their third meeting, Renko saves Irina from KGB poison, administered by hypo in the Moscow Metro. Because Irina uses her body to connect the sleuth and the killer, she's a natural choice for catalyst: "What two men better deserve to be alone than a killer and his investigator? Men who approached each other from the opposite side of the dead—also from the opposite sides of a bed."

2. *Resource Base.*

In a passage of narrative summary, explore your catalyst's connections to the resource base. If you had chosen Irina Asanova as catalyst, your passage might start out something like this: "Irina is my catalyst. She enters the story dressed like Cinderella in ripped vinyl boots and a shabby coat. In the first few moments she uses the sleuth for a punching bag. She's beautiful; she's blind in one eye. For Irina, America is the resource base. To get to America, she attaches Osborne to Valerya, who connects him to six sables from the Fur Center in Irkutsk. To get to Osborne, Irina bewitches him with her body, her love magic. The killer wants Irina's body so bad he brings her to America, dressing her in gold and fur. She has changed on the outside— using American makeup to hide the scar left by the KGB—but on the inside she . . ."

As you write, let your mind land on specific detail: What is the catalyst wearing when she enters the story? Is she encased in mink and dripping with diamonds? Is she wearing a borrowed wardrobe because hers is too shabby? Is she wearing a shabby coat and ripped boots?

What does the catalyst do in that first entrance? Does she

function as a gatekeeper, opening the door between the sleuth and the killer? Does she come awake from a pretty dream and scream when she finds a body next to the bed? Does she display her elegant legs, those smooth body parts that symbolize wealth and leisure and power? Does she flash money around? Does she buy something really expensive? Does she steal a sandwich from a tray?

What does the catalyst want? Does she want a piece of the resource base? Does she want to protect the resource base? Vivian Regan, a female who has not produced children, protects her kid sister, who appears nude not only in photos, but also in the sleuth's bed. This flagrant nudity (flagrant in 1940) suggests that the kid sister is a resource, a nubile female bursting to breed.

If the catalyst is already in control of a resource base, what does he want now? Conway Jefferson, the catalyst for *Body,* wants the killer who killed his Cinderella. When he finds out the killer's identity, Conway agrees to help the sleuth bait her trap. Conway is not only protecting his resource base, he's using its power for revenge.

If you apply the same test to Royce Fowler, the catalyst for *Fugitive,* the answer is different. Royce Fowler's resource base is the family motel. Because the killer hates the motel, she kills her mother, sweeping her out of the way of a quick sale once Royce dies. When Royce intrudes on the killer at the climax, he's carrying family photos of Mom, trying to patch the family back together again. His clumsy attempts to control his killer daughter save the sleuth's life. Payment for Royce is his daughter's loss of her foot, a symbolic sacrifice filled with irony, since her dream was to run away from Royce forever.

3. *Profile.*
When you have finished exercises 1 and 2, use a character profile to gather your insights about the catalyst. With a profile, your goal is to discover motive. The movement is from basic information like name, sex, age, income, wardrobe, etc., to need and desire—what the character wants. If you can focus on need

and desire, you'll develop an agenda for the character. Agenda, action taken to achieve a goal, generates a situation that creates a scene that pulses with drama. We'll be dealing with scenes in more detail starting on Weekend 10, but for this weekend you can work smarter if you start thinking about the dramatic situation now. Let's start our profile of Irina with basic information:

Name: Irina Asanova

Sex: Female

Age: Irina's in her early twenties.

Income: She's a poor girl, a Siberian Cinderella.

Body/Figure: Irina is slender. The sleuth admires her legs.

Scars/Wounds: Irina has a scar on her cheek. She's blind in one eye. The scar came from an operation that was botched on purpose to leave a mark, the brand of the KGB.

Wardrobe Indicators: When she enters the story, Irina's dressed like Cinderella—torn vinyl boots and a shabby coat. In the middle of the story, she wears a bedsheet with nothing on underneath. The lovers make love. At the end of the story, possessed by the killer, she wears gold and fur.

Wants/Needs/Desires: Irina wants to escape Siberia. She wants to stay warm. She wants some new boots. She does not want to fall in love with the sleuth because it spoils her plans: getting to America. She needs the sleuth's love.

Enemies: Irina's major enemy is the KGB. An American at heart, she hates the Soviet bureaucracy.

Skills/Education/Training: Irina's educated. She knows the work of Anton Chekhov. She's trained as a lawyer, so she knows the law. Her main skill is debate. Her terse words stab like daggers. When the KGB agents come for her, Irina swears to implicate Renko: "I can drag a friend down with me or I can drag you. I've thought it over. I want to take you."

Function in the Story: Irina is a femme fatale, a death goddess who presides over the sleuth's execution of the killer, and also a fatalist who sees death everywhere. If you fall into Siberian water, Irina says, you have two ways of freezing: first, you can freeze to death if you stay in the water; second, you can freeze to death if you climb out. Death, death, death.

Best Dialogue Line: Moments after the sleuth executes the killer, Irina is about to depart the bloody sable compound, leaving him in the cold while she escapes to America and eternal warmth. She cries. She stops crying. She takes a deep breath. "For snow like this," she says, "I should have felt boots."

4. *Scene Cards.*
Develop scene cards for the catalyst. On each scene card, jot notes about time and place, temperature and season, light and shadow, objects in the scene. Are the objects new? Or are they resurfacing from a previous scene? Jot notes about who else is in the scene. Who talks to whom? What is the subject of their dialogue? Jot notes about wardrobe as an indicator not only of temperature and season (bikinis for the heat; parkas for the cold, and so on), but also as a clue to economic and social status.

Hints for scene cards could be hidden in the work you have already done. For example, if you were tracking a Cinderella character like Irina Asanova from her entrance to her exit, you could use wardrobe items to help you generate scenes. Taking wardrobe insights from the character profile, you would create three scenes:

• *Siberian Cinderella.* Irina enters the story as a set dresser for Mosfilm Studios. Her wardrobe (shabby coat, ripped boots, et cetera) displays her poverty. Dialogue rises from the boots: "You see the director of this film? He promised me a pair of fur-lined boots if I slept with him. Do you think I should?" When the sleuth lights her cigarette, Irina mocks him. Before the sleuth exits, Irina asks him for another cigarette. A beneficent sleuth, he gives her the pack.
• *Bedsheet Beauty.* Reviving from her near-death experience in the metro, Irina wears a bedsheet to greet the sleuth. In a classic case of twisted love, Irina hates the sleuth and still loves him. Following the union triggered by the bedsheet, the sleuth treats her like a hostile witness (probing her connection with Osborne and Valerya), so she stabs him with more words: "We're still enemies."

- *American Princess.* In New York, Irina forces Osborne to force the FBI to force the KGB to bring Renko out of Russia to America. When she appears to Renko, she's wearing Osborne's gold. There's a fur coat in the closet. In a fancy apartment furnished by Osborne, there's a full wardrobe for America.

Since Irina as femme fatale presides over Osborne's execution at the sable compound in New Jersey, you would add her to your card for "Killer Confrontation." Since she doesn't die in the Moscow metro, you would create a rebirth scene where she comes back to life. Irina is the star player in the sleuth's final re-creation of the crime in the shabby rooms where Valerya lived with Kostia in a Moscow suburb. A good catalyst generates scene cards like "Final Re-creation of the Crime" for the last half of your book.

Because Renko's lust for the truth shatters their love, Irina falls into the clutches of the sleuth's boss, Andrei Iamskoy. Because one of her needs is revenge on the KGB, Irina shoots Iamskoy. As we'll see in the plotting section, her action at the university fountain not only satisfies her lust for revenge; it also closes the first two acts of *Gorky Park*. When an important scene surfaces on one of your cards, mark it so you'll remember to check it out later. Give it a name—something like "Iamskoy's Blood" or "The Drowning Pool"—and label it as a possible "Key Scene" in red marker in bold letters.

With four characters created, you're ready to start plotting.

Weekends 5–9
Plotting

Plot is an arrangement of parts, the way you choose to put your book together. The story happens in chronological order: A comes before B and B comes before C and C comes before D, a logical sequence of ABCD, et cetera, according to the way things actually happened. The plot is the way you reorder the events to create suspense, to set up your mystery, to hook your reader into reading.

To see how this reordering works for your tale, identify the parts of the story and then play with them, shifting some parts out of order. Part A, for example, is the murder, the killing that jump-starts your sleuth to take on the hunt for the killer who must pay. Part B is the discovery of the body. Part C is reporting the crime, letting the world know the awful truth. Part D is bringing the sleuth onstage at the crime scene, ready to hunt.

The Body in the Library, for example, starts with Part C, a housemaid in a country manor reporting the crime to her mistress, who sends her husband to check it out. Part B, the discovery of the body by the butler, has already happened offstage, as the mistress of the house lay dozing. Part A, the murder, happened last night. Strangled with a sash in another location, the victim was then moved to the hearthrug at Gossington.

Moving the corpse is smart plotting: if the corpse is misidentified, leading the police astray, then your sleuth has a chance to solve the crime.

Plotting is your chance to rearrange chronological events to create suspense, the way Christie does in *Body:*

Chronological Events	Christie's Rearranged Plot
A—Murder	C—Reporting by Maid—Includes B
B—Discovery	B—Discovery by Butler in Back Story
C—Reporting	D—Crime Scene/Sleuth Onstage
D—Crime Scene	A—Murder in Component Parts

Starting the story with Part C, reporting the crime, with Parts A and B hidden in the recent past, is a plotting device. Because of the disruption of the linear sequence of A-B-C, the reader is left in suspense about how things happened. Suspense about what happened (murder) and why it happened (motive) gives the writer a reason to bring the sleuth into the story, Part D. The reader learns about Part A—how the killer killed the victim and why—as the sleuth re-creates the crime. When you plot, you subdivide Part A, the actual murder, into its component parts (motive, opportunity, stalking, killing, disposal, et cetera), and then you string out the components as clues along the killer's trail.

Gorky Park opens with Part D, the sleuth entering the story at the crime scene. Part C, the reporting of the crime, happens before the book opens. Part B, the discovery of the body, is reported in a terse summary on the first page of the book: before the book opens, a park guard leaves the path to relieve himself and finds three frozen corpses. The guard reacts by freezing: "Then he saw them, himself half undone, as it were, and just about froze too." Discovery and reporting and sleuth coming onstage happen in April, creating a time gap that has to be filled. Part A, the murder of the three corpses, took place in February, more than two months ago. Finding out what happened between February and April will lead the sleuth into the past.

Choosing where to start your book is easier if you know what happens when you subdivide Part A, exploding the moment of the murder, using specific scenes to contain murder weapons and wounds and wardrobe items. Scenes are like building blocks; they help you to structure your book. From your work on character for Weekends 1–4, you already have a dozen or more scene cards with names like "Crime Scene" and "First Encounter" and "Re-creation of the Crime" and "Victim's Lair." With your scenes contained by scene cards, you can spread them out and play with the order of events. For a standard size mystery, a double-spaced manuscript of 250–300 pages, you will need around thirty to forty scenes.

The choices you make now about arranging your plot determines the scenes you need to create next. To keep the order of events clear in your own mind, you create cards that take you into the back story:

A—*Murder:*   three hours ago.
B—*Discovery:*   deep night, by the Major.
C—*Reporting:*   the Major calls the sleuth.
D—*Crime Scene:*   the sleuth enters the story.

· · ·

For dramatic effect, you might start your story at Part B, pumping shock into the discovery of the body by an innocent child. Part C, reporting the crime, could subdivide into several component parts as the circle of communication expands. Part D, the sleuth entering the story, brings order out of chaos.

If you choose to start your book with Part D, the sleuth entering the story at the crime scene, then you make room in the plot for several scenes where the sleuth re-creates the crime. You need to be clear about your purpose in plotting. When you choose to keep the violence and blood of Part A offstage, away from the eyes of the reader, you make a plot decision to replay the killing again and again, re-creating it as new evidence surfaces. When he first re-creates Osborne's killing in Chapter 2, the sleuth of *Gorky Park* has never heard of Osborne. Because he doesn't know the names of the victims, he names them. GP1, a male Europoid, is named Beast. GP3, a female Europoid, is named Beauty. GP2, a male Europoid with red hair, is named Red. The clue that surfaces here is leather on the slug that killed Beast. The killer fired through a leather bag held against Beast's chest. The leather bag is missing from the crime scene.

The mystery reader wants answers to the same questions you've been asking yourself these last four weekends: Who died? Why did they die? Who killed them? What was the killer's motive? What weapon was used? Where is the weapon? Who will catch the killer? How will the killer pay?

Because the reader wants answers, a complete picture filled in bit by bit, the writer holds something back. When you conceal something from the reader at the crime scene in Chapter 1, you give yourself an opportunity to reveal it later. The leather bag not found at the *Gorky Park* crime scene in Chapter 1 surfaces as tiny traces of leather in a laboratory report; this enables the sleuth to develop the leather bag theory in Chapter 2 when he re-creates the crime with his two detectives. The leather bag as a physical object turns up in Chapter 12, deep in the book, after the sleuth's helper has been murdered. In Chapter 12 the writer uses the leather bag as one element in male bonding, as the sleuth recruits a replacement helper.

Scene cards help you keep track of details. On your card for Part A, the killing scene, you might jot something like this: "Showing the prescient foresight of a death god, Osborne kills Kostia first. Kostia's big, dangerous; he needs to be nullified. Holding the bag against Kostia's chest and smiling like a buddy, Osborne fires. The slug goes through the leather bag. After killing, Osborne tosses the bag down the sewer."

• On your card for Part D, the sleuth at the crime scene, you would note "Killer's leather bag missing. Leather traces on the slug dug out by KGB Officer Pribluda."

• On your card for the first re-creation of the crime, you would note the role playing, the casting of the two detectives, the sleuth's focus on the leather traces, the assumption that the missing leather bag held food.

• On your card for the recovery of the bag later in the book, you would fix the setting, an early morning along the banks of the

Moscow River, divers working, the sleuth on the bank with his replacement helper. With two main characters onstage, you might jot down dialogue lines. The sleuth asks: "Who was James Kirwill?" Because of your work on Weekends 1–4, you know the connection is familial; you know the answer. The replacement helper answers: "He was my brother."

Making notes on scenes as they surface from the material gives you a growing stack of scene cards. As you order the parts of your plot, ideas pop about character and motive and clues and atmosphere. Jot these ideas on your note cards. Before the note card is filled, you will have ample material for writing the scene. With a stack of scene cards and notes on more scenes, you're already plotting the book. The next five weekends will guide you to a coherent plot.

You'll begin on Weekend 5 by developing a back story that re-creates the crime. In *Gorky Park,* for example, the February murders precede the April discovery by two months, but the killer first tasted blood a quarter of a century ago when he killed three German officers for laughing at him in wartime Leningrad. Osborne's first taste of blood comes from the back story: Leningrad, snow, cannibalistic Russians, the burn of scornful laughter.

The body in the library at Gossington arrived last night, before the story opens. The body in *The Silence of the Lambs* (Part B, discovery of the corpse) doesn't surface until deep in Act One. The body in *The Big Sleep*—it surfaces at the climax of the book—was dumped into the sump before the book opens. The body in *"F" Is for Fugitive* was killed on the beach seventeen years ago.

Back-story work helps you decide how to arrange things for your reader. Before you start writing, you must create a step-by-step chain of events for the crime that starts your story. As the story unfolds, your sleuth re-creates the crime by digging up the past. The past that gets dug up comes from the writing for this weekend.

On Weekend 6, you'll develop key scenes and Aristotle's three-act structure of beginning, middle, and end. Key scenes at the beginning and end frame your plot, giving you a sense of closure. A key scene marks the middle of your plot, the halfway mark, the point of no return. A key scene marks the high point of your plot, where the action peaks, where a blood sacrifice occurs. Key scenes are handy for closing off Acts One and Two.

On Weekend 7, you'll use a plot diagram to clarify the plotting ideas you have developed so far. The diagram is a simple line that rises to simulate rising action that peaks at a climax. The diagram is a way of visualizing parts of your plot—like taking a Polaroid snapshot that shows you in pictorial form how the parts connect, how they work together, what's been left out.

On Weekend 8, you'll springboard from the plot diagram to generate a subplot for your mystery. The main plot is the quest for the real killer, the one who must be made to pay; the subplot is a secondary story, a kind of plot "beneath" the plot. Writers use subplots for comic relief—Christie's cops stumbling about on the false trail—and also to create texture in the book. Texture is important for giving the reader a sense of weight and gravity.

On Weekend 9, you'll collect the ideas and insights into a synopsis. At this early stage of the writing, you'll create a working synopsis to use as a blueprint for writing. When you finish the book, when the killer is caught and the victims have been avenged, you'll write a more polished synopsis that helps you sell the book.

You'll write the working synopsis in five parts: Back Story; Act One; Act Two, first half; Act Two, second half; and Act Three. Writing a synopsis gives you a vision of the story as a whole. Using narrative summary, you write your way to the end; writing to the end gives you a sense of closure.

· WEEKEND 5 ·
BACK STORY

To write an entertaining mystery, one that buzzes with suspense, you must know the past that contains Part A of your story—the killing place that creates the crime scene that brings the sleuth into the mystery.

To secure the past, you create a back story. As we suggested earlier, the term *back story* means the specific events in the past that control the story in the present.

In *The Body in the Library,* for example, the dead blond victim just reported by the maid (but not yet verified by the master of the house) is downstairs on the library hearthrug because of events in the back story. The victim's blond hair, a rinse-and-dye job from the back story, is the first clue to surface in the book. The dramatic device used by the writer to bring the blond hair into the story is a brief monologue delivered by the master of Gossington, Colonel Arthur Bantry. About to become the Prime Suspect, Colonel Bantry opens the investigation by making light of mystery novels like the one he's appearing in right now: "You know, Lord Edgbaston finds a beautiful blonde dead on the library hearthrug. Bodies are always being found in libraries in books."

The Colonel's brusque comment in Gossington's master bedroom takes place in the present. The book has started; this is Scene One, Chapter 1. The comment, a veiled denial, is triggered by an event from the past: last night, a killer killed a victim. The body found in the present raises questions about the past: Was the victim killed on the hearthrug at Gossington? Was she killed somewhere else? If she was killed somewhere else, how did she arrive at the library? What time did she arrive? What was the conveyance, the means of transport? Was there more than one killer? If she was killed someplace else, how much time elapsed between the killing and her arrival? How was she killed? And why?

As the book unfolds, information from the back story is used to develop the plot. In Chapter 2 of *Body,* for example, following that single clue—the blond hair of the corpse—leads the police to question the designated scapegoat about a look-alike blonde. Surprised to see the look-alike blonde when she comes onstage walking, talking, and very much alive, the police scrub her from the victim list. Since the look-alike blonde is not the victim, the search goes on. As more clues surface, popping up from the past into the present, the blond hair will fade in importance as a plot device. To write this brief interrogation of the scapegoat early in Act One, the writer must know *now* what the reader doesn't know *yet*—information buried in the back story.

The red herring that Christie uses to open her second Miss Marple mystery—Colonel Bantry's brusque reference to beautiful dead blondes; the blond hair in Constable Palk's first police report; the arrival of the look-alike girlfriend (alive) while the police question the scapegoat about her death; Dolly Bantry's breathless repetition of "A blonde. A beautiful blonde"; the sleuth's first assessment of "unnaturally fair hair"—rests on a firm foundation of back story.

The back story you develop for your mystery is aimed at the murder that creates the crime scene that brings the sleuth onstage, a familiar call to adventure. As the sleuth probes the past, the back story opens up. Before you can bury the clues for your book, you develop a solid back story by focusing on concrete physical detail: time and place, weather and lighting, transportation (arrival and departure of victim and killer), choice of weapons, et cetera.

Guidelines to Writing Back Story

You work out back story in three steps. *Step One* is to gather materials by grubbing around in the past. As you dig up the past, a back-story checklist (see below) will trigger your creativity. *Step Two* is to decide what happens first in your back story and what happens next and what happens after that. *Step Three* is writing a narrative summary.

1. *Checklist.*
The sample checklist that follows asks questions that set up the crime, the motive, and the method. The work that you have done on character will be helpful here. Using the checklist provided with the exercises, the writer fills in the blanks. Sample answers develop back story for *Murder on Drake Island,* our write-along mystery:

Time: What time does the killing occur? Is it night or day? Morning or noon?

Filling in: The killer killed Lacey Anne around 1:00 A.M.

Place: Where does the killing occur? Is it inside or outside? If outside, on land or water? Desert? Parking lot? Snowy place? If inside, what sort of compartment? Room? Cockpit? Automobile? If a conveyance, is it moving or standing still?

Filling in: The victim is killed in the mud at a curve on South Beach Road, about a mile from Baxter's Bungalow, her home.

Lighting: Describe the light source. If daylight, is it sunny or cloudy? If we're inside, how dark is it? How does the killer see?

Filling in: It's dark in the night in the rain. Light comes from the headlights of the death van.

Weather: Describe the weather during the killing. Stormy? Calm? Raining? Snowy? Warm? Hot? Cold? Freezing? How do weather conditions contribute to the murder? What's the temperature?

Filling in: The weather is cold and rainy. The rain slacks off as the killer finishes slitting the victim's throat. The killer wears a rain slicker and rubber rain boots.

Arrival: How did the killer get here? Car? Boat? Plane? Bike? Train? Motor scooter? Skis? Skates? What time does the killer arrive? How did the victim get here? Did she arrive with the killer? Did she have to wait? Was the killer already here, waiting?

Filling in: To reach the crime scene, the killer drove a Marina Café delivery truck with four-wheel drive. The victim arrived in the death van with Julius Bugliosi, the designated scapegoat.

Departure: How does the victim leave the crime scene? Is she moved from one site to another? How does the killer leave? Any last-minute rituals before leaving?

Filling in: Lacey Anne leaves the crime scene in a crime-lab van. There is no morgue on the island; she is taken to the treatment room of the emergency clinic. The killer leaves the scene behind the wheel of the death van. After parking the van near the scapegoat's hotel, the athletic killer jogs back for the Marina Café vehicle.

Struggle: Is there a struggle preceding the murder? A tussle between victim and killer? How even are the odds? If there is a struggle, what clues develop here?

   Filling in: Lacey Anne struggles, but the killer is too strong for her. Julius does not struggle because he's been knocked unconscious when the van ran off the road.

Death Instruments: What murder weapon is used? Where does it come from? Is the choice of weapons random—something grabbed up at the last minute—or a matter of careful choice? How does the killer dispose of the weapon? If there is more than one weapon, describe how it is used by the killer.

   Filling in: The killer kills Lacey Anne with the same scalpel she used on Victims One and Two. The scalpel was stolen from the pathology lab at the university. The scalpel is kept in the killer's desk drawer in her office at the Marina Café.

Wounds: How is the victim wounded by murder? Is this a bloody murder or a bloodless one?

   Filling in: The victim's throat is slashed. Also her wrists. Her womb is removed, a serial-killer trademark in this case.

Wardrobe and Makeup: How was the victim dressed for murder? Was there a costume change? Before the murder? After? Why was there a costume change? How was the killer dressed? What wardrobe items—clothes, jewelry, hairpins, et cetera—were left at the crime scene? Was makeup used to alter or disguise the corpse? Were other means used to disguise the corpse?

   Filling in: For her evening performance, Lacey Anne wore a lace tunic over a spaghetti-strap chemise of pale silk. After stripping the corpse, the killer fitted her with a leather thong bikini, with a triangular patch of silk covering the crotch.

· · ·

The objects you discover using this checklist will change the way you write each book. As you develop the checklist, you'll realize the importance of a single detail. For example, the murder weapon:

• *Gorky Park.* The murder weapon in *Gorky Park* is a pistol. A leather bag is used to muffle the shots. The time is twilight. The month is February, so the killer knows the bodies won't be found until the thaw. The murder weapon is foreign made; the caliber, 7.65mm, is not Russian. The assumed non-Russian pistol is an early clue that the killer is American.

• *The Big Sleep.* Rusty Regan was killed with Carmen Sternwood's little pistol. He's too big for Carmen to move, so she gets help from her big sister, Vivian, who calls Eddie Mars, her criminal buddy. The murder weapon from the back story becomes the central image at the climax, when the sleuth hands over Carmen's little gun loaded with blanks. She reveals her true killer self when she shoots at the sleuth.

• *"F" Is for Fugitive.* The murder weapon is a belt. The belt belongs to the scapegoat, Bailey Fowler. The killer is Bailey's sister, Ann Fowler. The victim dies because she's pregnant. The secret father is the heartthrob of Ann Fowler, who loves from afar. A quarrel between Bailey and the victim blossoms into a fight on the beach. When Bailey stumbles away, drunk, his sister moves in for the kill. The murder weapon from seventeen years ago surfaces in Chapter 23 in a sleuth's dialogue line: "Maybe she was jealous of Jean and wrapped a belt around her neck."

• • •

2. *Chronology.*
Creating a chronology helps you organize the material from your writing on Weekends 1–4 when it's combined with the detail from the checklist. The example below continues our work for *Murder on Drake Island:*

1. *Graduation Night.* Annie Lee Baxter, a rich girl, is impregnated by Edward Severance, a married man. Rushed to Mexico for an abortion, Annie Lee defies her parents by choosing to keep her baby. To cover up the bastard child, father Major Philip Baxter concocts a fake marriage certificate with a non-existent Mexican.

2. *Automobile Accident.* An automobile accident in Mexico kills Annie Lee and her mother. The Major, losing his legs, is confined to a wheelchair. With feelings of guilt and love, he raises his granddaughter, born out of wedlock two months before the death of his daughter.

3. *Killer as College Call Girl.* Working her way through college as a high-priced call girl, the killer falls in love with Baxter's Bungalow on Drake Island. Inhabited by the rich old man and his granddaughter, the bungalow is the resource base that represents the sanctuary of the good life to the killer, who grew up in poverty.

4. *Killer Snares Edward.* Rejected as wife material by the Major, the killer marries Edward Severance, now divorced.

5. *The Marina Café.* With financing from the Major, the killer opens the Marina Café. One autumn day, the sleuth, newly arrived, wanders in for a *caffelatte.*

6. *New Town Marshal.* The killer connects the sleuth to the Major, who hires the sleuth to tutor Lacey Anne. Helped by the Major, the sleuth becomes the new town marshal.

7. *Music Lessons.* To help a down-and-out opera singer, the Major pays for music lessons for Lacey Anne. She surprises everyone by revealing a world-class voice.

8. *The Trust Fund.* After a bout of sickness, the Major establishes a trust fund for Lacey Anne. If anything should happen to him, the trust takes control of the Baxter millions.

9. *Plotting the Murder.* Threatened by the trust fund, the killer realizes she must act now to grab the resource base. She will kill Lacey Anne, framing a scapegoat to take the blame. As a member of the Festival Committee, the killer signs Julius Bugliosi and his band for this year's festival.

10. *Victims One and Two.* To set up a serial-killer pattern, the killer murders two teenagers. The place of the murders is the mainland, close to gigs by Julius and his band, Reggae Nouveau.

11. *Music Connection.* The killer convinces the rich old man to allow the granddaughter to rehearse with Julius's band. The old man reluctantly agrees. With her lovely voice, the granddaughter captures the hearts of the band boys because she produces the Sound that can make Julius and the Reggae Nouveau famous. Another instance of the victim as resource base.

12. *The Death Van.* To secure Lacey Anne's voice for future concerts, Julius drives through the rain for a midnight meeting with the Major. Beside him in the death seat, smoking a joint, is Lacey Anne.

3. *Narrative Summary*

Writing a narrative summary transforms the material into prose that could become useful as you write the book. Since you're writing about the victim, begin with identification: "The body on South Beach Road is Lacey Anne Baxter, the granddaughter of Major Philip Baxter." Then you add motive, why she was killed: "Lacey Anne was killed to give killer Myra Jane Severance a clear shot at the Major's wealth."

Victims die because they get too close to evil. You probe the past to explore the path that brought the killer and the victim to the same place: "When Annie Lee Baxter died, the Major realized that he had only one surviving blood relative: Lacey Anne. The Major's guilt at causing his daughter's death makes him seek relief with the killer, a college-student call-girl. On her first visit to Baxter's Bungalow, the killer wants to live here, wake up here in the morning, drink her coffee looking out through wide windows to the sea. There's only one person standing in the way: Lacey Anne Baxter."

The back-story summary you write now can inform the story at various stages. To close off Act One of our write-along mystery, the police arrest designated scapegoat Julius Bugliosi. "Can't remember a thing," says a cop. "Swears on a stack of Bibles he's not guilty. Yeah, sure."

What the reader *sees* in the book is a scapegoat named Julius being framed and led to the slaughter for a crime he did not commit. What the writer *knows* goes deeper: Julius's arrest is the killer's payoff for a plan she set in motion months ago. Because she knows the Major so well, the killer anticipates his thirst for quick action—a manhunt to catch Julius. If the manhunt mushrooms into a lynch mob, so much the better. The killer gets another victim's head to hang from her trophy wall.

After you have written the summary, you can rework sections of the back story to develop scenes later in the book. When the police arrest Julius at the end of Act One, the writer sets up an exoneration scene for Act Three. "The killer had to know anatomy," says the sleuth. "Julius plays a hot trumpet. But he doesn't know a scalpel from an electric guitar."

In Act Three, when the killer's love of dissection surfaces from the back story, the sleuth knows whodunit. The next step is baiting the trap.

WORKING THE NOVEL

Exercises

1. *Checklist.*
Develop a back-story checklist by answering questions like these: What time does the killing occur? Is it night or day? Morning or noon? Where does the killing occur? Is it inside or outside? If outside, on land or water? Desert? Parking lot? Snowy place? If inside, what sort of compartment? Room? Cockpit? Automobile? If a conveyance, is it moving or standing still? Describe the light source. If daylight, is it sunny or cloudy? If we're inside, how dark is it? How does the killer see? Describe the weather during the killing. Stormy? Calm? Raining? Snowy? Warm? Hot? Cold? Freezing? How do weather conditions contribute to the murder? To the clues? What's the tem-

perature? How did the killer get here? Car? Boat? Plane? Bike? Train? Motor scooter? Skis? Skates? What time does the killer arrive? How did the victim get here? Did she arrive with the killer? Did she have to wait? Was the killer already here, waiting . . . ?

These questions (there are more in the Guidelines) help you gather material about the past of your main characters. The questions are divided into categories—time, place, lighting, weather, arrival and departure, et cetera—but the categories are intended only as a suggestion, to make sure you gather lots of material. If an insight pops about lighting, and you're into the section on murder weapons, make a note to yourself. When the brass ring sweeps by, grab for it.

2. *Chronology.*
Organize the checklist material into a chronology of events. Keep the events connected to the murder. The first event in the chronology *for Murder on Drake Island* is Edward Severance's impregnation of the victim's mother. Seeking an abortion, the Baxters head for Mexico. After losing his wife and his legs in Mexico, the Major pays the killer for sex. Visiting Drake Island, the killer covets the bungalow. The victim created by Edward Severance dies because she blocks the killer's access to the Major's resource base.

3. *Narrative Summary.*
Write a narrative summary that covers the major events in the back story. To harness the power, and the inexorable logic, of cause and effect, use words like *because* and *since* when you write: "Because Annie Lee Baxter died, the Major felt guilty. Because he felt guilty, he hooked up with Myra Jane Wallace, a college call girl, who helped him forget his guilt. Because he hooked up with Myra Jane, the Major put his granddaughter in harm's way." After some heavy repetition, try a new tack with the writing. Go to motive: "Since the killer's deeper wish is to own a beach house and because Lacey Anne stands in her way, the killer removes her. Because the killer doesn't want to be

caught, she chooses a scapegoat to take the heat. Tuning in to the victim's voice, the killer chooses a musician as scapegoat. . . ."

· · ·

Taking the time to develop your back story creates material for structuring your plot, from Chapter One to the wrap up that ends the book. As your back story shapes up, you focus on key scenes.

· WEEKEND 6 ·
KEY SCENES

Key scenes give you a framework for your mystery. In *Murder on Drake Island,* our write-along mystery, the book opens with the report of a dead body. In fictional terms, this is a problem in search of a solution. The search gives the book structure.

The book ends, of course, with the solution: after framing the scapegoat, the killer killed to gain access to the resource base. The solution closes the book by tying up the loose ends of victim and killer, motive and method. The innocent dupe is saved from harsh and undeserved punishment; society can get back to normal. With the book framed by opening and closing scenes, the reader feels a deep sense of satisfaction.

When you divide your book into three acts—to create a beginning, a middle, and an end—you use key scenes the way a playwright uses the curtain, the way a screenwriter uses a fade-out, to close off a section of the story.

The scene that ends Act One is plot point one. The scene that ends Act Two is plot point two. These terms are shorthand for the writer.

Dividing your killer chase into three acts marked by key scenes helps you manage the material, the lines of dialogue, the character descriptions, the monologues and dreams and police profiles, the actions that drive the story. Act One is the setup. Settings are developed; doorways open to admit characters into the story. Because of your work on back story, your characters make their Act One entrances flashing their agendas. The agendas clash, producing conflict. Because of conflict, the reader keeps reading.

Act Two is the complication; the book thickens here. As more characters enter the story, the writer becomes a stage manager, a set designer, a director, a dialogue coach. In Act Two, the threads of the plot multiply—more corpses, more bad guys, sleuth in danger, sleuth in love, and so on. Because Act Two expands, getting longer to accommodate growth, you might need to divide your story at the midpoint. "Midpoint" is exactly that—the middle of Act Two, the center of your book.

Act Three is the resolution. It contains the climax, the high point, the moment in the book where everything comes together. In most mysteries, the climax is the scene where the sleuth (or sleuth substitute) confronts the killer, where good faces evil.

Based on a linear structure in three acts, the quest for your killer has six key scenes: opener, plot point one, midpoint, plot point two, climax, and wrap-up. Act One is framed by the opener and plot point one. Act Two is framed by plot points one and two. Act Three is framed by plot point two and the wrap-up.

Let's explore what might happen in a key scene.

Key Scene Happenings

Opener.
The opening scene hooks the reader. *Gorky Park,* for example, opens at the "Crime Scene" with the sleuth entering the story. There are two hooks to grab the reader: first, the three frozen corpses with their faces and fingerprints carved away; second, the intruder, the KGB's Pribluda. Because of back story—Pribluda executed two political prisoners six weeks ago—he becomes a Prime Suspect in this case.

The Big Sleep opens with the sleuth crossing a threshold into the big-money hothouse world of Sternwood Manor for a classic first encounter with the killer, Miss Carmen Sternwood. The client is Miss Carmen's father, General Sternwood, a sick old man who hires the sleuth to take care of a blackmailer who's gouging Miss Carmen for extortion money using nude photos. The hook is mythic, echoing a situation from the Grail Legend: the sleuth is a knight errant summoned by the dying king to set the wasteland kingdom right again.

Plot Point One.

Plot point one ends Act One. It's a good place for a miniclimax that tweaks the story with action, the way Raymond Chandler does in *The Big Sleep*, by killing off the blackmailer, Geiger. Crossing another threshold into another happy home in greater Los Angeles, the sleuth finds the killer giggling, doped, and naked except for a pair of earrings. A nice twist here: the killer had a reason to kill Geiger; but she didn't do it. For *The Big Sleep*, the death of Geiger (at plot point one) closes Act One and ushers in Act Two.

Plot point one for *Gorky Park* is a classic study in how to bring a killer onstage. The killer is John Osborne, American fur trader. Traces of Osborne have surfaced earlier in the form of documents and surveillance tapes, distant trumpets sounding the arrival of an ancient, primitive king. When the killer enters the bigwig party bathhouse, he dominates the scene. He can dominate because he has killed. Already alerted by these early warnings, the sleuth smells money and power and blood sacrifice.

· · ·

Caveat Scriptor—Writer Beware

Midpoint is the center of the book. *Midpoint* is the fulcrum of Act Two. For most writers, Act Two is the tricky trouble-spot, the place where things go wrong. In the heat of creation, you might be tempted to zoom past midpoint. Stop. Slam on the brakes. Slow down.

Midpoint is big. Spending time here now will make your writing easier later.

Midpoint.

Midpoint for your book might take one scene; it might take three or four. Four scenes comprise the midpoint of *Gorky Park*. In "Male Bonding," the sleuth gets a new helper, William Kirwill. Digging up his own past, Kirwill explains about his parents, Jim and Edna, who aided refugee Russians in their home in New York. In "Metro Rescue," the sleuth rescues Irina Asanova from the KGB. In "Rebirth," Irina escapes death and the sleuth learns she was blinded in one eye by a KGB surgeon in the back story. In "Digging Up the Past," the sleuth learns about Osborne's execution of the German officers in Leningrad a quarter of a century ago. Midpoint is an excellent place to use back story to thicken texture.

At the midpoint of *The Big Sleep*, the nude photos of the killer (Miss Carmen Sternwood) have fallen into the hands of a small-time hustler named Joe Brody. Waving her little gun at Brody, the killer demands the photos. Showing his muscle, the sleuth disarms Carmen. Midpoint peaks when an intruder, doing Carmen's work, shoots Brody the hustler. The intruder is a boyfriend of Geiger, the blackmailer whose nude photos of the killer (photos taken in the back story) started the sleuth on his quest.

Plot Point Two.

Plot point two closes off Act Two. The book is very thick here. If you're weaving several threads, plot point two is your chance to tie off a thread or two to end a subplot (for more on subplots, see Weekend 8) before starting Act Three.

That's what Martin Cruz Smith does with his plot point two in *Gorky Park*. The setting is the fountain at the University of Moscow. Iamskoy, the sleuth's boss and a high-ranking officer in the KGB, holds a gun on Irina while Osborne's helper, the German Unmann, tries to drown her. The German stabs the sleuth; then the sleuth stabs the German. When Irina shoots Iamskoy with the sleuth's pistol, she caps off a subplot of deceit and deception that began in Chapter 1. And since Iamskoy is KGB—he engineered Irina's near death in the Moscow Metro at midpoint—she exacts payment for KGB torture in the back story that left her with a scar and one blind eye.

The main event at plot point two of *The Big Sleep* is a scapegoat replacement. In order to keep the real killer, Miss Carmen Sternwood, from being punished, the sleuth delivers a substitute scapegoat figure named Lash Canino. The sleuth kills in self-defense—Canino shoots at him—and also to avenge the death of Harry Jones, a small-time snitch. With Canino dead, *The Big Sleep* moves to Act Three and the climax.

Climax.

The killer quest peaks at the climax. The killer is confronted. Masks are ripped off, revealing the face of evil beneath. At the climax to *The Big Sleep*, for example, the sleuth hands a gun to the killer. It's a trap: the gun is loaded with blanks. As the killer aims at the sleuth with intent to kill, her beauty mask falls: "She showed me all her sharp little teeth and brought the gun up and started to hiss." As the clock ticks, the young woman transforms into a death crone: "The hissing sound grew louder and her face had the scraped bone look. Aged, deteriorated, become animal, and not a nice animal." The climax closes when the killer wets her pants.

Gorky Park climaxes in a classic movie shootout. The setting is Osborne's sable compound in New Jersey. When the shooting starts, the sables from the back story—the sables that traveled from Siberia to Moscow to Leningrad to Finland, arriving in New York before the book opens—leap against the cage doors, screaming to get free. The sleuth's confrontation with the killer is presided over by Irina Asanova, the femme fatale, age nineteen. Everyone else is dead.

Wrap-up.

The wrap-up for *The Big Sleep* is the sleuth's lesson on scapegoat replacement: because Marlowe delivered Canino the killer, Vivian Regan—the killer's big sister—can whisk the killer away. "Will you take her away?" asks the sleuth. "Somewhere far off from here where they can handle her type?" Vivian Regan is an accomplice. Familiar with the back story, Vivian knows her little sister killed Rusty Regan. In sending the two sisters away together, the sleuth exacts a gritty revenge.

The wrap-up for *Gorky Park* is a trade: the sleuth will give himself to Russia in exchange for Irina's American adventure. This barter ritual—a willing exchange of one's own body for that of another—lends a certain selfless nobility to the act. The best wrap-up has the sleuth giving something up.

Guidelines for Creating Key Scenes

1. *Back Story.*

In mystery writing, the past explains the present. Figure 1, for example, shows how you can use back story to generate each key scene. For the opening scene, we use back story—the scapegoat and victim are ambushed by the killer on the rainy beach road—to plant the naked body in the mud, ready for discovery at the crime scene. At plot point one (the scene that ends Act One), the police capture the scapegoat, Julius Bugliosi, who has been framed by the killer in the back story, when she plans the murder of Lacey Anne.

The killer is beautiful, artistic, well groomed. She plans a murder with the same smooth efficiency she uses to operate her restaurant, the Marina Café. The next key scene, midpoint, takes place in her office at the café when she barters with Armand DuPre, trying to get her name as coauthor on his crime article. In this scene, the killer re-creates the crimes from the point of view of a male killer. The scene is built on a foundation of details from the back story— her student days at the university, dissecting cadavers; her lust for Baxter's Bungalow; the purchase of thong bikinis from Tamara's in Atlanta when she was a call girl working her way through college.

In plot point two (the scene that ends Act Two), the sleuth is forced to arrest Edward Severance, who has confessed to killing his daughter, Lacey Anne. Edward's arrest explodes from the past, from that night sixteen years ago when he impregnated Annie Lee Baxter. An abortion would have set Edward free, but Annie Lee stood up to her parents and had her baby and then she died, leaving Lacey Anne to grow up on the island where she could run into her secret father walking along the street.

At the climax of *Murder on Drake Island,* the killer and sleuth are brought together by back story. Visiting Drake Island for business purposes (paid-for sex with the Major), the killer fell in love with Baxter's Bungalow. Escaping to Drake Island for personal reasons (a failed love affair, writer's block), the sleuth becomes town marshal. The killer is evil; the sleuth is good. The setting for the climax is the big living room of Baxter's Bungalow: two females and a male driven by events in the past slam into each other at a crossroads in the present.

The curved lines on Figure 1 connect key events in the back story (Weekend 5) to key scenes in the structure of the story.

2. *Plot Diagram.*

Use a diagram to locate your key scenes in the plot. The simplest diagram is a line that rises to suggest action rising to a climax. Follow our model in Figure 1. Use vertical lines to separate Act Two from Acts One and Three. Use a short line topped by a bubble to identify your midpoint.

3. *Scene Cards.*

Use index cards to jot notes about your key scenes. If the scene cards already exist—the payoff for your hard work on Weekends 1–5—tag them as key scenes now. Jot notes that will help you write the scenes later:

• *Scene Card for the Opener:* Focus on objects. A scene card for *Gorky Park* would list objects like snow, death masks, vans, Volga autos, frozen clothing, headlights, trees. A scene card for *Murder on Drake Island* would contain mud, rain, wounds, the thong, the death van, the Major in his Suburban, the sleuth in her parka.

• *Scene Card for Plot Point One:* Focus on setting and emotion. A scene card for *Murder on Drake Island* would describe Baxter's Bungalow, the castle of the rich old man, who's organizing a manhunt for the scapegoat. As we saw on Weekend 4, in the Catalyst chapter, the house where the rich old man lives is rigged out like the quarterdeck of the *Pequod,* Ahab's doomed vessel in *Moby-Dick.* Objects include the wheelchair, the quarterdeck, the jawbone tiller, and the authentic rigging. As the sleuth follows the Major out of the

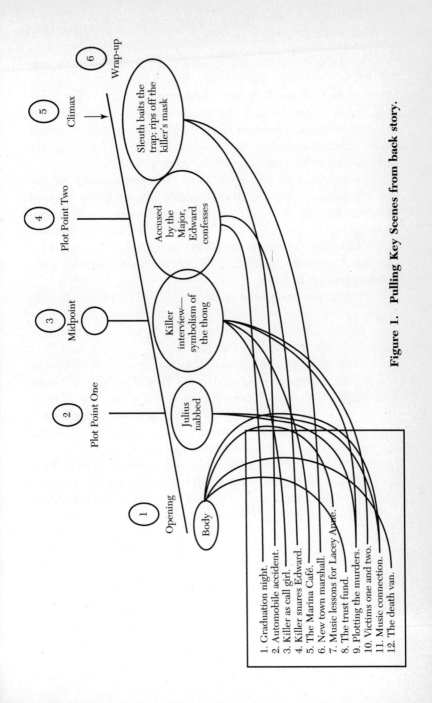

Figure 1. Pulling Key Scenes from back story.

Opening · 1
Plot Point One · 2
Midpoint · 3
Plot Point Two · 4
Climax · 5
Wrap-up · 6

Body

Julius nabbed

Killer interview—symbolism of the thong

Accused by the Major, Edward confesses

Sleuth baits the trap; rips off the killer's mask

1. Graduation night.
2. Automobile accident.
3. Killer as call girl.
4. Killer snares Edward.
5. The Marina Café.
6. New town marshall.
7. Music lessons for Lacey Anne.
8. The trust fund.
9. Plotting the murders.
10. Victims one and two.
11. Music connection.
12. The death van.

bungalow, she gets a call telling her the scapegoat has been captured.

• *Scene Card for Midpoint:*   Bartering for access to the scapegoat, crime writer Armand DuPre types on his laptop while the killer analyzes the symbolism of the serial murders. Objects in this scene include the laptop, food magazines, dirty coffee mugs, the customer list from Tamara's, and the meat mallet.

• *Scene Card for Plot Point Two:*   The past surfaces for Edward Severance when the Major accuses him of killing his own daughter. Because he did not admit to the pregnancy, the dead wife, or the living daughter, Edward believes he killed Lacey Anne. The sleuth locks him up for his own safety in the Village donjon, a jail cell with Caribbean furnishings. The key scenes in Act Two come from digging up the past.

If you go for action—the shoot-outs in *Gorky Park* and *The Big Sleep*—use plot point two to whisk a character offstage. Chief Prosecutor Iamskoy dies at the university fountain. Lash Canino dies in the countryside outside Los Angeles.

• *Scene Card for the Climax:*   Focus on the killer. The killer in *The Big Sleep* transforms into a Death Crone. The killer in *Gorky Park* laughs at the sleuth from the lip of the grave. The killer in *Murder on Drake Island* brings her scalpel to Baxter's Bungalow.

• *Scene Card for the Wrap-up:*   The sleuth gives something up. In *Gorky Park*, Renko refuses America, trading his skin for Irina's freedom. In *The Big Sleep*, Marlowe refuses money. In *Murder on Drake Island*, the sleuth refuses the Major's offer of money, safety, good food, good music, the good life. She's resigned her town marshal job. She's got a book to write.

WORKING THE NOVEL

Exercises

1. *Scene Cards.*

On an index card, write, "Opener." This is the card for your opening scene. On a second card, write, "Plot Point One." Keep going until you have six scene cards, one for each key scene: opener, plot point one, midpoint, plot point two, climax, and wrap-up.

What you write on the scene card comes from your back story: information from the past that creates detail about action and setting that sets up dialogue. If you were making notes for *The Big Sleep,* your scene card for plot point one would contain something like this: *"Setting:* Geiger the blackmailer killed at his home. Nude killer, zonked on booze or dope, is a witness. *Action:* The sleuth gets her dressed and out of there. *Objects:* No nude photos at the scene." Your midpoint card would read: *"Action:* Killer waves gun at Brody. *Motive:* Wants nude photos. *Object:* Sleuth grabs gun. Intruder zaps Brody."

2. *Diagram Showing Key Scenes.*

Using a linear diagram that rises to show rising action, transfer information from the scene cards to make a picture, a visual display of the turning points and high points of your plot. Pictures of the plot are more fun if you don't try to be neat. Messy is good.

Frame the story with your opener (crime scene, first encounter, sleuth at home, et cetera) and your wrap-up. Then add key scenes: plot point one, midpoint, plot point two, climax.

When you finish adding key scene names, add information from your back story. If you were building a plot for *Body,* you would have a Witness Interview at plot point two. The witness interview would trace the victim's path to the killer lying in wait at the killing place.

Conway Jefferson's airplane accident forms plot point one. A burnt-up body combines with a carefully crafted Dirty Old Man analogy and "the plan that went wrong" to make up the midpoint.

3. *Narrative Summary.*

To explore the insights you have reached thus far on your plot, summarize each key scene in a short paragraph. As a model for your summary, reread the summaries from the opening of this chapter. If you need a place to start, copy down this sentence, adjust it to fit your story situation, and then keep writing: "At plot point two of my mystery, my sleuth kills to save her own life because she is mired in the stink of corruption up to her eyeballs and . . ."

· WEEKEND 7 ·
PLOT PICTURE-DIAGRAM

A plot diagram is a picture of your plot as it moves from bare bones and yawning gaps where nothing happens toward the balanced poise of the finished book. Pictures of the plot give feedback signals without killing the creative process with harsh judgments. A plot picture now is like a snapshot of your story at its birth. More plot pictures— one when you start and one when you finish and a couple during the writing—are Polaroid snapshots that track your progress.

The Writer's Secret

Drawing pictures on the page of your notebook or with a graphics package on your computer screen gives you an overview of your novel. An overview enables you to write with the confidence that comes with well-plotted preparation. A plot diagram, like the names you assign to each of your scenes, is the writer's trade secret, intended for your eyes only.

You don't share writer's secrets with outsiders like family and friends. You don't reveal the plot picture to your literary agent or your editor in New York. Creativity is a small blue flame. It takes only a puff of wind—one tiny criticism—to blow it out. Show your admirers the finished book, but as you write, sweating over the words, keep those secrets safe and keep the blue flame burning. A diagram of your plot is worth 75,000–80,000 words, the average length for today's mystery novel.

Plotting is a logical, linear activity that works by cause and effect: a corpse surfaces; the sleuth takes up the chase; the trap is set; the killer pays. A plot picture charts this cause and effect along a rising line divided into four parts: Act One; Act Two, first half; Act Two, second half; and Act Three. Because the four parts are roughly the same length, plotting now with a picture in mind helps you control your story with estimates based on a page count. If your book is planned out for 300 pages, and if your plot picture tells you Act One should have peaked at page 75, and if you have reached page 113 of the manuscript with no whisper of plot point one, you heed the signal flashed by your plot picture. You don't stop plotting. You do make a note to compress. Your goal is to reach the end, to know the ending.

With the rising line divided into four parts, you load up each part with detail: character, scene names, murder weapons, wardrobe items, money, jewelry, furs, masks, and so on. Drawing a picture of your plot shows you, on paper, where certain characters enter the story; and also where they exit. Characters like Andrei Iamskoy who tote their own subplots (The Corruption of Mother Russia by Capitalism) must be capped off so they're not left hanging about when you reach your climax where the sleuth confronts the killer. As we pointed out earlier, Iamskoy exits the book when Irina shoots him at plot point two of Gorky Park.

Your first plot picture shows you where you are with the story, how much thinking you have already done, how much work there is yet to do. You draw subsequent plot pictures as the writing progresses, as your stack of scene cards grows, as your characters grow deeper, as your subplots converge. Your first plot picture contains basic information that helps you get organized: three acts, six key scenes, characters entering the story, characters leaving the story, eight or ten scenes connecting the key scenes, and time.

Caveat Scriptor—Writer Beware

This first plot picture is so easy to draw—five minutes, ten at the outside—that it's also easy to bypass. Some writers love words but consider plot diagrams unnecessary and unwriterly. Remember this: Like any creative ritual, the act of drawing embeds the book's structure in your brain. The act of writing scene names, transferring them from scene cards to the diagram, gives you one more chance for a quick insight into the structure of the scene. (Scene building starts on Weekend 10.)

Scenes are the building blocks for your novel. Don't miss this opportunity to sketch out a structure for your story. You might think of it as a frame on which you drape your scenes. The structure you sketch this weekend could solve a writing problem later, when you hit Weekend 20, or 30, or 40. A solid plot structure could help to sell your book to agent, editor, publisher, bookseller, customer, fan.

Guidelines—Plot Picture

Sketch out the basics quickly: Acts One, Two, and Three. Add the six key scenes (opener, plot point one, midpoint, plot point two, climax, wrap-up) and then add information about the entrances and exits of your major characters—killer, victim, sleuth, catalyst.

As a shorthand device, we use the term *onstage* for a character's first physical entrance into the story. A character might be previewed for the reader in the sleuth's head ("She thought of X's skull face, lank black hair, teeth, thin lips like a skinning knife . . .") or in a dialogue line ("I say, have you seen Señor X?"), but your focus in bringing the character "onstage" should be on the physical presence. John Osborne, the *Gorky Park* killer, appears as a tourist in travel documents and as a voice on surveillance tapes, but these are previews, an early warning preparation for his actual physical entrance into the story.

This first entrance is important because it's your chance to develop character presence, that sense of weight, the urgency of character agenda that drives your story. Because it's so important, bringing a character into the story requires preparation. You need to create a threshold—a doorway or some stairs or a barrier like a desk or a vast expanse of room or desert to cross—and you need solid character description (wardrobe, jewelry, gesture, face, figure, hairdo, et cetera).

Osborne's threshold in *Gorky Park* is a gate: "Arkady felt the gate opening." Except for a gold ring, Osborne is naked. He carries a white towel. His flawless all-over tan reinforces the killer's deep connection with the sun. When you bring a character onstage, a good dialogue line adds stability to the entrance. The subject of the killer's first words—"Absolutely gorgeous. . . . I won't dare eat one"—is canapés, food, eating, Osborne's power to devour if he so chooses. It helps to have a dialogue line that bites deep.

Osborne's entrance as the "Killer Onstage" marks the end of Act One and the beginning of Act Two for *Gorky Park*. The key scene that anchors this part of the plot, as we learned on Weekend 6, is plot point one. With the killer's entrance, the sleuth's problem shifts from who (the identity of the killer) to how (devising a strategy to nail him).

A diagram helps you make early decisions about entrances and exit points for each major character. The writer uses exit points on the diagram to clear the stage, making room for the final resolution at the book's climax. As you write deeper into the book, exit points can change to match the needs of your story. Use this first plot picture to get organized. It's easy to change later.

Before we explore the actual diagram, here are some examples of entrances and exits from other mystery writers:

• *"F" Is for Fugitive.* Killer Ann Fowler, the dark sister of scapegoat Bailey Fowler, comes onstage in Chapter 1 when her father hires the sleuth to save Bailey. Ann exits at the climax, spewing blood from her wounded foot.

• *Edwin of the Iron Shoes.* Cara Ingalls, the killer in this Marcia Muller mystery, comes onstage in Chapter 4 as the keynote speaker at a real estate convention. Following a lengthy confession, Cara exits the stage at the climax.

• *The Big Sleep.* Carmen Sternwood, the killer who will not become a scapegoat, comes onstage in Chapter One and falls into the arms of the sleuth. Carmen exits at the climax, after shooting blanks at the sleuth.

Drawing Pictures to Generate Ideas

As your major characters come onstage, attaching themselves to the plot picture, you generate names for the scenes. At this early stage of plotting, your goal is to get juicy ideas, insights about the plot and the characters.

If you have minor characters that play important roles—like Andrei Iamskoy in *Gorky Park* and Basil Blake in *Body*—attach them to your plot picture now. Iamskoy's entrance in Chapter 1 ushers in a scene common to the mystery genre—the sleuth groveling before a superior who holds more power in the police bureaucracy. A handy name for this kind of scene is "Brush with Authority." Basil Blake comes onstage for a brief "Suspect Interrogation" in Act One, but you could also call it "Basil Grilled by Cops." His exit from the story comes in Act Three.

• *Time.* If time is important in your story, add information about time to your plot picture. Christie's *Body,* a speedy killer quest, opens the morning after the murder, which took place around ten o'clock. Without a break for lunch or dinner, the setting shifts to the Majestic Hotel, where the police interview witnesses and lose the trail. It's daylight when Sir Henry recruits Miss Marple. It's daylight of an endless afternoon in Christie World when Miss Marple interviews Florence Small, the Girl Guide, late in Act Two. For Christie, darkness is the symbolic time for death: the killings and attempted killings take place at night.

If your sleuth is wounded, you'll need to figure in healing time. Arkady Renko, the sleuth of *Gorky Park,* gets stabbed at plot point two, the curtain that ends Act Two. The month of the stabbing is April. For the next thirty pages, the writer compresses time. Summer passes; Renko saves Pribluda, no longer the Prime Suspect, from the peat fire. In October, the KGB flies Renko to Leningrad, to the Fur Palace. The sleuth, healed from his physical wounds, is ripe for exacting payment from the killer. By the time Renko gets to New York, the month is November. It's snowing. The November snow mirrors the opening of the book on that cold April morning in Moscow, where a passive sleuth viewed those three corpses through a veil of cigarette smoke.

• *Objects.* A linear structure like a plot picture is also helpful for tracking objects that might become clues. The faces of the victims in *Gorky Park* were flayed with a skinning knife. The killer skinned faces to protect his sable empire the same way he skinned sables to fatten his resource base. Until a character uses it for a purpose, a knife is an object. Using that knife, the killer flays the faces of all three victims, making identification difficult. To identify the victims, the sleuth follows the ice skates worn by the female victim to Irina, the owner of the skates.

The white spangled frock worn by the corpse in *Body* is important. It surfaces in a list of details at the crime scene: "Her thin body was dressed in a backless evening dress of white spangled satin; the face was heavily made up, the powder standing out grotesquely on its blue swollen surface. . . ." Near the end of Act Two, Miss Marple uses costume analysis to crack the case. If you were writing *Body,* that white spangled dress is an object that belongs in the plot picture.

Figure 2—Character, Object, Time

Figure 2 is a model for traffic control as you organize your cast of characters. When characters enter the story in hordes, your diagram helps you keep them from stumbling over each other. Figure 2 shows *Murder on Drake Island* opening with the Crime Scene. The body has been discovered. The sleuth is on the scene. The Major, who discovered the body, waits for the sleuth in his Suburban. The state police sergeant arrives to start a Turf War over jurisdiction.

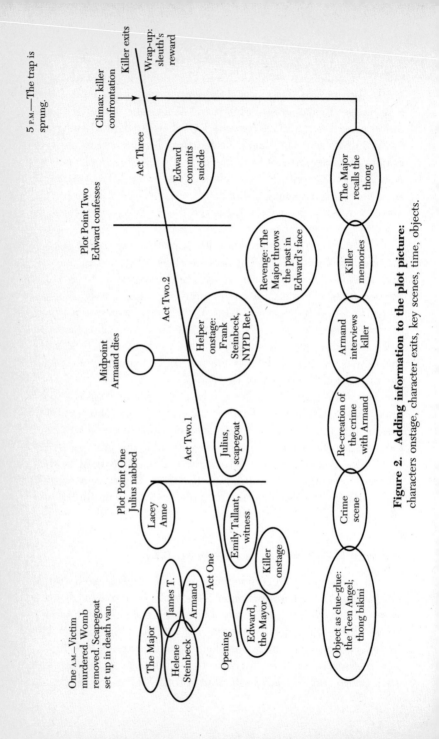

Figure 2. Adding information to the plot picture:
characters onstage, character exits, key scenes, time, objects.

The scene climaxes with the arrival of the sleuth's helper, Armand DuPre.

The killer should come onstage in Act One as the sleuth starts her investigation. Armand DuPre, who dies at midpoint (Weekend 6), is the key to one of our subplots because he discovers the source of the sexy thong undergarment worn by the victim. Subplots, important for plotting, will be covered on Weekend 8.

With the major characters onstage, you bring on minor characters and more walk-ons in Act Two. If the catalyst did not enter the book in Act One, make sure you bring him on in Act Two. Edward Severance, husband of the killer, enters in Act One to worry the sleuth about adverse publicity and cash flow. Edward confesses at plot point two. He exits in Act Three when he commits suicide.

Julius Bugliosi, the designated scapegoat, drives the van in the back story. Julius is captured at plot point one. He enters the book in Act Two, when he is interviewed by the sleuth. The sleuth's dad, Frank Steinbeck, NYPD retired, enters in Act Two after a call for help from the sleuth. James T. Worthington, the state police sergeant who wants jurisdiction over the Teen Angel case, enters at the crime scene and exits in Act Three.

Emily Tallant, friend of the victim, is a walk-on who packs a punch. As Emily traces the movements of her friend Lacey Anne from the Baxter Bungalow to the Pirate's Cove, the sleuth knows the Major is involved in a minor cover-up. The witness interview with Emily sends the sleuth to the Baxter's Bungalow to confront the Major, who's keeping secrets.

Figure 2 shows the killer exiting at the climax in Act Three. Figure 2 shows the sleuth still onstage at the end of the book, having a drink with the Major.

When the diagram gets crowded, and if you still have information to add, enclose it in bubbles. Figure 2 uses bubbles to track the thong undergarment from the crime scene to midpoint, where it connects to the back story. By tracing the source of the thong, the sleuth gets her first real intuition about the true identity of the killer. The bubbles in Figure 2 help you track an important object when there's no room on the rising line.

Figure 3—Generating Scenes

Because they have agendas driven by needs, major characters generate scenes when they enter the story. This agenda information belongs in your plot picture. If your first plot picture is too crowded to include scenes, you sketch another one. Figure 3 focuses on the scenes generated when characters cross paths with one another.

The sleuth crosses paths with the victim to create the "Crime Scene." Armand DuPre buys the sleuth a cup of coffee at Myra's café, where he shares information that helps her "Re-create the Crime." When the killer intrudes on the meeting, the scene is "Killer Onstage."

The sleuth's questioning of Emily is a classic "Witness Interview." The sleuth's encounter with the mayor over the dangers of bad publicity on Labor Day Weekend is a "Brush with Authority." In the first half of Act Two, the sleuth questions Julius Bugliosi in a "Suspect Interrogation" scene. "Victim's Lair," in that same cluster of scenes in Act Two, is generated when the sleuth crosses paths with the dead victim, a meeting of past and present in Lacey Anne's room.

Figure 3 shows the sleuth crossing paths with two other policemen. In Act One, as she shows her grit and lack of experience in the struggle with James T. Worthington, the scene could be called "Turf Wars." The entrance of the sleuth's dad, Frank Steinbeck of the NYPD, is "Helper Onstage" and comes in Act Two.

When the Major finally connects the thong to his half-forgotten encounters with a much younger Myra Jane Wallace, the scene could be called "The Major Recalls the Thong." As you create names for scenes, try to have fun.

When you sketch out your plot with a diagram, don't be afraid to be messy. Creativity is a messy business. The goal is to get a picture of your story inside your head. Vivid names help to make vivid pictures. With the plot picture working inside your head, you'll generate more insights about the book.

· · ·

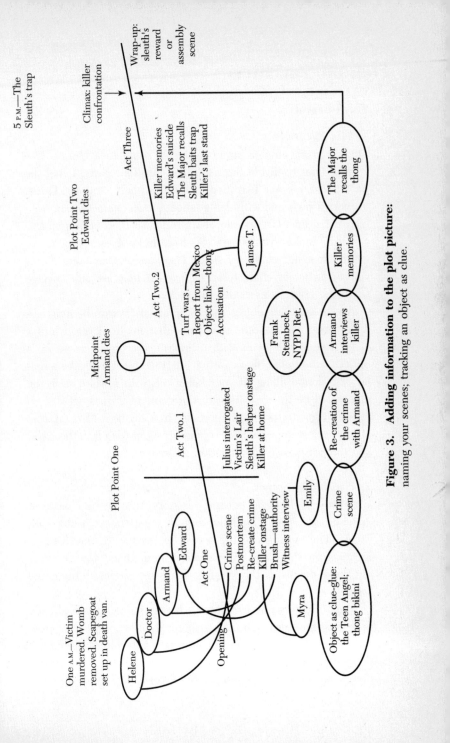

Figure 3. Adding information to the plot picture: naming your scenes; tracking an object as clue.

WORKING THE NOVEL

Exercises

1. *Plot Picture.*

Draw a rising line to simulate action rising to a climax. Use vertical lines to divide the rising line into four parts. Label the parts: Act One, Act Two (first half, second half), and Act Three. Working slowly and with deliberation, attach character names to your rising line. Group your characters near their entry point. If you like, enclose your characters in little bubbles.

Attach major characters first. Then minor characters. Show where the major characters exit, even if they are still onstage when the book fades at the wrap-up.

Add at least one object—weapon, money, wardrobe item, vehicle, body part, photo, et cetera—that might develop into a clue. If your killer kills with a firearm, the object might be a bullet. If the bullet blows away teeth, the object might be a molar or a dental filling. If your killer kills with a white sash, the object will be the sash itself or the garment it goes with.

Add time if time is important. In Christie's Miss Marple novel, time is important for separating night (death in the dark) and day (discovery, investigation, killer-quest).

2. *Generating Scenes.*

Each time a character enters your story, you have a chance to generate a scene. The killer entering generates "Killer Onstage." The entrance of the corpse makes the "Crime Scene." Details from the crime scene come from the back story. Following these details as they surface leads the sleuth through the book.

Make a new scene card for each new scene. If you already have a scene card, add information about connections: How does your "First Encounter" connect to a "Witness Interview" that opens Act Two? How does your first "Suspect Interrogation" connect to your quest for the killer?

3. *Plot Insights.*

Write a couple of paragraphs about what you see in your plot picture. If you take the time to do this writing, you'll make an important first step: writing a synopsis. You can begin this writing with a simple observation: "Act One looks really crowded. . . ." Another way to open might be: "The killer doesn't come onstage until the end of Act Two. Better fix that now. Thank God for diagrams."

Have fun with this writing. Be kind to yourself, especially if you think you can't draw.

· WEEKEND 8 ·
SUBPLOTS

A subplot is a secondary story that accompanies the main plot or story line, thereby adding texture to the book. *Texture* is your reader's perception of richness in the material that makes the book a pleasure to read. The writer develops texture by a careful process of weaving. In the structure of the mystery, the main plot is the quest for the killer; the subplot, usually developed around a false trail leading to the scapegoat, provides contrast in tone, mood, atmosphere, or momentum.

Subplots take planning.

In *The Body in the Library,* for example, Christie's main plot shows the sleuth tracking the real killer; the subplot, for contrast and comic relief, shows the police blundering about on the trail of an "assumed intruder." From bad leads and wrong evidence, the writer develops a laughable killer profile that points the finger of guilt at the designated scapegoat framed by the clever killer.

You can see the subplot at work by focusing on two scenes from *Body:* 1) the "Victim's Lair" scene near the middle of Act Two; 2) and the sleuth's "Costume Analysis" near the end of Act Two.

1. *Victim's Lair.* In Act Two of *Body*, nearing the midpoint, the stack of witness interviews leads the police to search the victim's room at the Majestic Hotel. This scene, heavy with details of wardrobe and makeup, shows the police blundering about, fouling up the investigation:

- They make incorrect re-creations of the crime.
- They overlook clues when they search the victim's room.
- They build a slanted killer profile.
- They make prejudicial remarks about professional girls. (The implied judgment is that painted ladies ask for trouble and they get it.)

This elaborate scene in the Victim's Lair, a room without a view, is a way station in the police subplot. The main plot of *Body* is the hunt for the killer. Catching the killer, making him pay, is the reason readers read mysteries. It's what audiences want to see in their mystery films. Deep in Act Two, to energize the plot, Christie brings back a wardrobe item introduced early in Act One—a beautiful example of *conceal* and *reveal*.

2. *Costume Analysis.* In the second half of Act Two, as the book nears plot point two, Miss Marple becomes really selective as she narrows the focus on the victim's wardrobe, using a wardrobe item planted at the crime scene as an indicator of the dating behavior of young girls. To the police, the victim is a working girl, a painted hussy who asks for trouble and does not dress like a lady. To Miss Marple, who sees pattern, there's something amiss with the wardrobe item. While an upper-class girl would choose an evening frock for a date inside the hotel and sportswear for outside, the victim would not: "[She] wasn't a lady," muses the sleuth. "She belonged to the class that wear their best clothes, however unsuitable to the occasion."

Christie uses her subplot—the plot beneath the plot—for contrast: the police subplot in *Body* (a mechanism for comic relief) makes the police look bad so that the sleuth looks good.

The police look bad in the subplot when they overlook clues. The clues in the Victim's Lair scene are items of makeup and wardrobe, a working girl's survival kit, her magical machinery of transformation. The victim is dead, leaving behind her survival ritual symbolized by the items in the room: face creams, skin creams, eyeliner, stockings, dance costumes. The victim's lonely room at the Majestic was a staging area, a dressing room for an actress who transformed herself, through the magic of makeup and costume, from working class dance hostess into a fairy-tale Cinderella. Before she died, the victim was a working-class girl clawing her way up the social ladder.

Near the end of the Victim's Lair scene, Inspector Slack, speaking for the police, makes a bigoted class-related value judgment that misses the urgency of the victim's desperate ritual of transformation: "But these professional girls," intones Inspector Slack, "they do exhibition dances, and one night it's a tango, and the next a crinoline Victorian dance, and then a kind of Apache dance . . . and of course the makeup varies a good bit."

When you develop a similar scene for your story—police bumbling to make your sleuth look good—try anchoring your subplot in a dramatic device like a police monologue that radiates similar short-sighted prejudice.

Subplot works in tantalizing cause-and-effect to develop both humor and suspense. Because the police cannot see into the back story, they overlook Christie's clever transformation ritual. Because they cannot perceive the need for disguise (the makeup ritual), they fail to understand the wardrobe item that the sleuth notes at the crime scene. Because they don't understand the clue that's placed before them, they manufacture an inaccurate killer profile. As the final element in the profile, the police lock on to a photo of the scapegoat planted in the victim's purse by the killer in the back story. It all adds up to bad police procedure. The bad police procedure in Act Two causes the arrest of the scapegoat in Act Three.

Police foul-ups in the subplot in Act Two whisk them off the story's stage in Act Three, leaving room for the sleuth to complete the main plot. To mark the police exit, Christie gives Inspector Slack another speech, a monologue about murderer madness that peaks to comic crescendo: *"Mad—sex and blood lust—lucky this girl's es-caped. What they call recurring mania, I expect."* As it rises to a climax, the Inspector's monologue displays a police mind that still hasn't figured out who did what to whom.

This is an excellent strategy for your mystery tale: while the subplot leads the police away from the killers along the wrong trail, your sleuth, by contrast, can be hot on the right trail. To develop your subplot, use specific scenes loaded with specific physical detail from the scene cards.

Guidelines for Using Subplot

1. *Subplots come from back story.*

Figure 4 shows Julius Bugliosi entering the story in Act One, stepping into a dialogue (the Major wants Julius arrested) from the back story. After an absence of a few hours between the crime scene and plot point one, the diagram shows him getting arrested: the killer's scapegoat plan has worked.

Before the book opens, the killer coats Julius and his van with mud and blood from the crime scene, part of her scapegoat plan. The van, a band trademark, allows the police to identify Julius be-fore he can get off the island. Once Julius is caught, Act One is over and the scapegoat subplot is well underway.

The Teen Angel corpses from the back story—Victims One and Two—are look-alikes for Victim Three, Lacey Anne Baxter. Al-though they were not performers, Victims One and Two were rock music groupies. Both were last seen at concerts where Julius and his band were booked.

As the jaws of justice close around the scapegoat, the story turns into a race between plot and subplot. In the subplot, the police, certain of their killer, rush forward to force a confession from Julius. In the plot, the sleuth pushes ahead through a labyrinth of clues and red herrings, trying to nail down the real killer.

In Act Three, with his memory returning, Julius places Myra Jane in the audience at the concerts where Victims One and Two died.

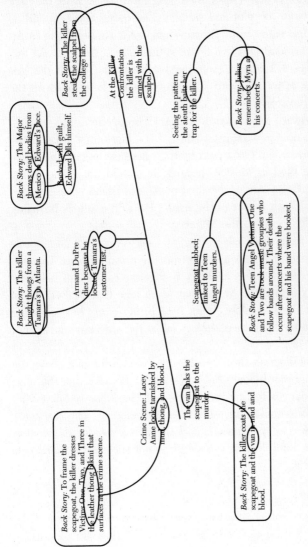

Figure 4. Subplot Comes from Back Story. The false trail of the scapegoat quest is below the line. The Teen Angel garb from the main plot is above the line. In mystery, an object from the back story often leads the sleuth to the killer. The objects in *Murder on Drake Island* are the death van and the leather thong undergarment. The police subplot, which leads to the arrest of Julius at plot point one, is meant to distract the reader as the police blunder about on the false trail.

Figure 4 uses curved lines to connect information from the back story to scenes in the plot and subplot. The thong bikinis found on all three victims came from Tamara's, an erotic supply depot in Atlanta. When Armand DuPre interviews the killer at the Marina Café, his knowledge of Tamara's customer list means he has to die. Armand's death, as we saw with key scenes on Weekend 6, forms the midpoint of the story.

When Edward Severance dies in Act Three, committing suicide in the Village donjon—a filmset jail that is a big tourist attraction—he is driven by his guilt as a secret father: because he got Annie Lee pregnant, she died in Mexico; because he would not acknowledge his daughter, Lacey Anne, she died on Drake Island.

Edward's death is part of the main plot: as the killer's husband, Edward blocks access to the Major.

Material from the back story allows us to create a memorable killer confrontation. The Major controls the resource base. To catch the killer, the sleuth needs his help. Before she can get his help, the sleuth must convince the Major that Myra Jane is the killer. When she arrives at the bungalow, Myra Jane brings along her scalpel, a plot device stolen from the pathology lab at the university during her student days.

Drawing a diagram similar to Figure 4—with the plot above the line and the subplot below—helps you create better scenes because you feel the danger felt by the scapegoat. The killer is smart. The scapegoat is vulnerable, but not altogether innocent. The scapegoat subplot for *Murder on Drake Island* is entertaining for the reader, but dangerous for Julius. If the sleuth is not successful, Julius gets the gas chamber.

2. *Subplots come from character.*

A character enters the story, surprising you with how well he handles himself. You give him a change of clothes, an identifying vehicle or weapon, a few lines of dialogue, a small toehold in a scene. The character works so well that you give him another scene, and another. The character helps the story—he's humorous, angry, very professional, and extremely competent when he kills to save the sleuth's life—so you keep him working, from Act One all the way into Act Three.

This character, like William Kirwill in *Gorky Park,* now has his own subplot. Kirwill explodes into the story in Act One, when he is spotted playing a flashlight on the crime scene. Kirwill, whose powerful presence onstage guarantees him a subplot, can enter the story with such confident gusto because the writer fully developed his back story. As the sleuth learns in Act Two, Kirwill's parents were caregivers for Russian refugees: "If it was Russian and crazy, it had a home in New York City—our home." He enters the story in Act One as a tough New York City cop on a personal quest for absolution: he blames himself for driving his brother Jimmy out of America. When the brother is killed in Moscow, his murder forces Kirwill to take on his own personal killer quest. Kirwill wants the killer to pay. When he fails to exact payment in Act Three, his subplot is over.

Most subplots must be capped off before the climax in Act Three. In *Gorky Park,* Kirwill dies when he runs his own revenge play on Osborne. The faithful dogs alert Osborne; Kirwill kills the dogs; Osborne kills Kirwill, roping his corpse to a tree. Like a threshold guardian in the world of the dead, Kirwill guards the entrance to the killer's lair. The Kirwill subplot ends here, a figure of a dying god from ancient times, entrails dusted with snow.

3. *Subplots come from objects.*

The painted bird that inspired the title for *The Maltese Falcon* is the central image in the Holy Grail subplot used by the writer to conceal the real killer, Brigid O'Shaughnessy. The quest for the falcon from the distant past drives the story in the present, generating several interesting scenes and fascinating characters such as Caspar Gutman, the fat man who lusts for the bird. While Gutman gets away, the sleuth chooses Brigid as the scapegoat who must pay for killing the sleuth's partner, Miles Archer.

Like Christie and her police subplot, Hammett uses the bird to distract the reader from the quest for the killer.

This management of plot and subplot is the key to entertainment. In the main plot, the sleuth nails the killer: "I'm going to send you over. The chances are you'll get off with life. That means you'll be out again in twenty years. You're an angel. I'll wait for you."

While the sleuth tracked the killer, the painted bird subplot entertained the reader: Joel Cairo, Caspar Gutman, the Knights Templars, et cetera.

4. *Subplots come from theme.*

In *"F" Is for Fugitive,* a big subplot is a Search for Lost Fathers. Finding the fathers enables the sleuth to crack the case.

1. Lost Father number one is Royce Fowler, a sick old man who hires the sleuth to save his son, Bailey Fowler, before society sacrifices him as a scapegoat. In the main plot, the sleuth quests for the killer, Ann Fowler, Bailey's sister.

2. Lost Father number two is Dwight Shales, the principal of the victim's high school. Shales, burdened by a sick wife, eased his burden by impregnating the victim. When Shales shunned the victim to protect his reputation, the victim asked a medical doctor for an abortion.

3. The medical doctor is Lost Father number three. His name is Dr. Dunne. In the book, he enters the story as the very proper proprietor of the local health spa. In the back story, the good doctor not only refused the victim's abortion request, but he also failed to confess, to own up to his own paternity: he was the victim's dad.

The Lost Father subplot in *Fugitive* functions as a cover-up. Framed by his sister for the killing that happened seventeen years ago, the scapegoat is about to pay for a murder he did not commit. To crack the case, the sleuth digs up the past, uncovering the Lost Father, Dwight Shales. Shales, coveted from afar by the killer, is the motive for murder: to save Shales's reputation as high school principal, Ann Fowler killed the victim to silence her about the unwanted pregnancy.

In *Fugitive,* Grafton uses the Lost Father subplot to cover up the motive for the crime: the killer plans to split, to leave town with Dwight Shales. Getting arrested ruins her dream.

• • •

WORKING THE NOVEL

Exercises

1. *Back Story.*
Back story is a perfect source for subplots. Review your work on back story from Weekend 5. Jot down details that might develop into subplots. Your detail might be a wardrobe item, like Irina's ice skates in *Gorky Park,* or a character that emerges from the wings ready to work, like Hannibal Lecter in *Lambs.*

Write a brief narrative passage on possible subplots in your novel. To get started, you might play What-If: What if Character X gets one more scene? What if she says something like "What do you want from me?" and starts a dialogue? What if she's wearing a bedsheet? A sable? A sunsuit? A tennis outfit? Prison dungarees?

2. *Scene Cards.*
Use scene cards to track your subplot through the structure of your novel. If you have more than one subplot—*Fugitive* has one subplot for Lost Fathers and one for money, the missing $42,000—code each subplot with a separate color.

You might use red for character: Kirwill from *Gorky Park;* Jame Gumb in *Lambs.* You might use green for money: the missing $42,000 in *Fugitive;* gold and fur in *Gorky Park.* You might use blue for objects: the painted bird in *The Maltese Falcon;* murder weapons in *The Big Sleep;* Irina's ice skates in *Gorky Park.* You might use yellow for themes: Lost Fathers in *Fugitive;* Corruption in *Gorky Park* or *The Big Sleep;* Christie's comic Keystone Kops in *Body.*

Make sure you name each subplot. Have fun with your names.

3. *Plot Picture.*

Organize the scenes in your subplot with a simple diagram. You might try redrawing Figure 4, the model for this chapter. Above the rising line you print scenes from the main plot. Below the line, you print scenes from the subplot. In a mystery manuscript of 250–300 pages, a subplot needs half a dozen scenes.

Use what you have learned from your study of the mystery genre: a walk-on character who enters the story twice becomes the focus of the police investigation based on wrong information supplied by the killer. Fix the beginning and the end of the subplot; then add scenes in the middle.

With your subplots down on paper, you're ready to write a narrative synopsis of your story.

· WEEKEND 9 ·
THE WORKING SYNOPSIS

Synopsis is a narrative summary of your plot. Writing the synopsis is an act of power, of being bold on paper. It organizes your thoughts, your characters, your clues, your scene cards. Because it reaches from start to finish, a synopsis gives you a span of control over your entire plot. The act of writing generates insights about motive, character, evidence, and scene.

The synopsis you write on Weekend 9 is a working synopsis, a bare-bones beginning that gives shape to your story idea. Its purpose is to guide you into the writing. Like scene lists and scene cards, the working synopsis gets you over the bare spots in the plot. Writing the synopsis now takes you to the end of the story, where you experience the sensation of closure. In an hour or two of steady writing, you capture the book. There are loose ends, sure, but the working synopsis gathers up most of the story.

The working synopsis is different from a selling synopsis. The selling synopsis is a marketing tool; it helps you sell the book. When the book is done, all the *t*'s crossed, all the *i*'s dotted, then you write a selling synopsis to grab an agent who finds you an editor who works for a publisher who will publish your mystery.

The working synopsis is a map, a chart that guides the writing. We suggest that you write two drafts this weekend. In draft one you feel the sweep of the story on its way to closure. In draft two you focus on the problem areas. For most writers, the main problem area is Act Two, the yawning middle of the book. In your rewrite, it's a good idea to spend more time on Act Two before you tackle Acts One and Three.

To get you started on your own synopsis, we've worked up a model based on our write-along mystery, *Murder on Drake Island.* Our synopsis is divided into a back story and three acts. Back story is your foundation, the source of buried clues, hidden motives, secret lusts, rabid hungers. The back story that starts our example is an expanded version of the work we did on Weekend 5, when we started plotting. In the back story, you draw on the work you did for character on the first four weekends. Following the sample synopsis are the usual guidelines and writing tips.

WORKING SYNOPSIS FOR MURDER ON DRAKE ISLAND

Example: Back Story.

In the back story, Major Philip Baxter loses his legs in an automobile accident in Mexico. The Major, who owns Drake Island, South Carolina, has come to Mexico to oversee an abortion for his daughter, Annie Lee Baxter. Refusing the abortion on religious grounds, Annie Lee gives birth to a beautiful baby, blond like her mother and with her father's facial features—pale blue eyes and the nose of a French aristocrat—who receives the name Lacey Anne. The Major and his wife falsify documents for a bogus marriage to a fake father, Luis Carlos Ortega, an engineer for Pemex.

Two months after giving birth, Annie Lee and her mother are killed in the same automobile accident that cripples the Major. The father's real name—Edward Severance—dies along with Annie Lee. Guilt ridden over the loss of both his wife and daughter, the Major changes the child's name from Ortega to Baxter. The last remaining Baxters live as father and daughter at Baxter's Bungalow, a huge house of twenty-five rooms on a rocky island promontory that looks across the white beach toward Florida, Cuba, the Yucatán.

For female companionship, the Major pilots his speedboat to the mainland, where he pays a thousand dollars a night to call girls. His favorite lady is a college student working her way through a course of premed studies at the university. (Her favorite subject is anatomy. She gets off on dissection—cutting up dead things.)

The college student call girl is a blond goddess named Myra Jane Wallace. Statuesque and beautiful, she reminds the Major of his dead daughter. The hunger in her eyes comes from losing both parents—her mother left home; her dad died. Raised by an aunt, she was sexually assaulted by the uncle.

When the Major entertains Myra Jane at Baxter's Bungalow, she falls in love with the house, the beach, the expensive ocean view. Lounging in a peignoir, she can easily envision herself presiding over the empire as Young Mrs. Baxter. No way, says the Major. He's an old man. He'll never marry again. Seeing it all slip away—the bungalow, the good life, the fortune—Myra Jane explodes into a blind rage. She latches on to Edward Severance, recently divorced. To stay close to her dream, Myra Jane marries Edward. At the wedding, the Major offers her money for sex. He misses her body. And her pecan pies.

Bored with Edward, Myra Jane softens the Major up with his favorite food—pecan pie—and offers him a deal: she'll take care of his sexual needs if he will finance the Marina Café. The Major agrees. For a couple of years, Myra Jane is happy. The café is a success. The Major needs her pecan pies. But her world collapses when Lacey Anne, coming home from a music lesson, catches them in flagrante.

Cursed by Lacey Anne's interruption, Myra Jane is barred from visiting the Bungalow. Again, threatened by the loss of the resource base, Myra Jane develops a hot hate for Lacey Anne. She's beautiful, svelte, smooth of hair and skin.

Lacey Anne turns sixteen. The Major, planning for the future, shows Myra Jane a new will. If anything happens to him, the Baxter fortune goes into a trust for Lacey Anne. The problem is clear: Lacey Anne stands in Myra Jane's way, spoiling her chances, ruining her life. It's time to take action.

Her plan has the simplicity of madness. To make room for herself in the Bungalow, she will kill Lacey Anne. To lead the police astray, she will build a pattern of serial killings. To satisfy society's lust for justice, she will choose a fall guy, a scapegoat to take the blame. In the process, she will get rid of Edward.

The scapegoat she chooses is Julius Bugliosi, a young musician from Juilliard with a band called Reggae Nouveau. Victims One and Two are chosen because they resemble Lacey Anne. They are young, blond, with that coltish sexiness that Myra Jane was forced to bypass in her tough teen years.

The victims are rock groupies. Their latest music industry crush is Julius and his Reggae Nouveau. To place the mark of the serial killer, Myra Jane spread-eagles her victims, simulating the servile passivity of the missionary position in sexual intercourse, and then she removes the womb. Cutting excites her. Because she lost her own womb in a botched abortion, Myra Jane hates motherhood, pregnancy, babies, the ugliness of giving birth. In a wild associative nightmare, she imagines her mother as the victim, imagines cutting into the womb. Being a Death Crone makes the killer feel very powerful. This is better than sex.

Victim Two dies on the mainland after a music event. Because of the pattern, the media brand Myra Jane the "Teen Angel Killer." After two hot newspaper stories, Armand DuPre, a crime writer, gets a book deal. The working title of Armand's book is *The Teen Angel Murders*.

As part of her scheme, the killer persuades the Major to pay Julius for a tryout for Lacey Anne. Give the child a thrill, says the killer. Test all those years of voice lessons. With her Sound, Lacey Anne is a surprise hit. Julius wants the Sound because it binds his musicians together as a unit. On their way to talk business with the Major, Julius and Lacey Anne are waylaid by Myra Jane, the killer in rubber boots. With Julius knocked out, Myra Jane forces Lacey

Anne to strip. Then she follows the steps taken for Victims One and
Two.

Myra Jane smears Julius with mud and blood. She drives him
back to the Village, where she parks the van a block from his motel.
In his fugue state, Julius can't remember what happened.

At the curve in the road, the Major and Ripley find the body of
Lacey Anne Baxter, the third Teen Angel victim. The Major calls the
sleuth, waking her up. Then he calls Myra Jane Severance, his only
close friend on the Island.

Example: Act One

The sleuth arrives at the crime scene to find the Major waiting in his
Suburban. Lit by the high-beam headlights, the sleuth examines the
victim. The death wound is a slashed throat; the thong is obscured
by mud. Because she cared so much, and also because this is her
first corpse, the sleuth vomits.

Smelling of vomit, the sleuth is pressured by the Major to
launch a manhunt for Julius. While the sleuth argues for proper
procedure, James T. Worthington arrives to claim jurisdiction for the
state police. The sleuth has no experience; James T. wants this case
for his career climb. Trudging to her Explorer, the sleuth encounters
Armand DuPre, an old flame. Armand wants to trade information.
They make a date for later, at the Marina Café.

In a witness interview, a friend of the victim places her in the
death van with Julius Bugliosi. At the Marina Café, Armand blows
the sleuth's mind with his detailed knowledge of the Teen Angel
killings. As they are going over his customer list from Tamara's, a
supplier of erotic gizmos, the killer interrupts. She's just left the
bungalow. The Major and James T. are masterminding a manhunt
for Julius.

At Baxter's Bungalow, the Major admits to the sleuth that Julius
was headed to the bungalow to get permission to hire Lacey Anne as
songbird for the band. Feeling left out by the macho manhunt, the
sleuth exits. On her way back to the village, the car phone buzzes.
The state police have Julius. His face is bruised from a beating. He's
about to be airlifted to the mainland—out of the sleuth's reach.

Example: Act Two—First Half

A late summer squall prevents the state police from airlifting Julius to the mainland. Until the storm lifts, Julius is held in the Village donjon, a film-set jail built to amuse the tourists. Julius has lost his memory. A medical expert hired by the town council calls it a fugue state.

The weather clears. A court order from a local judge prevents the state police from taking Julius away. Armand DuPre cannot get access to Julius. Myra Jane is connected. Perhaps she can help Armand. They make a date for later.

Edward Severance, the mayor of Drake Island Village, pressures the sleuth to get Julius off the island. The sleuth has no expertise in murder. And the phone lines are overloaded with tourists calling to cancel their Labor Day reservations. It's expensive having him here.

Having a murderer in town is bad for business.

The sleuth phones home. She calls for help. Her dad is a retired cop, a New York City homicide detective.

At the middle of Act Two, Armand DuPre meets with Myra Jane in her office at the Marina Café. This is her deal: She will get Armand in to see Julius if she can have a joint byline on his next Teen Angel piece. Armand balks at first, then gives in when Myra Jane stuns him with blinding insight into the heart of the killer.

Jazzed by Myra Jane's games, Armand writes notes on his laptop. When she asks to see the list of customers who bought thongs from Tamara's, Armand says okay. Seeing her old name on the list—M. J. Wallace—Myra Jane kills Armand, crushing his skull, slamming him with a meat mallet from the kitchen at the Marina Café.

The sleuth's dad arrives from New York City. Mayor Edward Severance, testy about the falling-off of tourist trade, fires the sleuth as town marshal.

Example: Act Two—Second Half

Armand's body is found on the marina. Because this victim is male, and because he was killed with a meat mallet instead of a scalpel, the police assume the presence of a second killer loose on the island. From the force of the hammer blows, they surmise, the killer of Armand DuPre had to be a man.

Still working on the Major's cover-up, the sleuth sends her dad to Mexico. She researches serial killers on the Internet.

With Julius targeted as the Teen Angel killer, Major Phil offers $100,000 for information leading to the capture of Armand's murderer. The Major's reward stimulates a gory tourist trade. As the tension thickens on Drake Island, long lines for the ferry take shape on the mainland. Families clutching their beach gear. Students on their way back to college. Hunters. Militia troopers wearing camo fatigues. Travel agents, smelling blood money, slap together tour packages: Manhunters needed to catch the killer of Drake Island.

Myra Jane lies to the sleuth, saying that husband Edward lusted after Lacey Anne Baxter. To prove her point, Myra Jane has photos of Edward and Lacey Anne at a party. Edward, high on gin, is grinning like a satyr. The phone rings. It's the Major, offering the sleuth her job back. With all the tourists, she's needed for crowd control.

The sleuth's dad calls from Mexico. Lacey Anne's birth certificate shows no name for the father. Lacey Anne's date of birth means that Annie Lee Baxter was pregnant before she went to Mexico. The father, Luis Carlos Ortega, was a fake. If the Major could fake a father, what else is he faking? What is the Major covering up?

At Baxter's Bungalow, the Major accuses Edward Severance of murdering both Lacey Anne and her mother. They fled to Mexico, the Major says, because Edward was a coward who would not admit his paternity. The child went crazy over music, the Major says, because Edward would pass her on the street and not acknowledge his fatherhood. On the desk in front of the Major are photos of Lacey Anne and Edward, showing the likeness in the Severance nose. Edward drops into a deep depression.

The sleuth finds Edward in her chair at the town hall. He's drunk, deeply depressed. "I killed her," he says. "I murdered my own daughter." Worried about Edward, the sleuth pulls a deputy off crowd control for a suicide watch. When she looks into the donjon, Julius Bugliosi is gone. The state police have taken him to a holding facility near the Charleston station. The deputy beds Edward down in the donjon.

Except for a couple of drunks, the Village is quiet. She feels bad about Julius; he is no longer her problem. Labor Day is tomorrow. The sleuth hates crowd control. On her way home, she prays for rain.

Example: Act Three

The sleuth is tired. Her brain, filled to the brim, is spilling over. She pulls out a photo album to look at old photos of that summer she was beach pals with Myra Jane. Her memory work is interrupted by a visit from Myra Jane. Lulled by wine and the photos, the sleuth unburdens herself to Myra Jane, sharing her feelings about men.

Men are pigs, says the killer. And then she tells the sleuth about her own poverty-stricken childhood, a real Cinderella story. Mom left. Dad died. Myra Jane lived with Aunt Myra, who she was named for, and Uncle Vincent, who taught her about sex, who got her pregnant. A botched abortion took both fetus and womb. It's a good thing, not having a womb, says the killer. A womb is trouble. It cuts into your pleasure.

As Myra Jane reveals her childhood trauma, the phone rings. The caller is the sleuth's dad, who wants a meeting in Charleston. Julius is lucid again. Myra Jane leaves, looking serene. The Major has asked her to move into the bungalow. Edward is a loser. She feels pity for him; not love. The killer's plan has worked.

The sleuth borrows the Major's fastest boat to pick up Dad on the mainland. In a reflective mood, Dad plays What-If. What if the killer was a female?

At the state police holding facility, the sleuth stands aside while Dad uses his police expertise to gain access to Julius. His memory has returned. He denies killing Lacey Anne. She was his angel, the lady with the voice. When the sleuth shows Julius photos of Myra Jane, he shakes his head. As the sleuth exits, Julius asks to see the photos again. He thinks he remembers seeing Myra Jane at the concerts where Victims One and Two were killed. Julius likes blondes.

Back on Drake Island, the sleuth finds a package from Armand containing the customer list from Tamara's Boutique Erotique. Before she can examine the list, Edward Severance hangs himself in the donjon. Edward's suicide note admits that he rejected his daughter, Lacey Anne. That's why she was killed.

Armed with Tamara's customer list, the sleuth asks for the Major's help to trap Myra Jane. The Major says no way. She's his only friend. She did a lot for Lacey Anne. That gig with Julius and the band was Myra Jane's idea. He's going to marry her.

The sleuth re-creates the crimes: Victims One, Two, Three. The Major's face clouds. He doesn't believe her. The sleuth pulls out Tamara's customer list. The Major recognizes the name of M. J. WALLACE. The sleuth pulls out the thong worn by the corpse of Lacey Anne. With tears in his eyes, the Major says okay.

The trap is pure queen replacement. Myra Jane tried to replace Lacey Anne. Now the sleuth will replace Myra Jane. Pushing the Major along the marina boardwalk, the sleuth stops at the Marina Café. Myra Jane is not there, so the sleuth shares her news with the cashier: the Major is taking her away for a honeymoon; he will marry the sleuth, not Myra Jane. The Major has made a new will.

Myra Jane arrives at Baxter's Bungalow with a concealed scalpel. She accuses the Major of sleeping with the sleuth. The Major asks her to witness the new will making the sleuth his executor, with a provision for building a writers' retreat on Drake Island.

The killer goes berserk. Pulls out the scalpel. Slices through the Major's jacket. The wheelchair topples over. Holding her Glock 9mm, the sleuth enters the room. You won't shoot me, the killer says. You don't have the stomach for it.

Tears burst from the sleuth's eyes. The killer advances. The sleuth shakes all over. She can hear her teeth chattering. She says nothing. The time for talk is over. The killer argues the merits of sisterhood, the women against the men. Then, screaming her rage, she charges the sleuth.

The sleuth fires. The force of the bullet knocks the killer off her feet. She can't believe what happened. Like all death gods, the killer thought she was invincible.

The sleuth delivers Myra Jane to James T. Worthington of the state police.

The sleuth resigns from her job as town marshal. She's leaving Drake Island. Over drinks at Baxter's Bungalow, the Major makes his proposition. He's feeling real lonely. He will pay the sleuth money, lots of it, to stick around, live at the bungalow, be his companion. The sleuth refuses. Her writer's block is gone and she has a book to write. Thanks for the drink. Got to be going. It's time to hit those keys.

Guidelines for Writing the Working Synopsis

1. *Be kind to yourself.*
Because the book is not finished, and also because you know more about some stretches of the story than about others, the working synopsis will have strong spots and weak places. Imperfection is okay; to have gaps in your mystery synopsis won't kill you.

A working synopsis is a writer's tool, a part of the plotting process. If a weak place shows up, view it as an opportunity for your creativity. You can patch a weak place, shoring it up with narrative summary. The reason to write a synopsis now is to produce a feeling of closure by getting to the end. When you write, be kind to yourself, not critical.

2. *Divide and conquer.*
The easy way to write a long narrative piece is to divide it into parts. Follow the example in this chapter, which has five parts:

1. Back story
2. Act One
3. Act Two, first half
4. Act Two, second half
5. Act Three

Because of your work on Weekend 5, you have most of the back story worked out. One of the exercises was to write a narrative passage. You can add to that passage now because you know more about your plot.

Back story—events in the past that shape actions in the present—gives you the foundation for writing the rest of the synopsis. Divide your scene cards into four stacks. Flip through each stack, noting information like who's in the scene, the time and place, the atmosphere, the weather, the season, objects that could become clues, and what happens.

3. *Set a time limit.*

Professional writers often find they work better under the pressure of a deadline. Their focus is sharper as the deadline nears. They write with more power, more simplicity, more confidence. You can use this same deadline pressure by writing under the clock. Try this: allot one hour or less for a first draft; after a break, allot more time for your rewrite, but still use the pressure of the timer.

In your first hour, give yourself ten to fifteen minutes for the back story, ten minutes for Act One, twenty minutes for Act Two, and ten minutes for Act Three. You can work in the notebook or on the computer. The trick is to keep moving. Don't stop to think and consider and get hypercritical. Whatever you miss in the first draft you can pick up in the rewrite.

Taking a break is important. Rest. Drink tea. Meditate. Refresh yourself.

Before you rewrite, read through your first draft. Take notes as you read. Write down key words. If you work under the clock again, expand the times where the writing needs work. If Act Two is perfect, allot less time there and more time for Acts One and Three.

4. *Have fun with language.*

Because this working synopsis is for your eyes only, you have an opportunity to play with words. Repetition can be fun. Try starting half a dozen sentences the way we started this sentence, with the word *because,* which generates sentences about cause and effect: "Because the killer wanted the big house, she engineered a tryout for the victim with the band. Because the victim wanted recognition—something to cling to—she sang her heart out. Because she

sang her heart out, the scapegoat heard the sound of the big time.
Because he heard the sound, the scapegoat drove through the night
to barter with the victim's guardian. Because the victim climbed into
his van, she died in the mud and rain. . . ."

Your goal in this early, bare-bones synopsis is to gain insight into
the story, to help you write the book. When you're writing along, see
what happens when you open several sentences in a row with *and
then*, giving your language a biblical cadence:

"And then the victim wanted a shot at singing with the band.
And then she agreed to talk to the Major. And then the killer am-
bushed the death van on the road, a mile from home. And then the
Major went looking for his granddaughter. And then the killer . . ."

· · ·

WORKING THE NOVEL

Exercises

1. *Back Story.*
Before you plunge into writing the working synopsis, take a few
minutes to rewrite the events in your back story. As you rewrite,
allow your mind to play with the important connections between major characters, with time and place, and with objects
that you're turning into clues.

In the back story for *The Big Sleep*, Miss Carmen Sternwood
kills her brother-in-law. In the back story for *Body*, the killer
kills the victim, then frames the scapegoat. In the back story for
Fugitive, Ann Fowler kills a pregnant teen and frames her
brother for the murder.

If you're using a timer to create deadline pressure, take ten
to fifteen minutes for back story.

2. *Dividing the Writing.*
Divide your writing into four parts: Act One, Act Two (first half,
second half), and Act Three. Using these same four parts, separate your scene cards, one stack for each section.

Read through the scene cards quickly. If you're holding your breath, remember to breathe deeply as you scan your material. Try to withhold judgment. You're still in discovery; the writing here is adventuresome.

Write the synopsis in four sections, from Act One to Act Three. If you're using a timer to create deadline pressure, give yourself the same time for each section. When the timer beeps, stop. Move to the next section.

3. *Take a Break.*
Rest. Meditate. Take a walk. Run around the block. Ride your HealthRider around the room. When you have rested, read your first draft.

4. *Rewriting the Synopsis: Second Draft.*
When you rewrite, focus on Act Two first—most books fall apart in Act Two. Rewrite Act Two before you tackle One and Three. To create deadline pressure, use the timer. If you took ten minutes to draft Act Two, double the time for the rewrite.

Weekends 10–13
Scene Building

The main building block for your mystery is the scene. A scene is a single action or a series of connected actions taking place in a single setting in a finite period of time.

In the old days—the days of Agatha Christie and Sherlock Holmes, of Dorothy Sayers and Dashiell Hammett—mystery readers grew up reading. These days, they grow up watching TV. The crime dramas that grab viewers on television, from the sixties classic *Naked City*, to *Murder, She Wrote* and *NYPD Blue* and beyond, are constructed with scenes.

The first scene of your favorite crime drama, for example, might show the street, a figure running. The street is the setting. The running figure is Character D, a rookie cop known to the viewers from previous episodes. The camera uses lighting to show the time of the scene, whether it's night or day. The camera zooms in for a close-up of the face of Character D. Sweat on the forehead, fear in the eyes, lips raked back from white teeth.

Scene One lasts forty-five seconds. It ends as Character D, the rookie, rounds a corner, into the sound of gunfire. Character D goes down; the screen goes dark. When the camera makes a jump cut from the dark street to a lighted room, the viewer knows from setting that the scene is done, that a new scene is under way.

The street is an exterior setting. The room, an interior, is the setting for Scene Two. There are desks in the room, giving a feeling of clutter. The folks who work here inhabit a pressure cooker. On each desk a telephone, a scratch pad, case folders.

The walls of the room are pea-green. There are grilles on the windows, a crosshatched web of wire mesh. A phone rings and a receptionist picks up the phone. This is action, a ringing phone, a woman answering. The phone call is for Character A. When the receptionist says, "Line three, Detective," and Character A says, "Got it," that's dialogue.

Character A speaks into the phone. "Herrera," he says, "Homicide."

If you study what's happening on the screens of today's fast-moving world, you'll understand the power of the scene for your mystery. The scene is alive, excitement pulses on the screen, something's about to happen. What happens on the screen in a crime drama is the same thing that's got to happen in your book: characters with agendas, characters taking action in a setting, characters revealing conflict through dialogue and gesture.

One key to the scene is a thread. Screenwriters call this the "through-line." A through-line links action and reaction. The phone rings. The receptionist answers. That's action followed by reaction.

The call is for Character A, a detective in the Eighth Precinct. The caller is a snitch, calling from outside, from the street. The message is "Officer down." Because it's outside, and because the viewer just saw the rookie falling, there's a chance the call connects Character A to the rookie, Character D.

Sweat beads form on the forehead of Character A. The receptionist catches his eye. In earlier episodes, she's been dating the rookie. Now her face cracks, showing emotion. Character A makes a quick note, rips the page from his notebook. He slams the phone down. Tension explodes in the cluttered room.

Character B enters the scene, crossing the threshold just as Character A grabs his overcoat and a navy-blue muffler. The overcoat means it's autumn or winter or a cold wintry spring outside. The kind of muffler, an object in the setting, is an indicator of income, taste, character behavior, style, likes and dislikes, mind-set. If you change the muffler from navy-blue wool to slick gray silk, the wardrobe item conveys new information about Character A. Under the tough-guy mask, perhaps Character A conceals a streak of the dandy. Or maybe the muffler was inherited from Dad, a dandy in showbiz. If the muffler belonged to Dad, maybe it's worn like a hair shirt, a penance.

The thread here—phone ringing, phone answered, message for Character A, "Officer down," Character A responding, receptionist reacting—leads the viewer to the third scene in this sequence. Scene One is "Man Running." Scene Two, "The Squad Room," ends as Character A and Character B exit, going back across the threshold, from inside to outside. Since they exit together, they must be partners.

Scene Three of this sequence—the "Crime Scene"—takes us back to the street for a viewing of the setting where the officer went down. Scene One ended as Officer D was seen going down. The viewer heard shots but did not see the shooter. Only the setting remains. The setting forms the base for the crime scene, the platform for launching the story. The objects in the setting—wardrobe, weapons, body parts, et cetera—become clues that lead the sleuth to the killer. Because the viewer did not see what happened, there is suspense while we find out.

The Importance of Scenes

The mystery writer writes scenes because today's readers are also today's viewers: for them, stories are scene driven. The fact that you write scenes, using them to structure your book, does not eliminate the need for narrative summary. Because narrative summary is easy to write, and because it compresses time while it divulges important information, you will still use it as one of your writing tools. Narrative summary is especially useful if you have written half a dozen short scenes to close a time gap in your plot. Because this time gap showed up when you mapped out your book with a diagram, you're ready to close the gap when you get there. With planning, you eliminate nasty surprises. An excellent model for closing a time gap in the mystery is the "Shatura" section of *Gorky Park*. As we pointed out in the plotting section, the sleuth is wounded in May at the university fountain. The writer needs a time gap between May and November for four reasons:

1. The sleuth needs time to heal from his near-death knife wound.

2. The KGB needs time for an inquisition that places the blame, making the sleuth a scapegoat in his own murder case.

3. The Prime Suspect who opened the book, KGB Officer Pribluda, needs to atone for his sins by saving the sleuth's life. If Pribluda can change, there is hope for mankind.

4. The writer planned to close off his story where it began, with death in the snow.

Narrative summary is extremely useful when you're in discovery mode, hot on the trail of insight. When you write to complete an exercise for this book, for example, you're using narrative summary. One of the steps in scene building is to capture the essence of the scene by turning the material on the scene card into narrative summary.

But while narrative summary is useful at certain points in the book, it doesn't help you build a story with power and forward thrust. And because narrative summary is seductive, writers of fiction sometimes rely on it too much, writing page after page of lush prose that the modern reader, trained on television, can perceive as essay or lecture.

Writing in scenes for your book won't give you the same breathless pace of movies or television. But scenes keep the book going. A scene has its own internal structure. It begins, the action rises to a peak, it ends. When a scene ends, you write another scene. The purpose of the next four weekends is to help you make scene building into a craft, a writer's reflex. Scene building takes practice. You'll need to build half a dozen scenes before you feel truly comfortable with the craft. But the payoff from scenes, like the payoff from plotting, is big.

Parts of a Scene

As suggested by the fictionalized TV drama above, a scene has three component parts: action, setting, and dialogue.

Action is the man running along the street, the receptionist answering the phone, the sleuth grabbing his overcoat. Setting is the place, the street and its buildings, the room and its contents. Dialogue is the words spoken by two characters: Character E speaks and Character A answers.

To write a scene, you can build it from the ground up, starting with setting, and add action and dialogue. Or you can build from the inside, starting with dialogue or action, and add the other elements later.

The important thing is to separate the parts.

- *Dialogue.* Isolate the dialogue and work on that, amplifying the rhythm, the pulse beat of language that connects the two characters.
- *Action.* Isolate the action and add reaction and replace weak verbs with strong verbs and then have a friend read it, just the action sequence, while you listen.
- *Setting.* Isolate the setting—the time and place, the temperature and the season, the lighting that throws shadows—and work on its logic.

Example: If Character A wears a sweater in the office and if he grabs an overcoat before heading outside, there's a good chance you're not viewing an episode of *Miami Vice*. That's the logic of setting. If you reverse the logic of setting, upending viewer expectation by sending Character A bundled up in his overcoat and sweater out into a street seething with heat and humidity and naked nymphs cavorting in fountains, you're into farce, dream, or surrealist fantasy.

The work you've been doing on character (Weekends 1–4) and plot (Weekends 5–9) will feed into the work you do on scene building. Your characters wait to enter the story with agendas bristling. You know why the victim died and where the killer killed her. Because of your work on back story, you know what the characters were wearing at the killing scene. From your work on plotting, you know where characters enter the story, and where they exit. You know which characters are most able to carry subplots and who's going to die next.

The scene we've chosen to launch you into scene building is the crime scene. In most mysteries, the crime scene comes early in the book. If it's not the opening scene, as in *Gorky Park,* then it comes in right away, as in *The Body in the Library.* If this is your first mystery, we suggest you start the book with the crime scene. As your writing skill grows, you can play with the elements of mystery, shifting the crime-scene placement to suit your purpose:

• In *The Silence of the Lambs,* Thomas Harris holds back his crime scene—the sleuth's discovery of a victim killed by Dr. Lecter—so he can use it deep in Act One. The purpose of this scene in *Lambs* is to test the sleuth. The killer reveals himself as a death god. He wants to see how the sleuth handles his display of power. Will she freak out? Will she grow as a pro?

• In *The Big Sleep,* Chandler uses the crime scene as the setting for the climax, where Marlowe confronts Miss Carmen Sternwood, nailing her as the killer. The setting is an abandoned oil field down below the lofty heights of Sternwood Manor. By returning to the crime scene where she killed her brother-in-law, the killer thinks she can kill the sleuth and get away with it. But the sleuth has seen the killer's heart. Because he knows she'll try to kill him, he loads her little gun with blanks.

• In Sue Grafton's *"F" Is for Fugitive,* the crime scene is shoved deep into the past—"Seventeen years ago, Jean Timberlake's body had been found at the foot of the sea wall"—and then eased it out of sight, concealing it from both sleuth and reader: ". . . but the spot wasn't visible from where I stood." The work here in *Fugitive* is digging up the past, a Herculean task of hauling up the weight of seventeen years.

On Weekend 10, you'll use narrative summary to explore the dynamics of the crime scene. On Weekend 11, you'll study the function of dialogue in scenes. On Weekend 12, you'll study how action works in the scene. On Weekend 13, you'll combine setting with action and dialogue to round out the complete scene.

· WEEKEND 10 ·
CRIME SCENE

The crime scene is a sacred space, a place of unholy sacrifice created by killing. Killing transforms the victim into a corpse. Death is a transition, a passage from one world to another, from the known to the unknown, from light to dark. The residue of this transition is displayed to the reader in the crime scene. The symbolism of the crime scene is powerful: someone died here, in this sacred space.

The officials in charge of this sacred space are the police. They control access. Control gives them power, authority over everyone who wants access. Miss Jane Marple, Christie's spinster sleuth, must get help from her helper to cross the threshold into the crime scene at Gossington. The house belongs to Dolly Bantry. The crime scene belongs to the police. A member of the official police order, the stolid Constable Palk, is the threshold guardian. Like the eternal boatman who poles dead souls across the River Styx, the threshold guardian at the crime scene must be bought, tricked, or overwhelmed. In *The Body in the Library*, Dolly Bantry overwhelms the constable by reducing him from a man to a small boy. "Don't be stupid," she says, using her voice of schoolmistress, Grande Dame, and matron to the downtrodden.

This threshold, the invisible barrier that keeps the police inside and everyone else outside, is one reason to write the crime scene now, and to use it to open your story. As we suggested in the introduction, the action at this threshold produces dramatic conflict. The Crime Reporter wants in; the police block her way. When a character who wants something gets blocked, the writer has a chance to create drama. To create drama, the writer takes another look at motive and agenda. How badly does the Crime Reporter want inside? What will she pay? What will she risk? What will it take to make her give up and go home and get out of the rain? If she can't cross the threshold, is there another way to get what she wants? If there is another way, you have just triggered another scene.

For the Crime Reporter in search of a story, the corpse inside

the official police circle is the resource base. For this hungry jour-
nalist, a resource base is fodder for a news story. Good fodder means
she can keep working. Working means she can keep eating. Eating
means she stays alive.

For your sleuth, an individual who has experience with death,
the crime scene holds the key to the crime. Seeing a corpse who was
once an innocent victim ushers in a feeling of moral outrage. The
moral outrage sends the sleuth on the quest for the killer. An innocent victim has died; now someone must pay.

Guidelines for Writing the Scene

Because there are three parts to scene building—action, dialogue,
and setting—you can start with any part, write fast and hard, and fill
in with the other two. To separate those elements for study, you use
a scene profile. To gather the material for the scene profile, you
write a narrative summary. To write a narrative summary, you use
the scene cards you've been developing since Weekend 1.

Scene Cards. You created your first scene card—"Killer Onstage"—on Weekend 1. On Weekend 2, the death of your victim in
the back story created a scene card called "Crime Scene." On Weekend 3, with your sleuth coming into focus, you added more detail to
fill out the crime scene.

During the next few weekends, you have made more notes
about the crime scene. Some of the notes have been on the scene
card; some have been in the notebook. You collected these notes for
this moment, writing a narrative summary of your crime scene.

Narrative Summary. A narrative summary compresses your
crime scene into a paragraph or two. In writing it, you move from
action (what the characters do) to dialogue (what they say) to setting
(where they are). While you're writing, you make no attempt to separate the action from the dialogue, to isolate the dialogue from
the setting. That comes later. If a thought occurs to you in the narrative summary, you write it down. If your writing takes you inside the
sleuth's head, you write down what the sleuth is thinking. If
the writing moves you from the sleuth's head to the head of the
corpse who lies there dead, you write down what the corpse is think-

ing. You write quickly, moving through the scene, noting points of conflict where Agenda A clashes with Agenda B. You try to have fun as you make discoveries. Here's an example of a narrative summary for *Murder on Drake Island:*

The scene of the crime is a muddy turn in the beach road on the southern tip of Drake Island. The time is predawn, a black night cloaking a grim morning. The rain, which started around midnight, has stopped. The season is late summer, a weekday before Labor Day weekend.

Headlights of the sleuth's vehicle stab through the dark to light up a Chevrolet Suburban. A fierce light from inside the Suburban means the Major is smoking his cigar. The sleuth is nervous. This is her first murder case. She remembers her flashlight, but forgets her weapon. The weapon, a Glock 9mm, is kept in a holster bolted to the raised hump of the gearbox, within quick reach of the sleuth's right hand.

On the way to the Suburban to speak to the Major, the sleuth catches a glimpse of a light in tall sea-grass. The light goes out. She speaks to the Major. He points in the direction of the body. Probing the dark with her flashlight, the sleuth slogs through the mud to view the corpse.

The body is a young girl, naked, streaked with mud. The girl is Lacey Anne Baxter, illegitimate granddaughter of Major Philip Baxter, the cigar-smoking man in the Suburban. She is spread-eagled, her wrists and ankles bound by black ribbons to wooden tent stakes. Her throat is slit. And her wrists. Her eyes are wide open, her blond hair is fanned out around her head in an awful halo. Because the sleuth is an amateur—her job is traffic control on tourist-heavy weekends—she is not aware that this is a serial killing. The sleuth, who knows the victim, reacts to the sight of her corpse by vomiting. With knees weak from horror, she returns to the Suburban to speak to the Major.

The dialogue between the sleuth and the Major begins softly and ends on a harsh note. The Major, along with his man Ripley, found the body spread-eagled in the road. The Major talks as if he knows who did this—Julius Bugliosi, the Afro-American band-leader—and pressures the sleuth to make an arrest before Julius escapes from the island. The sleuth, new to murder, insists on proper police procedure: controlling access to the crime scene, preserving the evidence for the crime-lab people, who come from the mainland.

The power struggle between the Major and the sleuth is interrupted by the arrival of James T. Worthington, a detective sergeant in the state police. Worthington, on the island for a week's fishing, picked up the sleuth's call for the crime lab and raced to the scene. As a professional policeman, he's been following the Teen Angel murders—one in Orangeburg, another in Charleston. If he can break this case, it will jump-start him into a promotion. Assuming control of the crime scene, James T. follows the Major's finger of accusation and puts out an all-points bulletin for Julius Bugliosi, wanted for questioning. . . .

Ejected from the sacred circle of her own crime scene, the sleuth heads for her vehicle. She is behind the wheel when Armand DuPre raps on her window. Armand, a writer of true crime who's been tracking the Teen Angel killings for a big-city daily, is here because he picked up the call to the crime lab on his police scanner.

The sleuth stares at Armand. He is a vulture. But she does need a helper. She makes a date for ten, at the Marina Café, where they will share information on the killing. She shakes hands with Armand and drives off.

After writing the narrative summary, you organize the material by separating the information into parts. The tool used for separation is the scene profile.

Scene Profile. A scene profile, like a character profile, provides slots you fill with details. Each slot in the scene profile—setting, character, dialogue, action, secrets, et cetera—queries your brain for an answer. Under the action slot, for example, you might write something like this:

"Action: Kneeling beside the corpse to shine her flashlight into the face, the sleuth reacts by vomiting." Under the slot for setting, you might write this: "Closed Circle: A parabola of light made by the headlights of the Major's Suburban. Mud, a naked corpse, ruts made by tires. When the sleuth intrudes, the Major keeps the lights burning. The yellow crime scene ribbons will go up when the crime-lab techs arrive."

At this stage of the writing, a scene profile is handy for breaking up narrative summary, separating it into the parts of a scene, giving you material to convert into drama. When you rewrite the book, scene profiles are used again as analytical tools to help you understand what a scene does.

To create a scene profile, you start with a slot for character. Who's in the scene? Why are they here? What are they wearing? What are they not wearing? What agendas are they working out? Since your main purpose for making the profile now is to separate the parts, you include slots for setting, dialogue, and action.

Under setting, you note time and place, temperature, and season, lighting (sunlight, moonlight, klieg light, shadows, et cetera), and important objects like weapons, money, body parts, and so on. Under the slot for dialogue you note the subject, what the characters are talking about, as well as the tone. If Character A defends (a passive tone) while Character B attacks (an active, offensive tone), you are exploring tone of voice as a clue to power—who has the upper hand in this scene.

Under the slot for action you note the core action—the KGB major cracking open frozen coats—and then the smaller actions or reactions. The sleuth's reaction to the cracking of clothing is to light a cigarette. If an action leads to a ritual, create a slot in the scene profile to explore the meaning of the ritual. For example, when the sleuth of *Gorky Park* lights his cigarette, he hides behind the smoke. The reason he hides behind the smoke is to keep himself under control. The KGB major outranks the sleuth. If the sleuth stays in control now, if he can continue to hide behind the smoke until the major leaves, he'll live to fight another day.

The scene profile is a flexible tool; the slots can change to fit the size of the writing task. In the *Gorky Park* crime scene, you might use a slot like "Objects Onstage" to develop a close-up of the corpses. Your entry under the slot for "Objects Onstage" might read like this: "The faces have been flayed. The act of flaying was done with a special knife. The knife, which is missing from the crime scene, turns up at the climax. The owner of the knife is the killer,

John Osborne. He uses the knife to skin sables. And to gut William Kirwill."

The slots in the scene profile are expandable. They function like file folders to contain what you need for your story. Because you can add extra folders, your profile can expand, grow longer, contain more powerful detail. The slot for the crime-scene setting on Drake Island might subdivide into a slot for lighting; lighting might lead the writing toward mood and atmosphere as the sleuth eyes the corpse from a distance:

"Headlights of the Suburban cut through the darkness to light up something in the road. A sea of mud. Ruts and wallows. Mud pulls on the sleuth's rubber boots. Mud holds her tight as she walks out of shadow into the tunnel of the headlight. The corpse is naked. Her body is streaked with mud. The bright headlights make deep shadows on her throat. A dead sea smell blows in from the east. Raindrops spatter the white flesh. If there was a vehicle, the rain has washed away all traces. The sleuth kneels down. The mud is cold on her knees through the blue jeans. . . ."

A checklist of slots you might include as you develop your scene profile:

- *Name of the Scene* (Crime Scene, Witness Interview, et cetera)

- *Position in the Structure* (Act One, Act Two, et cetera)

- *Character* (who's onstage, who's wearing what, who wants what from whom)

- *Setting* (time and place, temperature and season, lighting, objects like weapons that might develop into clues)

- *Dialogue* (subject of the dialogue, key words, tone of voice, power hierarchy for dramatic conflict)

- *Action* (core action, smaller actions and reactions)

- *Climax* (where the scene peaks)

- *Ritual* (a repeated action that might have symbolic overtones; example: lighting a cigarette to create a smoke shield to hide behind)

- *Plot Links* (an object in this scene surfaces in another scene: the tawdry dress in the crime scene might surface later in a sleuth analysis scene; ice skates from the crime scene lead the sleuth to the femme fatale, et cetera)

WORKING THE NOVEL

Exercises

1. *Placement.*
Using the diagrams you sketched for your plot picture from Weekends 5–9, review the position of your crime scene in the structure of the book. Are you planning to use the crime scene to open your story? If you open with the crime scene, following the model for *Gorky Park,* will your sleuth enter the story at that point? If you're delaying the crime scene until later (Christie's strategy in *Body*), make sure you have a strategic reason for holding off. Christie waits until she brings her sleuth onstage, delaying the reader's first view of the crime scene; delay, when timed right, builds suspense.

2. *Narrative Summary.*
Write a narrative summary of your crime scene. Touch on these items: character (who's onstage, who's coming on, wardrobe as an index to character and lifestyle); victim as focal point in the setting, and the subject of the dialogue; details in the setting that suggest mood or atmosphere; action that controls access to the sacred circle of death. Is the victim identified at this time? What traces did the killer leave behind at the crime scene? How old is the scene?

If you have discovered that you write better under time pressure, set your timer for ten to fifteen minutes.

3. *Scene Profile.*

Using the slots suggested in the Guidelines—Name of the Scene, Position in the Structure, Character, Setting, Dialogue, Action, Climax, Ritual, and Plot Links—build a profile for your crime scene.

Here's what you might do with a profile of the *Murder on Drake Island* crime scene:

Name: Crime Scene.

Position: The Crime Scene opens the book. Starts Act One.

Character: Sleuth Helen F. Steinbeck comes onstage wearing a rain parka and rubber rain boots. The Major sits in his Suburban, smoking a cigar. James Worthington, a sergeant from the state police, wears tourist clothes, string-tie pants, and a short-sleeve shirt from J. Crew, the mail-order clothier. The intruder, Armand DuPre, wears a reporter's trench coat.

The sleuth enters the story as an amateur. Tracking the killer, coming face to face with evil, transforms the sleuth. To survive the weekend, she must grow.

Setting: The time is predawn on South Beach Road on Drake Island, South Carolina. Headlights carve the dark. It's cold in the wind; the rain has stopped, leaving mud everywhere. The rain has wiped out all traces of the killer, tire tracks, footprints, even blood. The season is late summer. The corpse lies spread-eagled in the road, her body streaked with mud. The corpse is the central image. No murder weapon found at the scene.

Objects Onstage: Mud. Muddy boots, muddy tires, mud on the corpse. Black ribbon on her ankles and wrists, tying her to tent stakes. The sleuth's weapon, a Glock 9mm, is heavy and useless. Rain parka, rubber boots, warm socks, faded jeans. The Major's Chevrolet Suburban, cigar smoke, sad eyes, safari hat, the Major's powerful arms. The car driven by James T. Worthington. His Hawaiian shirt and thong sandals. His cheap plastic raincoat. The trench coat of Armand DuPre. His pad and pencil. Flashlights. Headlights. Black night.

Dialogue: The dialogue with the Major is about sadness and confusion: Who did this? Why Lacey Anne? The Major's desire to arrest Julius ratchets up the tension, creating dramatic conflict: the sleuth wants to follow procedure. She refuses to let the Major order her around. The Major accuses this Julius Bugliosi fellow. He's a musician, and therefore, in the Major's view, a logical killer.

The dialogue with James T. Worthington is about ability. He's experienced. The sleuth is an amateur. He assumes control of the crime scene, creating a closed circle, ejecting the sleuth. His message to the sleuth: Leave this to the pros and go back to beach patrol.

The dialogue with Armand DuPre is about sharing information. The sleuth needs a helper. She doesn't like Armand—for a short time, they were lovers—but she needs his help to crack this case.

Action: The core action taken by the sleuth is viewing the body. To get there, she exits her vehicle, goes back for her weapon, speaks to the Major, trudges through the mud, views the body, reacts by vomiting, cuts her eyes at Ripley's flashlight, trudges back to the Suburban, climbs in, feels the warmth, smells the cigar smoke, exits when she sees the vehicle of James T. Worthington. Ejected from the closed circle, the sleuth is leaving when she encounters Armand DuPre. She makes a date with Armand. She shakes hands. And drives off.

Climax: The scene peaks when the sleuth is ejected from the closed circle. This is her crime scene, but she can't get access. Being ejected means she has no power. She's an amateur, a female, a writer. Even though she slept with James T. Worthington a couple of times, that experience is worth nothing in the muddy expanse of the crime scene.

Ritual: The sleuth goes through the motions—driving to the crime scene, speaking to the Major, vomiting on viewing the body, soothing the Major, defending her turf—without knowing what she's doing. The sleuth is in a trance, a cocoon to protect her against the awful sight of the dead girl. Through the veil of her trance, the sleuth realizes that the state of the corpse— stripped down, streaked with mud, a single leather thong stretched across her belly—was a dressing ritual performed by the killer. The ritual is in code, a message from killer to sleuth. At this point, the sleuth is unable to decode.

Plot Links: The Turf War started by James T. Worthington at the crime scene will continue through the story. To gain control of her turf, the sleuth will be forced to grow. The Major's suspicions of Julius Bugliosi get him arrested as the designated scapegoat. Framing the killer, as we saw in the plotting section, is part of building the back story. The nosiness of Armand Du- Pre will get him killed at midpoint.

• • •

Your main focus in this scene profile is isolating the parts of a scene—dialogue, action, setting, ritual, et cetera—so you can expand and deepen each part as a separate element. Because the scene profile is so flexible, you may add information as it surfaces. In the example above, the slot for "Setting" spilled over into a slot newly created for "Objects Onstage." When you use the scene profile, it helps to stay fluid.

· WEEKEND 11 ·
DIALOGUE

Imagine you're watching the Movie of the Week version of *Murder on Drake Island.* The scene is that muddy road where the killer killed the victim, then removed her womb. The sleuth, wearing boots and jeans and a rain parka, parks her vehicle, then trudges through the heavy mud to the Chevrolet Suburban. Cigar smoke floats at her through the window. The tip of the cigar glows red against the Major's face. The sleuth feels like waiting. Waiting for dawn. Waiting for the crime-lab people. Waiting for the killer to give himself up. Waiting and waiting and waiting some more. This could be her opening dialogue with the Major:

> Hello, Marshal.
> Hello, Major. I got here as quickly as possible.
> You want to see her?
> Yes.
> You don't sound like it.
> I want to see her. It's my job.
> She's across there. In the goddamn mud. Look.

> [The Major flicks on the headlights. Across the rutted road, in a parabola of light, the sleuth sees an apparition. A ghost. A phantom. Before the sleuth can focus, the lights go off, leaving the red dots dancing on her eyelids. She climbs out, boots squishy in mud. Pulled by the beam of her flashlight, the sleuth trudges through the mud toward the apparition. It's not Lacey Anne. Not. Not. Not.]

Author Onstage

As the sleuth heads toward the corpse, a man in a turtleneck sweater and snazzy tweed jacket steps in front of the camera. This person is the writer-director of this particular Movie of the Week. The face of this writer-director fills the screen, shutting out the actors in the mud, while the writer-director delivers this monologue:

"Hi, folks. Let me take a moment to explain what's happening here. The subject of this conversation between my main characters is a serial killing. The victim is Lacey Anne Baxter and she's the granddaughter of Major Phil Baxter, played by Jack Tremaine, a great star. According to the script, we'll be bringing Lacey Anne back in Act Two. When Helene, played by Julia Rhodes, returns to the van, you'll be able to see some terrific conflict building over this scapegoat motif. The Major has this Julius Bugliosi character caught, tried, convicted, and strapped down in the chair. It's pitch-black out there, folks, and my crew gets credit for working overtime in the dark in three inches of rain. Rain works in the plot; it's very tough to film in. Well, okay, now that you know what's going down here, let's get back to the story."

Caveat Scriptor—Let the Writer Beware

In fiction, authors are tempted to intrude to explain their dialogue. When the writer steps in to explain things, it's called an "authorial intrusion." Authorial intrusion is like the playwright galloping onstage to stop the action so he can explain his play to the audience in the theater. It might seem important to the writer to explain the scene, but how does it sit with the reader? The theatergoer? The viewer of movies or television?

Judge for yourself. How do you react to this author explanation? Is it necessary? Or is it intrusive? Do you hit the channel changer? Do you stop reading? Do you leap up from the couch and head for the fridge? Is this lecture by the writer-director on the meaning of the dialogue an insult to your intelligence?

Explanation kills dialogue. Dialogue works because it clears the air. Dialogue is two characters talking. Character A speaks; Character B answers. Authors explain dialogue because they don't trust their characters. That's why we started you out on Weekend 1 with character: so you could get to know your characters. When you know your characters, they'll work for you, help you out with the plot. On Weekends 1–4, you groomed your characters, readying them to enter the story. When they enter the story, let them enter talking. Letting them talk does not mean Character A talks while Character B listens. That's an active lecturer and a listener about to doze off. Letting them talk means one-two, one-two:

> You look pale, Marshal.
> I feel sick.
> Take this handkerchief. Wipe your mouth off. Then get on your radio.
> The crime-lab people are on the way, Major.
> Get on your radio. Order a manhunt.
> A manhunt? We won't know—
> I know. It's that bandleader fellow. Julius.

Julius Bugliosi?

I appreciate your fine Italian accent, Marshal. But we're losing precious time here. Get on your radio.

We've got to follow procedure, Major.

I got you this job. I can take it away.

· · ·

The characters are talking in short sentences. The rhythm is one-two, one-two, your first key to writing good dialogue. This chapter shows you how to use the one-two rhythm to monitor your dialogue lines, to keep them short. Dialogue is not conversation; it contains more drama, more conflict. In real life, people may hog the floor with lecture and monologue. In a story, let your characters talk in short bursts. Fragments are good. Short sentences keep your reader reading.

Once you develop confidence in the short line, you'll use other patterns to make the dialogue work for your story. We'll show you those other patterns in the Guidelines.

Guidelines for Writing Dialogue

From your work on scene cards and scene summary and scene profile, you have enough material to write a brief dialogue. You know the name of the scene (crime scene). You know its location, whether it's indoors or outdoors. Location gives you objects to deal with, like the library hearthrug at Gossington or the snow that covers the bodies in the Moscow park. You know the characters and their roles and what they want from the scene. You know they'll talk about the corpse, what the corpse wears, the murder weapon, the manner and time of death, and perhaps the murderer. If there's a threshold and one character can't get across, there will be conversation as the outsider negotiates for access. Let's see how this plays out in the *Gorky Park* crime scene.

Recognition Line. Good dialogue starts with a recognition line that tells your reader what's going on. A recognition line acknowledges character presence in the scene. It also codes for rank, a

marker for the power hierarchy that exists between the two characters, the two main speakers in the scene.

If the sleuth of *Gorky Park* had opened the crime-scene dialogue with a line like "Yo, buddy," the informal tone would reduce
the power of rank. An informal tone is an attempt to level the playing field.

If the major had opened the dialogue with a rhetorical question
like "You here again, Slobodan?" or a brusque command like "Out
of my way, boy," the peevish tone smarts like a shove from a police
baton. The major has muscle in the vast Soviet bureaucracy, so he
flexes a lot. Perhaps the simplest recognition line is the one used by
the writer. The major says, "Renko," using the sleuth's last name but
not his rank as chief investigator. That single word thrusts at the
sleuth like a dagger. The sleuth parries with an adverb, "Exactly,"
turns his back, and walks away.

You follow the recognition line with more dialogue. When a
KGB photographer shoots pictures that develop themselves on the
spot, the major uses the speed of technology to enhance the power
of office. The major grabs the photograph and says: "What do you
think?" The sleuth's ironic answer ("Very fast") mocks the major's
shallow powers of detection by commenting on camera speed. The
rapid response, because it deflects the barbed question, reveals the
sleuth as a clever fellow.

These first few lines of dialogue lay out a grid of possible conflict for your scene. The major will demand, bark orders, and use his
power to control the investigation. The sleuth will defend, hide,
evade, dodge, and mock. The KGB major takes the active role; the
sleuth takes the passive role.

This polarity of active versus passive speakers is useful for writing your dialogue. When Dolly Bantry phones Miss Marple, she
takes the active role, getting agitated about needing help with the
dead body: ". . . you've got to come up at once . . . you're so
good at bodies." And Miss Marple evades, sliding behind her mask
of passive modesty: "My little successes have been mostly theoreti-
cal."

With your dialogue under way, with the passive-active voices
identified, and with the subject of conversation (death, murder

weapon, state of the corpse, jurisdiction, et cetera) nailed down, you can write better dialogue if you pay attention to specific patterns: 1) a one-two rhythm; 2) linking a dialogue line to an object in the setting; 3) echo words that repeat; and 4) hooking the dialogue to the past or to the future.

Dialogue Pattern 1. The One-Two Rhythm.

By keeping your lines short—compressing each line into a few words—you can write dialogue that simulates the cadence of real speech. Character A speaks; Character B responds. The pattern is efficient and easy to read. At the Crime Scene in *Body*, the sleuth mutters, almost to herself, "She's very young." The youth of the victim will become a clue, but instead of dwelling on the clue, explaining things to the reader, the writer has the helper answer with a tone of irritation ("Yes, yes. I suppose she is"). To make the insight, the sleuth will have to look below the surface of smooth-skinned youth.

Concealing information with the rhythm of one-two, one-two, is a handy device for your mystery dialogue. As the voices capture the rhythm, you can introduce new trains of thought. In the *Gorky Park* crime scene, for example, the passive sleuth knows Pribluda has killed before. The similar MO (short for *modus operandi,* or mode of operation) makes Pribluda the sleuth's Prime Suspect:

One: You always do the dirty work, Major.
Two: What do you mean?
One: Three people shot and carved up in the snow. . . . You don't want me to investigate this. Who knows where it could lead?
Two: Where could it lead?

In his response, Pribluda answers with an implied threat. He has the power. If the sleuth pushes too hard, he could end up a victim of Pribluda's ruthless power, in a KGB interrogation facility. Pribluda's aggressive tone carries this underlying meaning: Don't push your luck; don't follow up this "lead" or you're one dead detective.

As the dialogue lines gather on your page, you can use the pattern of question and answer to enhance the rhythm of one-two, one-two. In most dialogues in mystery writing, the questioner has the upper hand. In *The Body in the Library,* the policeman asks a question—"What was she doing in your library?"—that pokes through the air and through the landed-gentry shield of the library's owner, who has suddenly become a suspect. The suspect evades, dodging with an answer—"How should I know?"—that could conceal information vital to the case.

At the crime scene in *The Maltese Falcon,* a uniformed policeman blocks the sleuth's access with a question: "What do you want here?" The sleuth's answer—"I'm Sam Spade"—is the ticket to get him across the official police threshold, into the circle of death. Once inside, the sleuth opens up the murder with a question: "What happened?" The question from the sleuth elicits a quick re-creation of the crime from the policeman, who produces a murder weapon. Now it's the cop's turn to ask questions: "A Webley. English, ain't it?" While the weapon at the crime scene inspires the sleuth to a longer re-creation of the crime, his knowledge of guns ("Webley-Fosbery automatic. . . . Thirty-eight, eight shot") brings the police around to his room with more questions about guns.

If you place an object at the crime scene, and if you let your characters talk about it in a cadence of one-two, one-two, there's a good chance the object will generate a scene later in the story.

Dialogue Pattern 2: Linking to Setting.

The Webley-Fosbery pistol is an object in the setting of *The Maltese Falcon* crime scene. The writer uses the object to develop a brief re-creation of the crime: "I've seen Webley-Fosberys. . . . He was shot up here, huh? . . . The man that shot him stands here. . . . Lets him have it and . . ."

Watching the KGB officer crack open the first frozen coat at the *Gorky Park* crime scene, the sleuth emerges briefly from behind his veil of cigarette smoke to say: "You're destroying evidence, Major." Pribluda's response is action—he cracks open the other two coats. His exultant dialogue line ("Shot, all shot!") refers to the bullet holes in the chests, frozen wounds left by the killer in the back story. Pribluda's next dialogue line ("The men shot through the head as well") sets up the re-creation and destruction of Valerya's head in Act Two. Because the killer did not destroy the head of the female victim, the sleuth can pass it on to Professor Andreev for reconstruction.

The dialogue, by attaching to objects in the setting, selects information necessary to the plot: three corpses, five bullets; three bullets in the chest, but only two in the head. In a lab scene, one of the five bullets carries traces of leather from a leather bag; another bullet leaves traces of gutta-percha, a non-Russian material for repairing teeth. Linking your dialogue to objects in the setting helps you write a tighter book.

Dialogue Pattern 3: Echo Words.

As the KGB officer cracks open the third frozen coat at the *Gorky Park* crime scene, he tosses off an insult about the dirty work of homicide investigation: "Now that I've done the dirty work for you," he wisecracks to the sleuth, "we're even." Pribluda uses the *dirty work* phrase to explain his ghoulish coat cracking as heroic: for touching death with his bare hands, he casts himself as a hero, a brave comrade.

The sleuth, ever watchful, grabs the phrase, plucking it out of the air, then turning it back on the major: "You always do the dirty work, Major."

By repeating this simple phrase, the writer uses the dialogue device of echo words. If Character B uses a word or phrase, then Character A's answering line includes the word or phrase as an echo. If the characters are in an adversarial face-off, the echo twists the meaning of the phrase. When the Pribluda says "dirty work," he means that he's not afraid, implying the sleuth is fearful, afraid to face death. When he repeats Pribluda's words, however, the sleuth hauls up a dirty murder from the recent past, two bodies on the Kliazma River near a remote KGB facility, alleged to have been murdered by Pribluda.

Echo words function like musical notes in your writing. When a composer repeats a note, the listener remembers. The notes strike a chord. The chord resonates with familiarity. That familiar sound is unity, the same note cycling back. Echo words work the same way when they cycle back in the writing—they build unity with repeated sounds. Repetition of echo words binds your work together, weaving one tight passage after another. Repetition, one key to good writing, is the sign of a professional writer at work.

When the sleuth of *Gorky Park* challenges the KGB major about those earlier murders, and the major pushes back with his question about dirty work, the sleuth takes a chance: "You don't want me to investigate this," says the sleuth. "Who knows where it could lead?" The key word is *lead.* Pribluda's pushy response—"Where could it lead?"—challenges the sleuth's challenge by echoing the key word. Because he's careful to repeat a key word, the writer ties the two lines together.

Echo words keep your characters connected to the topic. When the cop produces the pistol at *The Maltese Falcon* crime scene, the writer uses the object from the setting as an echo word. The cop calls it a Webley. The sleuth echoes "Webley" but adds information to show the reader he knows about guns—he adds "Fosbery" and the caliber and the number of rounds—and then, in a musing tone, he repeats the name of the weapon again when he re-creates the crime.

Dialogue Pattern 4: Hooking to the Past or Future.

In the crime scene for Patricia Cornwell's *All That Remains,* the sleuth functions as an observer while the cops work through the objects from the setting. When a policeman asks how much money the alleged victim had, the victim's mother uses money and charge cards to dig up the past: "I gave her fifty dollars for food and gas. . . . She also, of course, had charge cards. Plus her checkbooks."

If a character makes a threat like "Tomorrow you'll be dead," that's a reference to the future. If a character says, "What on earth could she have been thinking to make that appointment with the film man?" that's a reference to an event in the past. If you're a reader, you probably read the dialogue without noticing these handy time hooks. But if you're a writer, you use these same time hooks to load your dialogue up with vital information.

That exchange between the sleuth of *Gorky Park* and the KGB major about where the dirty work could lead uses the present moment, the moment of the scene, to connect time past to time future: the dirty work done by the major in the past could lead to trouble for the major in the future. This is another strategy for writing dialogue—let your characters use time references to point backward, into the past, or to point forward, into the future.

Look again at the KGB major's echoing of the word *lead,* a verb that projects into the future. At the crime scene in Act One, with the major as the Prime Suspect, more accusations could lead to the sleuth's arrest, incarceration, interrogation, and death by execution. In Act Three, the sleuth is arrested, jailed, and questioned. He is guarded by the same KGB major. But in Act Three, with Osborne identified as the real *Gorky Park* killer, the sleuth and the major become comrades. The major's question in Act One, instead of leading to the grave, leads to rebirth as the sleuth, healed from his knife wounds, saves the major from burning up in a peat fire. When you write dialogue like this, the astute reader picks up on the cue and asks, "Okay, so where can it lead?" Echo words sound confident because they let the reader know that the writer knows where the story is headed.

Hooking dialogue to the future is an efficient way to close off your crime scene. As the KGB major leaves the *Gorky Park* crime scene, he barks a final order. If the sleuth uncovers something one minute, he's ordered to submit a report in the very next minute. The major uses a time reference to pound home his alpha-male KGB authority: "You understand, Investigator Renko? Whether you spend a year or ten years, the minute you learn something you'll call?"

In a speech bristling with future references *(a year, ten years, the minute, you'll),* the KGB major exits, closing off that section of the crime scene.

• • •

WORKING THE NOVEL

Exercises

1. *Writing Dialogue.*
Start with a recognition line like "What's your business here?"
Use the timer to put yourself under deadline pressure and write
for five to ten minutes from that first line.

Write short lines, one-two, one-two. For this first writing,
leave off the quotation marks and just write the lines. For this
first writing, leave off the attributions like *he said* and *she said*
and if you find yourself adding adverbs of authorial explanation
like *she said engagingly*, don't scold yourself but just keep writing.

Rest.

Read the dialogue. Dig into your lines, hunting for an object,
a time reference, an echo word. Use what you find to write
more dialogue.

Don't rest.

Scan the dialogue for time words, echo words, objects from
the setting. Start right there. Write more dialogue.

Writing more dialogue trains your writing ear. Your goal is
to become efficient. Starting out with a dialogue line is efficient.
If you started out your dialogue practice with a line like "The
roses grew thick around the Greek pillar, spilling out red blossoms like blood from a wounded bison," you'd have trouble
pulling loose from those long lines.

2. *Getting Feedback.*
If you need feedback on your dialogue, ask a couple of friends
to read the parts while you listen and take notes. Giving your
words away, passing them to someone else, is good practice for
a writer. Someone's going to have to read it sometime. Might as
well be now.

3. *Scene Building with Dialogue.*

Because it contains conflict—Character A's agenda clashing with the agenda of Character B—dialogue makes the perfect core for scene building. As you rewrite your dialogue, it's easy to add gestures—small actions—that reveal what the characters are holding inside. In the excerpt below, pulled from Weekend 3, the sleuth returns to the Suburban after viewing the crime scene. Her breath smells of vomit. Her stomach still rolls like a turbulent sea. The Major presses his agenda, finding the band-leader, getting him arrested. The secret buried in the subtext is the after-midnight meeting scheduled between the Major and the bandleader to decide the near future of Lacey Anne Baxter. Burying a secret is the first step in conceal-and-reveal.

For this exercise, we build off the dialogue in the Sleuth Speaks exercise for Weekend 3. In this dialogue, the lines are shorter; the Major is more direct with his agenda; the conflict has more bite.

Let's start with a quick setup:

[The door of the Suburban opens. The sleuth climbs behind the wheel. Cigar smoke makes her cough. The Major hands her his flask. Smell of whiskey as she unscrews the top. She drinks, a liquid burning, fire in her throat.]

You okay, Marshal?

It's awful. Terrible. Who would do such a thing?

A brute, Marshal. If you move fast, you can catch him.

What?

Have another swallow, Marshal. He's hiding somewhere on the island. But we've got to move on this before the bastard gets away.

Who are you talking about?

That bandleader. The king of reggae. Julius B.

Major, chill out.

Did you hear her sing?

Yes. Two nights ago. She was wonderful.

Did you happen to notice the leader of the band?

Yes. He played very well.

He killed her, Missy.

I've asked you before, not to call me Missy.

Sorry. Marshal it is. [The Major shoves his car phone at the sleuth. She shakes her head. Her knuckles are white as she grips the silver whiskey flask.] Here. Take this telephone. Dial some numbers. Get a manhunt going. Catch this murdering sonofa-bitch before he does it to someone else.

No.

Do it, woman. Or else.

Or else what?

· WEEKEND 12 ·
ACTION

Action in your mystery novel is what characters do. What they do to each other, to objects in the setting, to animals, and to themselves. At the crime scene, the Crime Reporter flashes her press card to the uniform guarding the perimeter created by the yellow ribbon. Flashing her ID is action. When the uniform shakes his head, his reaction shows the viewer the Crime Reporter won't get past the yellow ribbon.

It's different when Character A flashes his shield. The same uniformed cop nods. With one gloved hand he raises the yellow ribbon to shoulder height. He does not speak, but with a jerk of his head he indicates the presence of death. His eyes narrowed, Character A bends down, passing under the yellow ribbon. Inside the perimeter, Character A blows his nose on a white handkerchief. Outside the perimeter, the Crime Reporter stabs her reporter's notebook with a sharp ballpoint.

When you write action, you are not only moving the plot along—at the crime scene, your sleuth unearths clues that lead to other scenes—but you are also using action to reveal character.

When Character A's eyes narrow, he's reacting, showing emotion, maybe even pain. His buddy is dead; he feels it. Because he's a professional, he keeps going. His job is to run down the killer. If he whips out a handkerchief and then blows his nose, Character A could be stalling for time, stealing a minute in his tight pressure-cooker schedule to mourn the death of the rookie.

At the center of each scene, you develop a core action to grab the attention of the reader. At the crime scene in *Gorky Park,* a KGB major straddles a body that lies in the snow. With his bare fists, he cracks open the coat. He cackles as he reaches inside the frozen cavity to pull out a lead slug. Try this for your mystery: A high-ranking police official who straddles a dead body gets the attention of the reader.

There are three dead bodies frozen in the snow. The KGB major straddles the middle body first. The middle body is the female; the act of straddling, therefore, crackles with sexual overtones. The writer uses action to show the reader the KGB major is a brute, a grave robber, a ghoul. By destroying evidence, the major becomes the Prime Suspect.

When you write action, you complete the loop for the reader by adding a reaction. Pribluda straddles the body; he cracks open the coat with his bare fists; the sleuth lights a cigarette. The sleuth lighting his cigarette is a reaction to the violence of the cracked coats. As we suggested last weekend, action helps you lay out a power grid for your scene. You use action and reaction to inform the reader who's passive and who's active. Action shows the reader who's got the power and who recedes, dodging, backing away, hiding.

The core action of the *Gorky Park* crime scene is cracking open the coats to destroy evidence. Whether you're writing dialogue or action, repetition—saying it again, doing it over again—signals importance. What if Pribluda had made his exit after scooping up one fistful of token snow? What if he'd left the scene after cracking open only one coat? One cracked coat could be KGB horseplay, an annoyance to the investigating team. Three cracked coats mean business.

Patterned repetition of an action or a series of actions brings the order of time-limit to your scene. There are three corpses; the major cracks them open, one at a time; when he's finished cracking the third coat, he barks orders to the sleuth and takes his goons away. The major's exit changes the dynamics of the scene as the sleuth puts his militiamen to work: with the KGB major gone, the atmosphere of violent turbulence changes into organized searching.

This is the way to use action in your story. Open the book with an action that grabs the reader's attention. It doesn't have to be killing, murder and gunshots and blood; it should be dramatic. When the action has done its work, close off that section and move on, tracking the killer.

Because of the violence of Pribluda's actions, he becomes the Prime Suspect. Because he is the Prime Suspect, the writer builds a research scene where the sleuth uses courthouse records to dig up the past, the Kliazma River murders: "It's the Kliazma River all over again." The writer has planted a red herring in the crime scene. While the sleuth focuses on the KGB major, he is blinded to the real bad guy in the police bureaucracy, his boss, Andrei Iamskoy, the Moscow town prosecutor.

Guidelines for Writing Action

Core Action. Build your crime scene around a core action. The manic actions of the KGB major—digging, scooping, cracking, peeling—build a vivid picture in the reader's mind. Instead of saying, "The major had really gone crazy," the writer builds a picture to show madness in action.

The core action is strong because the verbs—*peel, crack, straddle, wash, discard, brush*—are strong. Whether you're a beginner or a seasoned professional, strong verbs are a must. In your first writing, you work fast. If you keep writing, the word pictures emerge like photos in developer, sharpening with each successive writing into a filmstrip running inside the reader's head. Once you define a core action, it's easy to develop a list of actions for your scene. In the list of actions below—the action sequence in the *Gorky Park* crime scene—each item has a strong verb:

- The sleuth *lights* a Prima cigarette.
- The Prima *tastes* cheap. Smoke *fills* the sleuth's mouth.

- The KGB photographer *shoots* pictures. The *bodies* levitate.
- The photographer's boss, a KGB major, *tramples* the snow around the corpses.
- The sleuth *runs* his fingers through his hair.
- The KGB major *discards* his gloves.
- He *straddles* the bodies.
- He *scoops* snow. He *brushes* snow away.
- He *straddles* the middle body. He *pounds* the frozen overcoat. It *cracks*. The major *pulls* it open. There is a dress underneath. The major *peels* open the dress.
- His job done, the KGB major *washes* his hands in the snow.

• • •

Strong verbs bring the writing to life. A clean line of strong verbs tracks the writing through this scene and onto the next scene.

Action and Reaction. The one-two rhythm of action followed by reaction is a pattern of cause and effect brought into fiction from the real world. In real life, if you prick your fingertip with a needle, the skin bleeds. You feel a prick of pain. "Ouch," you say. The *action,* pricking the finger, comes first. The *reaction,* felt pain and visible blood and perhaps a startled exclamation, comes second. Reaction makes the action seem real, solid, palpable. When the pain fades, you remember the blood.

When you follow an action with a reaction, you not only capture the reader with the logic of the real world; you also deepen your writing. Before you write action, it's a good idea to create an action-reaction chain. Using that same list of strong verbs you worked with before, you identify *action* and then *reaction:*

Action: The major scoops away snow.

Reaction: The sleuth registers the "death mask" on the corpse.

Action: The major cracks open the coat of the middle corpse.

Reaction: The sleuth spots the entry wound in the heart.

Action: The KGB photographer tracks the major cracking two more coats.

Reaction: The sleuth registers no fingertips, no fingerprints.

Action: The intruder washes his hands in the snow.

Reaction: The sleuth tries to pass the case to the KGB.

Action at the Threshold. Some mystery professionals like to mute the action at the crime scene. The sleuth observes; the medical examiner putters about; the clues surface in the mind of the sleuth; some clues are revealed to the reader; other clues are concealed.

If you choose to mute the action at the crime scene, the core action becomes a threshold crossing, getting the sleuth inside the closed circle of death, and then getting her out again. If you create a threshold, it's easy to bring in a threshold guardian. If your sleuth is part of the police machinery—a police officer like Inspector Luke Thanet in Dorothy Simpson's *Dead on Arrival*—he has automatic access: "[Thanet] ran through the pelting rain along the short, curving drive to the front door, where a uniformed PC in a waterproof cape was stamping his feet in a fruitless attempt to keep warm." The front door is the threshold. The uniformed policeman is the threshold guardian. Thanet says hello. The uniform answers in a tone of respect. As the uniform's superior, the inspector crosses the threshold into the crime scene without fuss.

If your sleuth is an amateur like Miss Jane Marple, however, she'll need a helper to get access to the crime scene. In *Body,* Christie employs two threshold guardians to delay Miss Marple's access to the corpse. The first guardian is Colonel Bantry, the master of Gossington; the second guardian is a policeman, Constable Palk. By plotting the sleuth's approach, Christie uses thresholds to imply movement—easing her sleuth past the threshold guardians deeper inside, into the sacred circle:

Threshold One—The Colonel blocks the sleuth. The helper orders the Colonel back to his bacon. When the Colonel hesitates, the helper shoos him back to the dining room. With the guardian under control, the helper leads the sleuth to the library threshold.

Threshold Two—The constable intercepts both sleuth and helper. Cajoling from her power position, the helper persuades the constable to let them in. The constable gives way. The helper points out the corpse. The sleuth views the body, nods her head. A police car arrives outside. The helper and the sleuth and the constable exit the crime scene.

Mythic Helper. If you want to keep your sleuth in the observer role, and if you still want to write action because it creates suspense, try using a mythic helper. One of the best mythic helpers is an animal. At the crime scene in *All That Remains,* for example, Cornwell uses a trained police dog in action to produce a cliff-hanger climax. The scene is a roadside rest stop at the edge of an interstate in Virginia. The center of the crime scene, drawing investigators like a neon beacon, is a red Cherokee Jeep driven by the victims—one young man and one young woman not present at the scene.

To build suspense, the writer places obstacles between the dog and the interior of the Jeep, the last trace of the victims at the scene. The first obstacle is a locked door; the second obstacle is the thunderous arrival of a helicopter carrying the mother of the female victim. The helicopter works for Cornwell the same way the KGB major works for the crime scene in *Gorky Park.*

An officer picks the door lock. The door opens. The police dog, an honored member of the search-and-rescue squad, sniffs the seats where the victims sat—and goes ballistic: "He yelped as if he had encountered a rattlesnake, jerking back from the Jeep, practically wrenching the harness from [the officer's] hand."

Action produces reaction: the police dog whimpers; he quivers; he defecates into the grass. The powerful reaction of the dog, a mythic helper, hooks the reader. What happened inside the red Cherokee? What did the dog smell to make him react that way? Where are the victims? What monster stopped at this lonely rest stop?

The crime scene that opens *All That Remains* peaks here, with the police dog recoiling from that single mystery sniff. The sleuth reacts ("a chill ran up my spine") because she's seen the dog work before, but the reader is kept in the dark. The writer will pick up on this lead—what the dog smelled to make him react with such violence—in the next chapter. But as the crime scene ends, the reader is left in suspense. A reader in suspense will continue reading.

· · ·

WORKING THE NOVEL

Exercises

1. *Narrative Summary.*
Develop the action of your crime scene in a passage of narrative summary. Identify the core action; use strong verbs. If you were summarizing the action for *All That Remains,* your passage might read something like this: "A uniformed officer blocks the sleuth's access to the crime scene. She's wearing civvies. He's a male and she's a female driving a Mercedes. To cross the threshold into the circle of death, the sleuth is forced to show her ID. The center of the crime scene is a red Jeep Cherokee. It's empty; the doors are locked; there are no victims visible. . . ."

When you're writing to discover, clues surface in the writing. Use clues to build suspense.

2. *Writing Action.*
Using strong verbs (*park, spatter, bites, pelt, raise, smell, sink,* et cetera), write out the action sequence for your crime scene. Start at the threshold and bring your sleuth into the closed circle and write about reactions like taste and smell. Let the words slow down as you wrap them around specific actions. If your sleuth is the Crime Reporter, you use specific actions at the crime scene to reveal the workings of her mind: "The sleuth parks her Explorer. Rain spatters the windshield as the wipers go quiet. Looking through the windshield, she focuses on the

Chevrolet Suburban, part of the Major's fleet of ground transport. She bites her lip as she climbs down. Raindrops pelt her face and she stops to raise the hood of the parka. The sea smells ugly tonight, like a garbage dump. She closes the door. Her feet sink into mud as she walks. . . ."

If the actions edge into description, keep writing. You can make any necessary changes later. If a new character takes over this part of the story, keep writing. You're after detail, movement, discovery. When you're writing to discover, don't stop to edit.

3. *Scene Building.*
Start with action, then add dialogue.

Action: "The Major's window rolls down. Smoke from his cigar smells heavy, thick, an expensive Cubano Especial imported by the Major's personal smuggler, a thin man named Estévan."

Add Dialogue:

> She's over there.
> Have you seen her?
> Hell, yes. Stop asking stupid questions and get to work.
> I know you're hurting, Major.
> She's been gutted, Marshal. Sliced open like a butchered deer.
> I'm sorry. Where is she?
> There. Right there.
> [The Major flips on the headlights.]
> All right. I'm sorry. Oh, God.

· WEEKEND 13 ·
SETTING

Setting is the term we use to cover time, place, season, weather, temperature, lighting, objects, and images. Objects in the setting at the crime scene become clues when you bring them back later in the book.

Setting at the crime scene determines character behavior. If it's rainy and cold, your sleuth dresses appropriately, like Inspector Luke Thanet, who wears a raincoat at the crime scene in *Dead on Arrival*.

If it's a cold morning and the bodies are buried in the snow, your sleuth wears boots and a heavy overcoat, like Arkady Renko in *Gorky Park*. The atmosphere in the park is dark, eerie, ominous. The time is predawn, before first light, as headlights from the KGB vehicles slice across the snow. Because the KGB major forgot his boots, he won't hang out too long at the snowy crime scene: "Neither the major nor his photographer had thought to wear boots. Maybe cold feet would send the KGB on its way."

When he uncovers the bodies, Pribluda scoops snow like a dog pawing at a grave. There are three bodies; when he finishes with the third body, the major makes his exit. When the major leaves, the dynamics of the scene change. With the aggressive intruder gone, the sleuth gets his militia to work combing the crime scene for clues. Three bodies, objects in the setting covered with snow, give the scene a timing device.

The way you describe your settings, the choices you make about detail, about what to reveal and what to conceal, determine the course of the book. At the end of a passage of description at the *Gorky Park* crime scene, the sleuth notes: "They were wearing ice skates." In a forensic lab scene later in Act One, the sleuth picks up the thread from the crime scene when he asks for the owner's name. Tracing the ice skates of the female corpse to their owner leads Renko to Irina Asanova, a script girl in a shabby coat and cracked vinyl boots: "We found your ice skates. . . . We found them on a dead person."

Because she is a femme fatale ("Dead," Irina says. "I feel better already"), she will change the course of the sleuth's life forever. If you were writing *Gorky Park,* you would have connected Irina's skates to Valerya when you developed the back story. Now that you're constructing a setting, the skates would already be on your list of objects from the past.

Setting gives your characters a stage to stand on, a place to act out their agendas, a season to dress for, a time of day to establish mood and lighting. If you build a stage in Seattle in November, there's a good chance it's raining, heavy gray stuff falling from the sky. The mood is dour, gloomy, oppressive.

Your characters, dressing in response to the weather, decide what to wear, and that helps you write detail: boots, rain parka, sweater, cap, bright colors to ward off the gloom, the layered look.

Guidelines for Setting

Showing versus Telling. Setting helps you to stay objective by using detail to convey information. Instead of *telling* and explaining, you're *showing* with careful detail. *Showing* means you use *word pictures.*

Example: Let's say your sleuth is just arriving at the crime scene. The time is early morning, a predawn black as night. Rain hammers down, pelting the windshield. The sleuth drives a two-door Explorer. On the doors are the words TOWN MARSHAL, DRAKE ISLAND VILLAGE. The interior is battered. An empty coffee carton from the Marina Café rests in the cup holder between the seats. To capture the mood of the crime scene, you might start with headlights slicing the dark:

> The headlights throw a long shadow across the rutted mud as the sleuth moves forward. Her lip trembles. Her legs are ancient trees hard as stone. The long shadow falls across the body. The sleuth turns on her three-cell. The corpse is naked, streaked with mud. Her eyes are open to the night, the gray mist, the cold wind. Her hair is fanned out like a halo. She is spread-eagled. Black

ribbons around wrists and ankles. Black ribbons looped to tent stakes driven into the mud. There are slashes on the throat and both wrists. The sleuth kneels down for a closer look. Mud is caked around the victim's midsection, across the pubic bone, between the unmoving thighs. A leather thong, thin as a shoestring and partly hidden by mud, stretches across her belly like a belt. Leaning over, clutching the heavy metal flashlight, the sleuth vomits.

The word picture contains clues. The trick is to use the picture to conceal something now that you can dig up later: the caked mud hides the leather thong bikini, the link to Victims One and Two. Before the sleuth has a chance to investigate, she breaks her concentration by vomiting. By writing this description now, the writer plants a picture in the reader's mind. By portraying the death of an innocent victim, the word picture forces the reader to react. When innocence dies, society wants someone to pay.

Showing is more professional and far more interesting to the reader than telling. It's also hard work. As you train your eye, however, you'll grab on to better details faster. Those details become clues.

Planting Clues. When you develop the setting for your crime scene, plant clues. When you plant a clue, hide it from the reader, concealing it now so you can reveal it later.

1. In *Body,* the writer plants a wardrobe item at the crime scene in Act One. The wardrobe item, buried carefully in a list of other details, conceals the identity of the victim. While Christie's cops track the wrong man, Miss Marple tracks the wardrobe item, waiting to reveal her deductions until her final re-creation of the crime in Act Three.

2. In *Gorky Park,* the writer plants death masks at the crime scene. The three flayed faces, two of them with their jaws blown away, conceal the identity of the victims. To reveal the face that traps the killer, the sleuth has the face of the female victim reconstructed. The reconstruction reveals the face so well that the sleuth's boss, Chief Prosecutor Iamskoy, destroys it with an ax before the sleuth can use it to reveal the killer's true identity.

3. In her opening chapter of *All That Remains,* Cornwell plants a missing purse in the reader's mind. Arriving at the crime scene in a helicopter that verifies her power position in government, Drug Czar Pat Harvey (the mother of the victim) clings to a missing purse to support her hope that the daughter is still alive: "Debbie would have been carrying a purse. Nylon, bright red. One of those sports purses with a Velcro-lined flap." As the mother pins her hopes on the missing purse, the writer adds detail to expand the purse as a container for emotion: "I gave her fifty dollars for food and gas," the mother says. "She also, of course, had charge cards. Plus her check-book."

The purse buried at the crime scene surfaces deep in Act One, when the victims turn up. A cop briefs the sleuth on the purse and the money that's left: "We found a purse," the cop says. "Forty-four dollars and twenty-six cents in it. Plus a driver's license." The driver's license belongs to the female victim from the red Jeep Cherokee.

Borrow this device—it's part of the pattern of conceal and reveal—for your mystery. The fifty dollars remembered by the mother at the crime scene has been reduced to $44.26. The writer uses simple subtraction to reveal the horror of the crime: because the killer did not kill for money, he kills for pleasure. A killer who kills for pleasure turns up the heat on the killer quest. Whatever the cost, he's got to pay.

Setting and Behavior. One way to create dramatic conflict is to bring your sleuth to the crime scene wearing the wrong outfit. Worn out from forensic analysis on a muggy Saturday, Dr. Kay Scarpetta returns home from her lab. She's looking forward to a lunch of Hanover tomatoes and chicken salad. A phone message intrudes, calling her to the crime scene.

Because of Dr. Scarpetta's casual wardrobe, a uniformed trooper blocks her access to the crime scene. As she digs for her official ME identification, the sleuth reflects on her wardrobe and on the power vested in symbols of authority: "Dressed in a stone-washed denim skirt, pink oxford cloth shirt, and leather walking shoes, I was without the accouterments of authority. . . . At a glance, I was a not-so-young yuppie running errands in her dark gray Mercedes. . . ."

If you were writing this threshold crossing for the crime scene, the wardrobe items would define the sleuth by exteriors like age (young middle age), income (the stylish Mercedes means money), and lifestyle (upscale yuppie in leather walking shoes, et cetera). The objects of identification from her purse define the sleuth as a professional: "Digging into my purse, I produced a thin black wallet and displayed my brass medical examiner's shield, then handed over my driver's license." The objects of authority enable the sleuth to stay calm. A female in a male world, Dr. Scarpetta operates with a cool deliberation reminiscent of Miss Jane Marple.

You use weather to tell the characters what to wear. You use wardrobe items to inform the reader about weather and setting. A sleuth in a skirt and shirt with no jacket means it's a warm day. The season happens to be early fall. The place is an interstate in Virginia. Setting helps you stay logical with the writing, even when you're writing fast.

Setting Checklist. Using the categories of time and place, season and temperature, et cetera, you develop a checklist for your setting. Jotting notes before you write is essential.

Sample jottings for the crime-scene setting in *Murder on Drake Island:*

Example—

Time: The time is predawn, the hour of complete darkness.

Place: South Beach Road on Drake Island, South Carolina, about a mile from Major Baxter's Beach Bungalow.

Season: Late summer, a weekday before the Labor Day Weekend.

Temperature: Chilly for this time of year. The Major wears a hunting vest. The sleuth wears a rain parka.

Lighting: The scene begins in full dark, moving slowly into the pale, ghostly light of an island dawn. Headlights from the Major's Suburban slash the dark. When her body casts a shadow, the sleuth turns on her three-cell flashlight.

Objects in the setting: Vehicles—the sleuth's Explorer, the Major's Suburban, vehicles driven by James T. Worthington and Armand DuPre. The Major's cigar. The sleuth's flashlight, boots, parka, jeans, Glock 9mm. Mud, rain, ruts in the road, windshield, car telephone. Body of the corpse: white skin, wounds, partly concealed thong bikini, black ribbon, tent stakes. Objects not at the setting: the scalpel; the death van; no footprints left by the killer.

Landscape Detail: Mud, rain, wet sea-grass, ruts, twisted trees, wind, headlights, car heaters, cigar smoke.

Corpses: One corpse spread-eagled in the mud. Arms outflung. Legs splayed. Hair a halo.

Evidence: Throat cut. Wrists slashed. The victim was bled to death like a sacrificial animal.

Sense perceptions:

Sight—headlights glint off the naked body; red glow of the Major's cigar; Ripley's intruder flashlight sweeping over the hood of the Explorer; rain mixes with mud and blood.

Taste—of the sleuth's vomit, green and foul.

Touch/feeling—the sleuth feels the pelting of the rain on her face. Not a cleansing feeling. She feels the warm whiskey going down.

Smell—cigar smoke; wind off the sea; vomit.

• • •

The information you jot down for your setting triggers your creativity: season defines weather (rain in late summer is cold, chilly); weather defines character wardrobe (late summer rain means parka, rubber boots for the mud, jeans); wardrobe defines character and agenda (the sleuth wears rain boots so she's planning to muck around at the crime scene); weather controls setting (the Major can't move around in his wheelchair, so he exercises his agenda—muscling the sleuth—from inside the Suburban); agenda defines action (if the Major muscles the sleuth this early, maybe he knows a secret that could help crack the case).

Your goal in writing setting is richness of detail. The crime scene starts the story. Even with massive planning, there's no way you can know exactly what you'll be needing on page 150, when you're deep into writing Act Two. Better to write fat now and trim it later than to write bare-bones lean and not have a rich choice of images and objects when you're at midpoint in your first draft.

· · ·

WORKING THE NOVEL

Exercises

1. *Narrative Summary.*
In a brief passage or two, summarize the setting for your crime scene. Example: "It is late summer on Drake Island, and rain falls heavily on South Beach Road, creating a sea of mud where the victim lies spread-eagled, a caricature of an angel. The power of wet mud dominates the crime scene. Wind blows off the sea, smelling of . . .

If writing under time pressure sharpens your prose, set your kitchen timer for ten to fifteen minutes.

2. *Checklist for Your Setting.*
Before you write the scene, develop a setting checklist. Use categories like time, place, weather, season, temperature, lighting, objects, landscape detail, sense perceptions, and so on.

3. *Building the Scene.*
Convert checklist and narrative summary into a setting for your crime scene. One easy way to start is to focus on the power of sense perception—the smell of rain, the taste of vomit, the powerful odor of a cigar—which leads the writing into action and

reaction: As the sleuth views the body from a distance, she stays cool. When she kneels down for a closer look, the sleuth reacts by vomiting.

Start with Setting—

Dark through the windshield. Dark ocean out there, to her right. A dark road sliced by headlights. The window of the sleuth's Explorer is open; one inch of wet air, smelling of seaweed and death, swirls in from the outside. The heater is on, the blower pumping against the chill.

Through the windshield off to the right, she spots the Major's big Suburban. From behind the auto glass comes the red orange glow of the Major's cigar.

Add Action—

The sleuth parks her Explorer. Rain spatters the windshield as the wipers go silent. She bites her lip as she climbs down. Raindrops pelt her face and she raises the hood of the parka. The sea smells ugly tonight, like a garbage dump. Her feet sink into mud as she walks. Halfway to the Suburban, clicking the flashlight on, she remembers the Glock. Soggy earth sucks at her boots as she goes back for it, feeling amateur stupid. Armed, with the Glock in her clip on belt holster, she shows herself at the Major's window. The window rolls down. . . .

Add Reaction—

Smelling the smoke from the Major's cigar, the sleuth chokes back her opinion on illegal contraband smuggled from Cuba.

Add Complication—

The Major got her this job. She needs the money. Her lip trembles. She hates the idea. Not Lacey Anne.

Add Dialogue—

Hello, Marshal.
Hello, Major. Are you sure it's Lacey—
Hell, yes, I'm sure. Go and see for yourself.
All right. Give me a minute.
You ready for this, Marshal?
I have to see her. It's my job.
Do your job, then.
All right.
She's across there. In the goddam mud. Look.

Add More Complication—

The Major flicks on the headlights. Across the rutted road, the
sleuth sees a hump in the mud. She blinks. The hump vanishes.
Wind bites her face. She turns to the Major. Feels tears starting.
She hates being an amateur. Hates being a female in a man's
world. Death is a man thing. She shakes her head.

Add More Dialogue—

I don't see anything.
It's my baby. He spread-eagled her. He raped her. Bled her
like a staked goat.

• • •

The crime scene is under way. As agendas clash, your conflict
sizzles: the Major versus the sleuth. He wants the head of Julius
Bugliosi. The sleuth wants to do things right. First, she must view
the body. Viewing the body—someone she knows—makes her
vomit. To compound the conflict, two characters wait in the wings:
1) James T. Worthington of the state police will intrude for the first
battle in the Turf War; 2) Armand DuPre, a writer with information
on the Teen Angel murders, will intrude to pose as the sleuth's
helper.

With your character work done, your key scenes sketched out,
and the sleuth facing problems, it's time to write that first draft.

Weekends 14–25
First Draft

Your main goal in the next twelve weekends is to write your first draft all the way through to the end. In the first draft, you write fast, speedballing along, skipping, leaping deep chasms in the plot, feeling the wind in your face. In the first draft you are a child at play in the vast field of your fiction, using technique to discover the shape of your story.

Don't think too much on this writing. Thinking comes later, when you write the second draft. Don't stop for research now. Don't stop to fix a sentence or to monkey around changing words or fixing clues. Don't stop to polish up a dialogue line. Don't worry about form or gaps or gaping holes between Acts One and Three.

Your internal editor, that judgmental voice inside your head, will urge you to stop. "Listen up, beginner," the editor will say. "You can't write a novel this way, without rewriting every word. It's too messy; it's too chaotic; I can't work this way. The time to rewrite is now. The time to fix those misspelled words is now."

Don't listen and don't stop. Keep the hand moving while you write scenes, and if you can't finish a scene jot down a couple of key ideas on your scene card and push on ahead to the next scene. Keep the creative imagination locked on that final image in that final scene where the sleuth is rewarded for making the killer pay.

Sink into the writing. Settle into the power of the words. Use this writing to discover motive and method for your characters. Go

again into closet and wallet and dresser drawer and mind and memory and poke around. Gather images from the characters' past. Hold
the images in your arms. Knit them into your book. Keep filling up
the well of your unconscious.

Try not to worry about what you are writing while you are writing. This is the first draft of your first mystery, your first attempt at
writing a book of 250–300 pages. You must have patience. Be kind to
yourself because you're learning as you go, making discoveries about
character and plot that you could never have made if you hadn't
come this far, preparing, laying the groundwork. You're growing as a
writer. Every day of writing increases your writing power.

Keep control of your writing by working in easy steps. For example, instead of tackling a full scene, start with a dialogue from a
scene card. Write the dialogue and attach it to some action and
watch the scene grow, almost by itself. Get into the story. Build a
setting and watch the lights come on and feel the temperature
change and bring on a character dressed by your wardrobe people
suitable for the occasion—Philip Marlowe in a powder-blue suit;
John Osborne in a golden tan—and let your action peak and write
an exit line and suddenly you've got a scene, which is a container for
drama, which is what audiences pay for.

Alternate your writing for this first draft between the computer
(or typewriter) and your notebook. If you're hot, the computer is
great for getting down those thoughts. When you cool off, write in
the notebook. As suggested earlier, if you work better with a deadline, time yourself with a kitchen timer to distract the internal editor. When you print your work out, file the pages in a manila folder.
Some writers code sections of the writing with colored file folders—
red file for Act One; blue file for Act Two, et cetera. If you spot
things that cry out for change, jot a note to yourself and keep writing. Your goal is closure, completing a first draft of your story all the
way to the end. Stopping to edit slows you down.

If you have to, push yourself to make it all the way to the end.
Stay up late and get up early and when you lose your way, map your
scene sequences on the plot diagram.

Mapping helps you step back for a breather so that you can
keep going.

The Next Twelve Weekends

You can divide your work something like this: You'll spend four weekends drafting Act One; you'll spend five weekends on Act Two; you'll spend three weekends on Act Three.

If you're following the guidelines suggested earlier, Act One will run around seventy manuscript pages. If your scenes average seven pages (some might be three pages, some might be ten), that means you'll need eight to ten scenes for Act One. Some writers find it helpful to contain scenes by numbers of pages. Make sure you name each scene.

In Act Two, which is longer, your scenes might deepen and also expand. You could use twelve to fifteen scenes here, which leaves you ten to twelve scenes to write for Act Three. As you move to the end of the book and closure—capping off characters, ending the subplots—you'll write tighter and tighter scenes. You're aiming for a novel manuscript of 250–300 pages, which, at this writing, will keep the cost of your hardback book low. The key to writing three hundred pages is to take small steps and keep a steady pace.

Your preparation is done—characters primed, acts framed by key scenes, scene cards laid out in a row, subplots beginning to emerge. This is a first draft. Remember that the scenes don't have to be perfect. If you can't write a scene, you add to the scene card and keep writing. There might be something up ahead to help you; if you don't write your way up there, you won't find it.

You're writing to reach the end while you fill in what you can. You can always fix things when you rewrite.

Let's move on to Act One.

• WEEKENDS 14–17 •
WRITING ACT ONE

The first draft of your mystery is an exploratory writing containing scenes, scene sketches, snatches of dialogue, snippets of action, new faces, and settings that are overwritten on purpose as you root for symbols.

As you write, speeding along, new characters (strangers never seen before) will come onstage. Since they're new, they won't have back stories. Since they don't have back stories, you're not sure of their motivation, where they're coming from, so you make a note to yourself, "During the Week: Prepare Back Story on Character F," and then you keep writing.

That's your goal in this first draft: to keep writing.

Give yourself room to grow while you produce a lot of manuscript. Make a list of scenes, keeping it fluid, to give yourself a track, a chain of events to follow. Act One is your setup, just as it was for Christie or Chandler or Hammett. Act One begins with your opening scene and builds to the first structural peak, plot point one. In Act One you introduce your characters, who come onstage brandishing their individual agendas. In Act One you set up your scenes, creating settings to establish place, time of day, temperature, season, and lighting. As you develop these settings, stay open to symbols and images popping up, physical detail you did not think of until it was unearthed by the writing. A short list of these details—a name on an ice skate, a tawdry white dress, bits of leather on a pistol slug, a photo of a society belle who wears only jade earrings—will help you bridge your writing from one session to the next.

In Act One you curb the internal critic and allow large actions to spring from the motivations of your characters. Flanked by his KGB goons, Major Pribluda charges onstage in *Gorky Park* to collide with the sleuth. Pribluda throws his weight around, but his crowning moment is exulting like a grave ghoul as he cracks open those frozen coats. Pribluda's dialogue line—"Someday this will be you"—caps the award-winning performance, and makes him the Prime Suspect for two thirds of the book, when he saves the sleuth's life after being saved by the sleuth from the peat fires in Shatura. Writing strong action in the first draft makes strong characters. Later in the writing, when you deepen the story, strong characters help you with the plot.

Guidelines for Writing Act One

Because of the careful preparation you've been doing for the last thirteen weekends, you've already assembled most of what you need for writing Act One. Some of your characters are onstage; others, dressed and expectant, wait in the wings. Your work on character—profiles and monologues and dialogues—reminds you what they're after in the story. You've recorded their speech and mentally video-taped their actions and gestures. You've poked around in their closets; you've probed their motives for being in the book.

You've built settings and packed them with physical detail. You've written key scenes built around action and motive. A quick look at your plot picture diagram will remind you of things you need to accomplish in Act One: introducing characters, getting them in motion, letting them interact with details of the case.

Before you start writing, take the time to organize your scene cards into a list of scenes. Name each scene. Then jot notes about action, dialogue, and setting. By spanning Act One, the scene list becomes a road map for your writing.

As an example to follow, here's a list of scenes for Act One of our write-along mystery, *Murder on Drake Island:*

Crime Scene
   Setting: A bend in the road to Baxter's Bungalow. Mud. Rain. Headlights. A chill wind from the east.
   Action: The Major harangues the sleuth to organize a man-hunt for Julius. Sergeant Worthington starts a Turf War over jurisdiction. Armand DuPre, Crime Writer, offers to trade information.

Phone Call One
   Setting: The sleuth's office in the Village Center.

Action: The death van is found near the hotel where Julius and the band are staying. Julius is at large.

Phone Call Two
   Setting: The sleuth's office.
   Action: The sleuth sends a deputy to bring in Emily Tallant, the friend of the victim.

Postmortem
   Setting: The treatment room at the Drake Island Emergency Clinic. White walls. Body bag. Cold lights.
   Dialogue: Time of death. Manner of death. Wounds.

Re-creation of the Crime
   Setting: The Marina Café. Coffee and rolls. Butter. Smell of fried meat.
   Dialogue: Sharing information with Armand DuPre.

Killer Onstage
   Setting: The Marina Café.
   Action: The killer in disguise intrudes on the sleuth and Armand.

Witness Interview
   Setting: The street outside the Marina Café. Foot traffic. Tourists gawking at shopfronts. A gang of skinheads.
   Action: The sleuth shows the photo of Lacey Anne and the skinhead.

Brush with Authority
   Setting: The street outside the Marina Café.
   Dialogue: Mayor Edward Severance, a slimy fellow, offers career advice.

Witness Interview
   Setting: The sleuth's office.
   Dialogue: Emily Tallant places Lacey Anne in the death van with Julius.

Guilty Old Man
   Setting: The Big Room at Baxter's Bungalow.

Dialogue: The Major reveals his after-midnight meeting with Julius. Because he knew of the Teen Angel killings, the Major blames himself for her death. Guilt piles up.

Scapegoat

Setting: The sleuth's vehicle on the road back to town.

Action: The phone rings. Julius Bugliosi, just nabbed by the state police, is being airlifted to the mainland for interrogation.

With the scene list in place, it's a good idea to compress the material with narrative summary as you tell yourself the story. An example follows:

Example: *Narrative Summary*

• The sleuth vomits at the crime scene. This is her first murder. She knows the victim, Lacey Anne Baxter. Major Baxter, Lacey Anne's grandfather and guardian, pressures the sleuth to arrest Julius Bugliosi. This is the first step of the scapegoat subplot. The Major keeps a secret—the after-midnight meeting scheduled with Julius to discuss Lacey Anne's future as a songbird for the band. The Major wants action. The sleuth wants to go by the book.

• James T. Worthington starts the Turf War: he needs a career boost. James T., a professional policeman, sees the pattern of the Teen Angel serial killings. Armand DuPre has been on the Teen Angel killings for a month. He can help the sleuth. They agree to share.

• Deputies locate the death van. Going by the book, the sleuth brings in Emily Tallant, the last person to see Lacey Anne alive, for a witness interview. Information from the postmortem: As the Major said, the victim was bled to death like a sacrificial animal. Her womb was removed. The instrument for removal was a surgical scalpel. There was no evidence of recent sexual intercourse. The doctor, a local man, has not followed the MO of the Teen Angel killings on the mainland.

• At the Marina Café, the sleuth barters with Armand DuPre. She gives him information on the postmortem; he fills her in on the MO of the Teen Angel killer—spread-eagled position, removal of the womb, leather thong bikini, black ribbons, et cetera. Victims One and Two were rock music groupies. The murders took place at night after concerts where Julius was billed. Was the Major right? Did Julius kill Lacey Anne?

• The sleuth's first attempt at re-creating the crime is interrupted by the entrance of the killer, Myra Jane Severance. She has just come from Baxter's Bungalow, where the Major is working with James T. Worthington to organize a manhunt for Julius.

• Outside the Marina Café, the sleuth interviews the skinhead who leers at Lacey Anne in a photo from last night. Edward interrupts the interview to pressure the sleuth to let go of the murder case. Let the state police handle everything. Get the investigation off the island before it ruins Labor Day cash flow. Merchants are growling, says Edward. The future of Drake Island is at stake. And after all, he says, the only experience the sleuth has with murder is between the pages of a book.

• From Emily Tallant, the sleuth learns how valuable Lacey Anne was to Julius and his band. Lacey Anne was taking Julius back to the bungalow to talk with the Major about letting her go on the road. Time to visit the Major.

• The Major admits Lacey Anne was bringing Julius for a meeting. It was a crazy idea. Lacey Anne was a child, very much underage. He planned to send Julius packing. They never arrived. Around two o'clock, the Major dozed off. When he woke up, the Major roused Ripley. They found the girl on South Beach Road. She was dead.

• The Turf War escalates as the state police attempt to airlift Julius Bugliosi to the mainland. The sleuth, going by the book, phones the Village magistrate for an injunction. The sleuth checks the sky. Black clouds moving in. Maybe the weather is on her side. She needs help from somewhere.

• • •

Follow this strategy for your book—closing off Act One with a twist in the investigation. With your scene list completed and a narrative summary for compression and control, you're ready to write the scenes that build Act One.

• • •

WORKING THE NOVEL

Exercises

1. *List of Scenes.*
Using your scene cards, develop a list of scenes that spans Act One. Follow the form used for *Murder on Drake Island*—focusing on action, dialogue, setting, et cetera—as you pin down clues that will drive your story. Creating this list frames a large section of the story between a designated beginning (opening at the crime scene) and a designated end (plot point one as the scapegoat is caught). If your goal is to write a book with thirty to forty scenes, then you'll list eight to ten scenes for Act One. If you list more than that, don't worry. You can compress them later, after you get a sense of the rest of the novel.

2. *Key Scenes.*
Act One is framed by your opening and plot point one. If you have written the key scenes (Weekend 6), take a couple of hours to expand them, adding new material: new clues, new actions, new sections of dialogue. To speed up the writing, profile these two scenes. The purpose of the profile is to isolate the elements of a scene—dialogue, action, and setting—so that they work together to build suspense.

3. *Narrative Summary.*
With Act One framed, summarize the main events in a couple of passages of narrative prose. A narrative summary increases your span of control over the material.

4. *Write the Scenes.*
Write the key scenes first—as bookends. Then write as many scenes as you can for Act One. As you write scenes, practice your writer's craft. If you start one scene with dialogue, start the next one with setting, loading up the physical detail to convey

mood, atmosphere, temperature, and so on. To get from one scene to the next, practice jump-cutting. Start a scene with action, *in medias res,* which means "in the midst of things." Play with technique to strengthen your writing muscles. Your writing goal is three to four scenes per weekend.

5. *Getting to Plot Point One.*
Keep to a schedule. With Act One framed by the opener and plot point one, and with your important scenes written, it's easier to fill in the gaps. If you reach the end of the third weekend with only half the scenes written, use a narrative summary to finish writing Act One. Your goal is to reach plot point one.

· WEEKENDS 18–22 ·
WRITING ACT TWO

As you discovered in the plotting section, Act Two is important because it's big, exciting, thick with complexity. When Act Two opens, most of your characters have entered the story. Your subplots are well under way. In Act Two, tough obstacles block the sleuth's progress in the killer quest.

Act Two is exciting to write because you keep gaining momentum as you push deeper into your story. Act One is your setup; Act Two, your complication, is where the story heats up.

Because Act Two is both intense and complex, you write it by cutting the problem down to size, halving Act Two at midpoint, and by framing it with plot points at each end.

The framing you did in the plotting section (Weekends 5–9) helps you manage the material that develops in Act Two. In *Gorky Park,* for example, Act Two is framed by plot point one (the killer coming onstage naked in the bathhouse) and Plot Point Two (Irina kills Iamskoy; the sleuth, wounded, drops into near-death). Because the killer is absent at the end of Act Two, the killer quest is not done. Because the killer quest is not done, you create a burning need for Act Three.

. . .

The Writer's Reward

The hard work you did on Weekend 6 (Key Scenes) pays off here, when you write the first draft for Act Two. With your midpoint fastened down, you can write with energy and confidence because you know where you're going with the words.

When you start generating scenes for Act Two, your midpoint might be a section of dialogue or a powerful action where the book changes direction. For example, the action that changes the direction of *The Big Sleep* is a vengeful execution by a walk-on character named Carol Lundgren. The victim is a small-time hood named Joe Brody. The execution takes place at Joe Brody's front door, with the sleuth present as an eyewitness. The killer has just left, without the nude photos of herself and without her little gun. The action sequence of Brody's execution is tight:

- The door buzzer rings.
- Brody growls—he thinks it's the killer coming back.
- He snatches up a Colt pistol.
- He marches to the door, twists the doorknob.
- Holding the gun against his thigh, Brody leans forward.
- There's one word of dialogue: "Brody?"
- Brody answers; the sleuth can't hear what he says.
- Two shots are fired.
- Brody's wounded body pushes the door closed.
- His left hand leaves the doorknob, slaps the floor.
- Brody dies clinging to his Colt.

With a fresh corpse to lock down his midpoint, the writer sends the sleuth out on the street to nab the executioner. They drive away from the Joe Brody crime scene to another crime scene, the home of the dead blackmailer—his name was Geiger—the small-timer who sent the nude photos to General Sternwood to trigger the killer quest.

Carol Lundgren, Brody's executioner, turns out to be the black-mailer's chum and roommate. Assuming that Brody killed his "roommate," the boy then executed Brody to get revenge. At Geiger's house, however, the sleuth detects Geiger's real killer: the Sternwoods' chauffeur.

A murder for the wrong reasons is an excellent strategy for your Act Two because it makes more work for your sleuth as he sifts through the complexities to relocate the lost killer trail. In *The Big Sleep*, the subplot of the nude photos leads the sleuth to solve the motive for Geiger's death: the Sternwood chauffeur killed the black-mailer to protect the woman he loved—the lovely daughter of the house, Miss Carmen Sternwood.

Planning links the parts of the book together. The Sternwood chauffeur who killed the blackmailer whose death drove Carol Lundgren to kill Joe Brody in a fit of sad revenge has already appeared in Act One on page one of Chapter One of *The Big Sleep*. Chandler plants the chauffeur in his description of the setting: French doors, emerald grass, a white garage, where "a slim dark young chauffeur in shiny black leggings was dusting a maroon Packard convertible." Driven by nude photos of his secret love, the chauffeur (a walk-on character with not a single line of dialogue) generates the midpoint for *The Big Sleep*.

At the postmortem following Brody's execution, the sleuth displays the photos of Miss Carmen and the blackmail notes sent by Geiger. As the nude-photo subplot ends, the killer quest heats up because the sleuth wants to protect his client's family: "I left out two things," the sleuth admits to himself. "I left out Carmen's visit to Brody's apartment and Eddie Mars's visit to Geiger's in the afternoon."

You use midpoint not only to change direction, but also to escalate the intensity of the killer quest. By concealing the killer and the crime king from the cops, the writer creates an opportunity to bring both of them back soon.

Miss Carmen, as you know from Weekend 1, is the killer. Without the sleuth's protection, she'll get the gas chamber. Eddie Mars, the crime king of the book, helps Carmen's big sister with body disposal in the back story.

This is a good strategy for your story: you hide something now so you can dig it up later. As Marlowe conceals Carmen and Eddie, the cops smell the stink of corruption.

As the novel shifts gears at the midpoint, the cops accuse the sleuth of covering up for the Sternwood family. The halfhearted accusation leads to a cop lecture, a warning that foregrounds what will happen in the second half of Act Two: "Those girls of his [Carmen and Vivian] are bound certain to hook up with something that can't be hushed [the death of Rusty Regan], especially that little blond brat." The cop ends his lecture with a wager—he bets the sleuth that Rusty Regan is part of the cover-up. The sleuth says maybe so, keeping his mouth shut to protect his client. The cop hands over the nude photos and the blackmail notes. This evidence, so important to the first half of the book, has faded in importance. Act Two, second half, is well under way.

Guidelines for Writing the First Draft of Act Two

1. *Lock Down Your Midpoint.*
Divide your work at midpoint. Write the first half, then the second half. Put labels on the movement of both halves of Act Two. For example, in the first half of Act Two of *Body,* the police interview witnesses at the Hotel Majestic. If you were diagramming Christie, you might print "Witness Interviews" as a controlling motif for this first half. The sleuth is offstage, thinking, waiting for access to the case, excluded from the closed circle of police procedure. While Miss Marple engages in her armchair sleuthing, Christie displays for the reader the sedate pace of police procedure. Midpoint in *Body* gets interesting when the sleuth reenters the story, a dramatic stage entrance where she develops her King Cophetua analogy (dirty old men and fertile young women) from the Burne-Jones painting,

"King Cophetua and the Beggar-Maid." Her audience for the analogy is Sir Henry Clithering, Scotland Yard, retired, called in by Conway Jefferson, to help the bumbling police.

Midpoint in *Gorky Park* is complex: two subplots (one based on Irina, one on Kirwill) converge with the main plot, the hunt for the killer. To make this convergence work, the writer creates three powerful scenes: 1) a "Male Bonding" scene between Renko, the sleuth, and William Kirwill, the sleuth's helper; 2) a dramatic "Metro Rescue," where Renko saves Irina from the KGB; 3) a bitter face-off between the sleuth and his father.

Let's summarize each scene:

• *Male Bonding—Kirwill Subplot.* The sleuth and Kirwill drink a vodka toast to Pasha Pavlovich, the sleuth's detective helper, murdered by Iamskoy: "Hey," says Kirwill, "here's to your dead detective, huh?" As the two cops (one Russian Muscovite and one American detective from New York City) bond over the dead body of Pasha, Kirwill joins the sleuth on the killer's trail.

• *Metro Rescue—Irina Subplot.* Renko leaves Kirwill to find Irina. In a ritual that replicates her sad Siberian past, Irina is snatched by KGB goons working for Iamskoy. Racing against time because a KGB goon with a pockmarked face has injected poison into Irina, Renko rescues her in the Moscow metro under Red Square. Coming out of near-death, Irina calls the sleuth an idiot. Seeing that she's okay, the sleuth digs up the killer's past by probing the memory of a sick old man.

• *Father And Son—Main Plot.* To research Osborne's killing past, Renko visits his father, a Soviet Army general (his nickname is the "Butcher of the Ukraine"), where he learns about Osborne's killing of three German officers in 1944, during the siege of Leningrad. "At the end," recalls the general, "the American [Osborne] took the Germans for a picnic in the woods with champagne and chocolates and shot them. For fun." This deadly pleasure-killing, with its falsification of reports and payoff of investigators, reveals the killer as a savvy corrupter.

2. *Use Midpoint to Change Direction.*

Things change at midpoint. The change in *Gorky Park* is marked by a new friend (Kirwill), fierce love with an ice-veined femme fatale from Siberia (Irina), and solid information on a previous kill (Osborne's execution of the three German officers) involving familiar ingredients—a corrupt payoff and a cover-up.

The change in *Murder on Drake Island* is marked by the killer's confession as she plays What-If with Armand DuPre. Armand, who's tracked the Teen Angel murders from the beginning, assumes the killer is a man. As she reveals herself, the killer has fun toying with Armand's frozen preconceptions—this is just the way she wants it—and the minute he understands, looking at her with new eyes, she kills him.

With Armand dead, slammed in the skull by a butcher's meat mallet, the police assume a second killer is loose on the island. The killer is overjoyed; she thrives on chaos and confusion.

3. *Dig up the Past.*

Act Two is the best place to dig up the past. You can hint at the past in Act One, but save the heavy excavation for Act Two. As the police in *Murder on Drake Island* narrow their focus to Julius Bugliosi, the sleuth peels back layers of the past. The Major's hiding something about the victim. The sleuth sends her dad to Mexico to find out what's hidden. The Major helps out by accusing Edward—he's Lacey Anne's Lost Father—of helping to get her killed. If Edward had been brave, if he had acknowledged his daughter, then she would not have had this crazy idea of singing with the band.

The Major does not know about the killer's scapegoat setup: to connect Lacey Anne to Julius. If you remember the plotting section, this information developed on Weekends 5–9, when we created the back story.

To dig up the past, you have to bury stuff first.

4. *Close Off Act Two.*

When you close off Act Two, get dramatic. Act Two of *Gorky Park* closes with a shootout at the university fountain. The sleuth saves Irina; Irina saves the sleuth. It's helpful to jot down the actions before you write:

1. Wielding a huge knife (a symbolic foreshadowing of the knife Osborne will use to kill Kirwill in Act Three), Iamskoy's goon stabs the sleuth.
2. Jerking the knife free, the sleuth stabs the goon.
3. Her hand steadied by the rage of revenge, Irina shoots Iamskoy, creating a fitting climax to the action.

If you leave something out at plot point two, you keep the reader reading. Two of the bad guys die at the fountain, but Osborne remains. Because the killer is still at large, there is a reason for Act Three.

To close off Act Two of *Murder on Drake Island*, Edward Severance confesses to causing the death of Lacey Anne. Depressed by a pressure-cooker session with the Major—who has discerned through photographs that Lacey Anne possessed the famous aristocratic Severance nose—Edward flips out. The guilt he has carried for impregnating Annie Lee Baxter gets to him. The daughter is dead, he feels, because he never claimed her as his own. He's a coward. He hates himself. He wants to die. The sleuth has her hands full with traffic control. To protect Edward for the time being, she locks him up in the Village donjon, a replica of a prison cell from a pirate film.

What the sleuth does not know in Act Two is that the killer wants Edward dead so she'll be free to marry the Major.

With Edward in the donjon, the weary sleuth heads for home and some sleep. If Edward loses his mayor's job, the sleuth could lose her job. She's worn out and sick to death and she still has not solved the murder of Lacey Anne Baxter.

· · ·

WORKING THE NOVEL

Exercises

1. *Divide Act Two.*
Cut your work in half by dividing Act Two at the midpoint. On your plot diagram, you might apply metaphoric labels ("Police Procedure," "The Plot Thickens," "Where's My Sleuth?" et cetera), that suggest possible themes for the first and second halves of Act Two. Below the line on your diagram, jot down ideas. New scenes belong on the diagram. And any new and surprising clues.

2. *List of Scenes.*
Following the form we used for Act One, create a list of scenes for both halves of Act Two. If your goal is to write a book with thirty to forty scenes (making an easy transition from book to film), then you'll list a dozen or more scenes for Act Two. Highlight scenes that dig up the past.

3. *Scene Cards/Scene Profiles.*
Using scene cards and scene profiles, develop plot points one and two, the key scenes that frame Act Two. Focus on midpoint, where you divide Act Two. One way to make your midpoint solid is to knit three or four scenes together in a sequence.

4. *Write the Scenes.*
The easy way to write the scenes is to start with a narrative summary—a ten-to-fifteen-minute writing if you use the timer to sharpen your focus with time pressure—and speed-write who's there and what they're doing and what each character hopes to gain.

If you name each scene as you write it—"Male Bonding," "Metro Rescue," "Victim's Lair," et cetera—you'll organize your work without breaking the creative momentum. When you have filled several pages with narrative summary, comb through your work to find more scenes. Create scene cards. Include the new scenes on your scene list. Don't stop to edit and rewrite.

5. *Getting to Midpoint, Then to Plot Point Two.*
Your first goal is to reach midpoint. If you don't finish drafting all the scenes, sketch the rest in narrative summary and stay on schedule. Reaching midpoint should give your momentum a boost. After that, you move on to plot point two. Work on the computer when you're hot; when the writing cools, take up the notebook. When new scenes appear, sprouting up from the landscape of your fiction, sketch them quickly on your scene cards and keep writing toward the end.

· WEEKENDS 23–25 ·
WRITING ACT THREE

Act Three is the closing movement of your novel. Here, with a climax that pulses with drama, you bring your action to a conclusion that satisfies the reader. If you were writing a love story, the lovers, having been split apart for much of Act Two, would get together at last. Since you're writing a mystery, the sleuth clears a final set of obstacles, traps the killer, and receives the proper reward.

Act Three is framed by this sleuth's reward scene and by plot point two, the scene which closes off Act Two. Because you have prepared, spending the time to sketch out your plot, taking the time to create scene cards and scene profiles, you can speed through Act Three, writing with a wild confidence that builds as you approach the confrontation with the killer, because three fourths of the book lies behind you.

A look at Act Three of *Gorky Park* offers some great strategies for your work. For example, following plot point two, where Irina kills Iamskoy and where the sleuth kills Osborne's goon, the lovers are separated, torn apart for interrogation by the KGB. With Osborne gone and Iamskoy dead, the sleuth becomes the prime suspect in Iamskoy's death. From his state of near-death, the sleuth is dragged back into the world like a baby being born: "Interrogation is largely a process of rebirth done in the clumsiest fashion possible, a system in which the midwife attempts to deliver the same baby a dozen different times in a dozen different ways." One of the rituals you can use to write Act Three is rebirth, bringing the story back to life by bringing the sleuth back to life to continue the hunt.

Irony blossoms in Act Three of *Gorky Park* because the sleuth takes on a subordinate role. Plunged into near-death by a knife wound, Arkady Renko is transformed into the scapegoat, forced to take the heat for the killer's sable smuggling. "You masterminded the conspiracy along with the American Osborne," intones a faceless KGB interrogator, "promising protection against the efforts of Prosecutor Iamskoy." The conspiracy here is not murder, not the taking of the life of the Moscow town prosecutor, but rather the Osborne-Iamskoy conspiracy to smuggle sables out of the country. This transfer of wealth threatens the security of an important economic resource base, creating a threat to Russia's age-old monopoly on fine sable fur. Society needs a scapegoat. For most of Act Three, the sleuth of *Gorky Park,* once a chief investigator for the People's Militia, assumes the scapegoat role.

Act Three is an excellent place for character transformation. As we pointed out earlier, readers like change. The way to display change in character is to borrow from Greek drama, where the actors wore masks. To change a character, you rip off the mask you placed on the character earlier in the story. Let's see how this character transformation works in *Gorky Park.*

Through summer and early fall, the sleuth is kept in a KGB facility somewhere east of Moscow. His watchdog is Major Pribluda, the KGB ghoul who intruded into the crime scene to crack open frozen coats to start the book with a cold graveyard shiver. At this facility, Pribluda bonds with his peasant roots, showing his vulnerable side as he transforms from a cackling inhuman monster-torturer into a human being with a heart. The KGB stone-soldier mask comes off when Pribluda kneels, pressing his ear to the earth: "I confess I joined the Army to get away from the farm . . . but at heart I'm still from the country. . . . This is peasant science. Hear the earth? You can hear how dry its throat is." Because Pribluda has changed from KGB ghoul into a stolid Russian peasant, Renko saves his life from a fire. Because Renko saves his life, Pribluda does not execute the sleuth, but instead sends him on to the Chieftains of Fur, who send him to New York to finish Act Three with a blood sacrifice.

Because you're writing a mystery—a genre with its own rules and conventions—you'll finish off Act Three by making the killer pay. If you were writing an existential novel with a Kafkaesque antihero, *Gorky Park* could end here, in a lockup facility with the sleuth trapped in a mirror maze of guilt, accusation, and self-loathing. He might die by lethal injection. He might starve to death calling for his shadowy femme fatale lover. Or the book might fade out with the antihero staring at the portrait of Stalin on the wall of his interrogation cell.

But this is a mystery you're writing. Someone has taken a life; therefore, someone must pay. Payment balances the scales; ritual sacrifice puts the world back in order.

In mystery, rules born of convention help the writer stay on track with the plot. If the killer is alive and well, his continued existence intensifies the sleuth's moral resolve to keep going; to run the killer to earth; to exact payment and punishment.

Instead of being executed by the KGB, the sleuth of *Gorky Park* will perform a designated execution for the KGB. The demands of plot take the sleuth out of his jail cell to America.

Act Three is also the place to give your reader a strong reminder of the power of the resource base, the object of desire that drove the killer to kill in the first place. In *Gorky Park,* that reminder comes in a rotten smell at the Fur Palace in Leningrad ("The Palace smelled of dead meat"), where a powerful KGB general outlines a possible end to the Soviet sable monopoly—Osborne has fifty sables now; in ten years his sable herd will have grown to two thousand—before sending the sleuth on his final mission. "Do you like to travel?" asks the general, with Russian irony. "Have you ever wanted to see America?"

• • •

The sleuth's task—executing the killer to exact payment—is made more complex by the collusion of the FBI and the KGB. On the surface, at least, the KGB wants what the FBI wants—one American smuggler dead, one Muscovite investigator dead, one Siberian Cinderella dead, six sables to go home. With the clockwork timing of a shootout on Boot Hill, the sleuth gets his man. Killing Osborne caps the book with the spilling of the killer's blood. For his reward, the sleuth will purchase America for Irina with his own blood. He will return home to the Soviet Union, to his life in a cage called Mother Russia. To this pale sleuth, Irina is worth the price.

Guidelines for Writing Act Three

1. *Prepare for Character Reentry.*

Who comes back in Act Three? What do they want? What do they do? What are they wearing? Whose side are they on?

In Act Three of *Gorky Park,* Irina Asanova reenters the story in a display of Osborne's fur and Osborne's gold to breathe life into the sleuth ("Irina's face pressed against his chest. As if she's blowing life into me, Arkady thought") and to propel him into a deadly maze of self-doubt and self-loathing: "Now they [Renko and Irina] were both whores."

After his escape in Moscow using Irina's scarf, Osborne reenters the story to confess—a final re-creation of the crime in the park from the killer's angle—and to display his economic power: clothes, an apartment, escape from Russia, a chauffeured limousine.

By replacing Osborne's chauffeur behind the wheel of the limousine, Kirwill reenters the story to guide the sleuth through the New York underworld (to a creature named Rats, who's found Osborne's sable compound in New Jersey), and to exit the story by dying.

In Act Three of *The Big Sleep,* the killer reenters, wearing the same blue outfit, to use the same gun to try to kill the sleuth at the same crime scene where she killed Rusty Regan. The rich old man reenters to make one last attempt at buying the sleuth's soul.

In Act Three of *"F" Is for Fugitive,* the killer reenters to have her foot blown off by her father's shotgun. The father, a sick old man, reenters in time to save the sleuth's life. The sleuth, while solving the case, becomes a sad witness to the killer's motive for wanting to leave the family: her father withheld his love.

In Act Three of *Murder on Drake Island,* our write-along mystery, the killer reenters to start Act Three in confession mode to tell the sleuth about her childhood. Dad left and Mom died and the killer had her first taste of intrafamily sex from Uncle Vincent, the husband of Aunt Myra Johnson. A botched abortion took the killer's womb away along with the unborn fetus. In a scene called "The Killer Goes to College," the killer reveals how much she loved being a student at the university. She was a whiz at anatomy, diagnosis, identifying rare diseases. In the pathology lab, she was a true artist. While her fellow students fainted during dissection, the killer saw only the pure light of discovery.

Edward Severance, the killer's husband, reenters in Act Three to commit suicide. Propelled by the Major in Act Two, Edward kills himself when his guilt trip gets too heavy. The sleuth's dad, who came onstage in Act Two, reenters the story in Act Three to help the sleuth gain access to Julius Bugliosi. Julius Bugliosi, the scapegoat, reenters in Act Three to place the killer at three concerts connected with the Teen Angel killings. Armed with this information, the sleuth asks the Major for help. His reluctance charged by a lingering bias against Julius, the Major reenters in Act Three to help the sleuth trap the killer.

2. *Increase the Pace of the Story.*

In Act Three of *The Body in the Library,* to prevent society from punishing the fall guy, Miss Marple swings into action. For most of Act Two, the sleuth hung out at the Majestic Hotel, sitting around, analyzing, conducting interviews over tea. Act Three opens with the sleuth in urgent motion, a threshold crossing that takes Miss Marple through a maze of gates and paths in her never-ending quest for the truth: "Miss Marple passed out through the French windows of her drawing room, tripped down the neat garden path, through a garden gate, in through the vicarage garden gate, across the vicarage garden, and up to the drawing-room window. . . ."

This series of threshold crossings in Act Three symbolizes the sleuth's quickening toward a solution of the case. Though not revealed to the reader, Christie's sleuth has penetrated the killer's heart, brain, and soul. She knows how the murder was committed because she has seen, with her sleuth's intuition, the plan that went wrong. She understands the power of motive. She needs one final piece of evidence before helping the police bait the trap to nail the killer. Each step Miss Marple takes has a purpose: from the vicar's wife, the sleuth obtains a disguise; the disguise (as collection agent for a local charity) gets her across the threshold into the world of the scapegoat. There she will find the clue, the last thing she needs to know before baiting the trap.

In *"F" Is for Fugitive*, Sue Grafton uses the same device—a series of threshold crossings—to speed up Act Three. The pace quickens at the Mineral Springs Hotel when the sleuth crosses the threshold into a spa to find Shana Timberlake, the victim's mother, dead in the hot tub. Here's a quick list.

- After ramming into Elva Dunne, the sleuth takes off. The cops are coming fast.

- She climbs the fire lane to a gate, another threshold. She takes a fall when she jumps the gate.

- She crosses a road, hides in some bushes.

- Heading for the stairway to the victim's house, she follows a chain-link fence.

- The fence leads her to the home of Dwight Shales, the Lost Father who holds the secret key to the case.

- Crossing the threshold into Dwight's house, the sleuth digs into his past.

• • •

3. *Conceal and Reveal.*

You dig up in Act Three what you buried in Acts One and Two. Because this is discovery writing, there's a good chance you'll run across clues when you write Act Three that you didn't know about earlier, when you wrote Acts One and Two. When a hot clue surfaces in the writing, don't throw it away. Instead, make a note to yourself, then take the time to bury it earlier in the book. If your detail pulls you into the past, bury the object in the back story. Here's an example of conceal and reveal from *Murder on Drake Island.*

Back Story—College Call Girl

Forced to earn money as a call girl to finish her college degree, Myra Jane Wallace discovers that she likes to dominate men, using the power of sex to bend them to her will. To enhance the erotic experience for her clients, Myra Jane uses special play-toys, most of them purchased in Atlanta, at Tamara's Boutique Erotique. She uses a thong to enliven the Major on their first date.

Back Story—Victims One and Two

Myra Jane kills Victims One and Two. Strips them naked. Dresses them in the thong bikinis to mark them as serial kills. She works by instinct, not thinking too much. The thongs are part of the pattern to lead the police astray.

Back Story—Crime Scene

Sticking tight to the pattern killings, Myra Jane dresses the dead Lacey Anne in the third and last thong. When the Major arrives in the Suburban, Lacey Anne looks naked and wet. She's spread-eagled in the mud. The rain has turned to mist. Mud is caked on the thong. Hampered by his wheelchair, the Major can't get close enough to see the body, so he sends Ripley. Before Ripley has a closer look, the sleuth arrives.

Act One—Crime Scene

The sleuth kneels in the mud, close enough to see the thong waistbelt against the white belly, the mud caked between the legs.

Before she can get a close look, the sleuth's emotions take over, forcing her to vomit. She returns to the Suburban without having had a clear look at the thong.

Act One—Re-creation of the Crime

At the Marina Café, Armand DePre establishes the thong as the signature of the Teen Angel Killer. The sleuth, a mystery writer with an inquisitive mind, thinks this is a silent message from the killer. Since she can't decode the message, the sleuth hits the wall here.

Act One—Killer Onstage

Myra Jane, looking beautiful and cold in her mourning black, enters the Marina Café to intrude on the sleuth and Armand. The Major's getting together a manhunt for that bandleader person, Julius. Out of the blue, the sleuth asks the killer for help with "alternative lifestyle clothing," and then tells her about the thong. The killer looks from the sleuth to Armand. Smiling, she shakes her head.

Act Two—Interview with a Killer

Near the climax of Armand's interview, Myra Jane has the answer to the sleuth's question: the thong is a verification of sexuality. In life, the victims wear virgin masks; under the masks, they are little whores. The thong is the emblem of honesty. As Armand composes a paragraph about the primal significance of the thong, the killer cracks his skull with a meat mallet.

Act Three—Package from Armand

A package from Armand DuPre, sent by special messenger from the mainland, contains a thong purchased from Tamara's in Atlanta.

Act Three—Help from the Major

Showing the thong to the Major, the sleuth triggers a memory of Myra Jane Wallace during her college call-girl days turning him on with the thong. Did he ever wear it? asks the sleuth. Never, says the Major. The sleuth now has leverage. The Major agrees to help trap Myra Jane.

Act Three—Killer Confrontation

Wearing battle dress, the sleuth confronts the killer in the Major's bungalow. She holds the thong in one hand and her Glock 9mm in the other. Failing to recruit the sleuth to her cause, the killer turns to mockery. You won't shoot, the killer says. I've read your books. Your detectives are men without balls. This is not a book, says the sleuth. She fires. The bullet slams the killer in the shoulder.

4. *Explanation, Abstention, Closure.*

How will you close your book? Who explains the solution? Where does the explanation occur? How is your sleuth dressed at the end of the story? How does the sleuth appear as the book ends?

In Act Three, the reader learns how the sleuth cracked the case. If the solution is concealed during the quest for the killer, it must be made clear at the end. The work you have done so far—on character, on plot, on scene building—provides you with the material to write an explanation that satisfies the reader. In a Christie-type mystery, the sleuth's explanation—it's the last scene in the book—can function as a moral beacon that guides the sleuth to the truth: "The truth is," explains Miss Marple, "that most people—and I don't exclude policemen—are far too trusting for this wicked world. They believe what is told them. I never do. I'm afraid I always like to prove a thing for myself."

The cops were wrong; Miss Marple was right. They followed the false trail while she nailed the real killer. Dressed in her best evening gown, Miss Jane Marple addresses four males of authority—three policemen and one rich old man—taking the moral high ground as she discloses how she cracked the case.

If you don't want to follow Christie—Miss Marple's final analysis in *Body* takes several pages of monologue—then try shifting the burden of explanation to the killer, the way Martin Cruz Smith does in *Gorky Park,* where Osborne confesses that he paused before shooting Valerya, because she was pretty: "I did hesitate before I shot her, you're correct." Stirred by Valerya, the killer shuts down the memory of killing with food, eating, digestion: "I find that confession gives me an appetite. We'll have something to eat."

A good lesson here for the mystery writer: if you write an explanatory confession scene and if you break the rhythm with a meal, don't let your sleuth eat. Even in Act Three, the proper sleuth abstains.

Whether it's food or sex, abstention defines the sleuth's moral stance. When he confronts the killer in *The Maltese Falcon*, Sam Spade gets her to lie one more time when she fingers her accomplice as the killer of Spade's partner. As Brigid lies, Spade closes the trap on her. He can close the trap now because he abstains, curbing his wolfish desire: "He looked hungrily from her hair to her feet and up to her eyes again." The key word, tapping in to the ritual of eating and incorporation, is the adverb *hungrily*. In Act Two, the sleuth tasted the killer's twisted love. The equation of sex to eating brings the closure scene to life. But Spade denies his appetites. By abstaining from this final taste of twisted love, he wins. Brigid gets sent over. She's the killer; the one who pays.

WORKING THE NOVEL

Exercises

1. *Character Fates.*
Before you start writing, check your character roster and your plot diagrams to see who reenters the story in Act Three. Work out the fate of each—what happens to the killer; the sleuth; the catalyst, et cetera—and make sure each character is accounted for.

2. *Conceal and Reveal.*
Following the form used in the Guidelines, track a detail buried early that you dig up later. Sables enter *Gorky Park* in Act One from food traces, chicken and fish blood on the clothes of the victims. The writer conceals by burying the detail. Live sables surfacing at the end of the book give the sleuth an edge on the killer (Renko maddens Osborne into missing his kill shot by throwing open those cage doors); they also provide a stunning image for closure: "black on white, black on white, black on

white, and then gone." Track one of your details from early in the book all the way to the end.

3. *List of Scenes.*
Working fast, create a list of scenes that spans Act Three from plot point two to the wrap-up. Making this list, printing it out on the computer, will provide you with a feeling of closure.

4. *Write the Scenes.*
In timed writings of fifteen to twenty minutes, write the scenes from your scene list, scene cards, and scene profiles. By now you should be writing full scenes, integrating the parts—action, setting, dialogue, narration—as you go. Your goal is three to four scenes per weekend. The key to Act Three is increasing the pace of the story as your sleuth presses forward toward a solution.

5. *Finishing the First Draft.*
Write as many scenes as you can. Work on the computer if you can. If you stall out, reenter the notebook. As you print each scene out, allow yourself to feel a sense of completion. Your goal is to push yourself to reach the end.

Weekends 26–38
Second Draft

In the second draft, you reshape your work from the first draft. You rebuild your settings. You rewrite dialogue and action. You probe your characters to clarify motive: Why does the killer kill? Why does the victim have to die? Why does the sleuth detect?

Probing character takes you to What-If questions: What if the killer was present at the crime scene when the book opens? What if the book begins with a first-encounter scene? What happens if the killer is behind bars when the story opens? What if the crime took place ten years ago? Fifteen years ago? Twenty?

When you write the second draft, you think and you brood over your work and you jot notes to yourself. You make lists of details. Lists of character traits. Lists of scenes. You work like a film director, dividing the scene cards into day scenes and night scenes, light and dark indicators of mood, atmosphere, and time passing. If you were making scene cards for *Body*, for example, you'd need lighting for only one night scene—the killer confrontation in a bedroom of the Majestic Hotel at 3:00 A.M.

The deeper writing on the second draft allows you to slow down and develop details. Getting organized on time markers like night and day gives you a tighter focus on light and dark, heat and cold. *Gorky Park* opens on a dark morning in April. It's cold out here. Headlights slice the dark, bringing the intruder onstage. The intruder is a night creature. When he leaves, dawn arrives, and with it a Russian spring: "The sun was really up now, alive, not the ghost disk that had haunted winter."

Using your scene cards, you follow a single character from that first entrance into the story in Act One through Acts Two and Three. When you rewrite a scene, you explore symbols planted earlier in the writing. A dress worn by the victim turns out to belong to someone else. Is the owner of the dress dead or alive? An ice skate worn by the victim leads the sleuth to a character that brings twisted love into your story.

When you write the second draft, you step away from the work, taking a breather, and you see a larger pattern at work. In the second draft, the sick old man from the first writing transforms from a walk-on character into a dying king. The dying king controls a resource base. The queen is dead. Who will replace the queen? Which character wants a slice of the resource base? To find out, you give the king some dialogue lines. By letting a character talk, the writer fastens on to new insights. "I thought of her as a daughter," says the sick old man. "She was Cinderella. I see that now. I played the role of Fairy Godfather. Who would brutalize such a lovely young thing? Do you think I killed her, Inspector?"

The last dialogue line reveals an old man riddled with guilt. He's asking for absolution, for forgiveness. In your first draft, you might have told the reader about it with narrative summary—"The old man felt really guilty about her death. He sat in his wheelchair staring out the window, thinking about her, hour after hour, day after day"—and now in the second draft you turn the narration into dialogue. Character X asks a question. A policeman answers. The dialogue rolls out like a magic carpet:

> "Do you think I killed her, Inspector?"
>
> "Did you kill her?"
>
> "Are you mad? Of course not."
>
> "Oh, I didn't mean that you might have delivered the death blow yourself."
>
> "Then what did you mean?"
>
> "Well, sir, I only meant that perhaps she wanted in here . . . and that perhaps you did not wish her in."

"And where is here?"

"Have you seen her room where she lived?"

"Inspector, I'm confined to this abomination eighteen hours out of twenty-four."

"But the room, sir. Have you seen her room?"

"The chair, man. Look at this chair and then tell me how."

"And her room, sir?"

"Her room? What about it?"

"Do you know its particular whereabouts, sir?"

"Dammit, man. You think I killed her."

• • •

You write dialogue to extract a scene from narrative summary because you know that showing is better than telling. You write dialogue so that you can hear the voices of your characters. Hearing the voices deepens your insight into mood and motive and agenda. By moving the line about guilt out of the author's head into dialogue, by allowing the old man to talk to someone instead of musing to himself, you not only reveal his inner state ("Are you mad, sir?" has a tone of edged anxiety), but you also give the police person a toehold in the scene. Contained by the scene, the characters propel the story forward, to the next scene. The old man wanted absolution. Instead, he gets an interrogation. How far will the policeman go? Will he arrange a visit to the room of the dead girl? That could be the next scene, the sick old man in his wheelchair in the victim's lair. A secret buried in one scene generates another scene where the secret gets dug up.

The police person in that scene smells a prime suspect.

Rethinking the Resource Base

What is the resource base? Who's greedy for a piece of it? How is the resource base in your story connected to the killer quest?

• In *Gorky Park,* John Osborne kills to protect his illicit empire of sables, and then uses Iamskoy, the sleuth's boss, as a substitute to stall for time. The killer's shrewd substitution ploy sends the sleuth to save Irina from Iamskoy at the university fountain, creating plot point two and ending Act Two.

• In *Murder on Drake Island,* Myra Jane Severance kills because she wants to be mistress of a beach house. The biggest beach house on Drake Island belongs to Major Philip Baxter. To get the beach house, Myra Jane frames Julius Bugliosi to take the fall for three serial murders.

• The scapegoat in Sue Grafton's *"F" Is for Fugitive* is Bailey Fowler, behind bars when the story opens for a killing seventeen years ago. The resource base is $42,000, illicit funds stolen in gas-station holdups around the time of the killing. The killer is Bailey's sister, Ann Fowler, a femme fatale with an overbite who kills her own mother in true Christie style, with a hypodermic needle. The sleuth unmasks the killer when she digs up the secret of the re-source base: the killer wants to escape the cage of her suffocating beach town; the $42K, ballooned by investments in IBM stock, is her escape fund.

Greed, one of the seven deadly sins, helps you make this impor-tant link between killer and resource base. In the moral structure of mystery fiction, greedy people die. On the trail of the killer, the sleuth scans the suspect list, sniffing the ground for greed. While the police grab the likely suspect, the sleuth knows the scapegoat did not commit the crime because he has no access to the resource base.

If you take the time to develop the resource base, you create a magnet for greedy characters. In your first draft, it's all right to mention greed in abstract terms—"From this perspective, the sleuth thought, Character G appeared to be an awfully greedy person"— but since showing is more powerful than telling, your job in the second draft is to create word pictures, letting the writing deepen with each word as you develop the resource base as the target for greed: "The air was thick, wet, steamy and larded with the cloying smell of tropical orchids in bloom. . . . The plants filled the place, a forest of them, with nasty meaty leaves and stalks like the newly washed fingers of dead men."

The sleuth has been called to adventure. The caller is a dying king, a rich old man who wants to save his daughter. The king is old;

his cold bones need heat; so he inhabits a hothouse filled with orchids: "I seem to exist largely on heat, like a newborn spider, and the orchids are an excuse for the heat." This hothouse is a garden of death, orchids, ponderous wealth.

Greed surfaces in this hothouse scene in the form of documents, promissory notes signed by the old man's daughter promising several thousand dollars to Character G. The documents are physical evidence that display the fruits of greed to the reader, showing instead of telling. Character G, the greedy party, is making an assault on the resource base. His assault weapon is blackmail. A clue surfaces in the handwriting of the daughter, which the sleuth characterizes as "moronic" and "sprawling." The out-of-control handwriting sets up another clue: the daughter will become a complication to the killer quest.

Character G wants money, a piece of empire; the old man who controls the resource base wants the sleuth to get Character G off his back. The sleuth's fee, twenty-five dollars a day, sets him apart from the thousand-dollar greed of Character G. In mystery fiction, money is one measure of morality. "No money now," the sleuth says to the butler who writes checks for the rich old man.

Rethinking Your Structure

Key scenes control your pace, so it's smart to rethink your structure before you rewrite. When you rewrite Act One, for example, study the scene you have chosen as your opening ("Crime Scene," "Killer Onstage," "First Encounter," et cetera), and then rewrite plot point one. With Act One contained, you can rewrite with confidence and power.

Our advice on rewriting key scenes for the second draft is to let them grow larger and more powerful. These are the turning points of your tale. Don't shut down the power when you rewrite. A key scene that gets a bit long is easy to cut. Cutting is the task of the final draft.

To develop your structure, combine scenes connected by a common thread, the way Martin Cruz Smith does in *Gorky Park*. In Act One, for example, scene work traces the sleuth's movements as he leaves the Crime Scene: he visits two labs, forensics and pathology, where he gathers data; he writes a report including the data; he reports to his boss, Chief Prosecutor Iamskoy, about the data; he digs up research on the KGB's Pribluda, the Prime Suspect who destroys evidence at the crime scene; he goes home to his wife, a party gymnast who will be replaced by Irina Asanova, a femme fatale from Siberia.

As you rewrite your second draft, jot down notes (names, roles, et cetera) of characters you're planning to replace later in the story. In *Body,* Sir Henry replaces Dolly Bantry as sleuth's helper; in *Gorky Park,* Irina replaces the wife as the love interest.

· WEEKENDS 26–29 ·
REWRITING ACT ONE

The key to a powerful and entertaining Act One—Act One is where you hook the reader—is Act Three.

Since you've just finished writing the first draft of Act Three, you know what it contains. You know which characters are present at the climactic killer confrontation. You know how the killer pays. You know the nature of the sleuth's reward.

Because Act Three is fresh in your mind, you know the objects that are needed for a successful resolution to a tale of crime and punishment: for example, the killer's little gun in *The Big Sleep;* Osborne's skinning knife in *Gorky Park;* one of Christie's trademarks, a deadly hypodermic; the shotgun and the photos of Mom in *Fugitive.*

With the specific objects in place, you are more aware of the specific settings you used for Act Three. As a reader, you know which settings are new to the story—the killer's sable compound in *Gorky Park;* the killer's bedroom in *Fugitive*—and which settings have already been visited by the characters in Acts One and Two.

For his climax to *The Maltese Falcon,* Hammett returns the reader to the sleuth's lair, first visited in Act One.

After confronting the killer in the played-out oil field—a quick car trip down the hill—the sleuth of *The Big Sleep* returns to Sternwood Manor, where the book began, to confront the killer's big sister accomplice. This is an excellent strategy for your book—ending where you started—because it creates closure for the reader. Back at the big mansion where he started his quest in Act One, Philip Marlowe sees that nothing has changed: "The main hallway looked just the same. The portrait over the mantel had the same hot black eyes and the knight in the stained-glass window still wasn't getting anywhere untying the naked damsel from the tree." Time has passed; people have died trying to get at the General's money through his daughters. At Sternwood Manor, the inhabitants are statues fixed in stone. Insulated by the General's money, the Sternwood girls can gamble and drink and pose nude and kill and get away without paying the price.

Writing Act Three—especially that scene at the climax—opens up your characters for rewriting Act One. You have lived with them through the first draft and now you know them. When you rewrite Act One, you use the insights from Act Three to sharpen your focus on character. The old man in *The Big Sleep* is a deadly spider in a deadly hothouse; the daughters of the house are deadly femmes fatales; young men who come courting (like Owen the chauffeur, like Rusty the soldier of fortune) are doomed to die for love. The sleuth lives because, like Sir Gawain and the seductive wife of the Green Knight, he abstains, rejecting not only naked flesh and elegant legs, but also money. If the writer knows from Act Three that the beautiful damsel is the killer, there is an opportunity to sharpen the focus on character when you rewrite Act One: "She had little sharp predatory teeth, as white as fresh orange pith and as shiny as porcelain." The key word in this character entry is *predatory.* The killer's teeth are for biting, tearing, eating, devouring men who displease her. The killer's young face is pale, the shade of the shroud: "Her face lacked color and didn't look too healthy."

Guidelines for Rewriting Act One

For insights on rewriting Act One, you apply Act Three as a guide. To begin, make some lists: a list of objects in a room, a list of wardrobe items in a closet, or a cast roster that sharpens up role definition as the characters enter the story.

1. *Roster Control.*

If you build a cast roster based on Act Three, you'll know which characters to concentrate on when you rewrite Act One. For example, which of your Act Three characters enter the story in Act One? If you were directing a film, you would want all of your actors—from major stars to lowly walk-ons—to be solid. It's the same for a crime novel. A solid character needs a purpose, a reason to enter the story. A cast roster marking character entrances gives you control over the rewrite.

Here's an example from *Murder on Drake Island:*

• *Sleuth.*   Helene Steinbeck enters in Act One, Chapter One, to answer the Major's call for help. (Rewriting Strategy: Focus on the sleuth now. Her strengths, her weaknesses, her back story.)

• *Killer.*   Myra Jane Severance enters in Act One, near the middle, with the news that the Major is organizing a posse to hunt down Julius Bugliosi. (Rewriting Strategy: Focus on the killer now. Strengths, weaknesses, back story.)

• *Victims.*   Lacey Anne Baxter enters the story in Act One at the crime scene. Lacey Anne, costumed by the killer in the thong bikini, stands in the killer's way, blocking her access to the resource base. Armand DuPre, the crime writer, enters the story at the end of the crime scene. Armand has information helpful to the sleuth. Edward Severance enters the story in Act One, with career advice for the sleuth. (Rewriting Strategy: Focus on Lacey Anne now. Back story on Armand now. Where has he been? What does he know? Focus on Edward now. Back story with Annie Lee, Lacey Anne's mom. Back story with Lacey Anne. He knows; she doesn't.)

• *Helper.*   Frank Steinbeck, NYPD Retired, enters the story in

Act Two as the sleuth's helper. (Rewriting Strategy: Save Frank for later, when you get to Act Two.)

• *Scapegoat.*   Julius Bugliosi enters the story in Act Two, when he is interviewed by the sleuth at the donjon, Drake Island's substitute for a jail. (Rewriting Strategy: Although Julius is the focus of the Major's anger, you can save him for Act Two.)

• *Cops.*   James T. Worthington enters the story in Act One at the crime scene to start a Turf War. James T. wants jurisdiction over this case, which could help his career. (Rewriting Strategy: Focus on James T. now. Do a profile and a sketch. A brief back story.)

• *Catalyst.*   Major Philip Baxter enters the story in Act One, waiting for the sleuth to show up at the crime scene. The Major's money—a vast and luscious resource base—provides the motive for the killer's murder of Lacey Anne. (Rewriting Strategy: Work on the Major now.)

• *Walk-ons and Red Herrings.*   Ripley's in the bushes at the crime scene. Deputies are around, but not talking much. Emily Tallant is important during her witness interview in Act One. (Rewriting Strategy: Work on Emily now.)

• • •

To extract helpful insights from your cast roster in the rewrite, focus on the climax first. In addition to the killer and the sleuth, is there a third character present at the killer confrontation? What are the characters wearing? What are they carrying? What do they want? Do they want the same thing in Act One that they wanted in Act Three? Are they moving faster in Act Three than they moved in Act One? Are they smoking the same cigarettes? Lighting them with the same orange flame? Do the characters at your climax in Act Three talk the same way—same cadence, same words, same tone— as they did when they entered the story in Act One? Have their voices changed? Is the killer deadly as a dagger in Act Three and silky soft in Act One?

Answering just one of these questions will jump-start your rewrite. For example, let's take the first question—"Is there a third character present at the killer confrontation?"—and use that to generate insights about rewriting Act One.

• *"F" Is for Fugitive.* The third character at Grafton's climax in *Fugitive* is Royce Fowler, a sick old man. Royce stumbles onstage carrying photos of Ori Fowler, the killer's dead mom. In Act Two, with Royce offstage, the killer murdered her mom to speed up the sale of the family motel, once Royce is dead. In Act Three, Royce is the active catalyst who saves the sleuth's life by grabbing the shotgun. The shotgun goes off, blowing away the killer's foot. In Act One, Royce just sits there, talking away. He enters the story in the sleuth's office as a client with a mission: to hire the sleuth to save his boy Bailey from the gas chamber.

Here's the lesson from Grafton's handling of Royce Fowler: because he has a job in Act Three (grabbing the shotgun, saving the sleuth by wounding his daughter), and because the writer knows that Royce is a catalyst who makes things happen, his presence onstage in Act One is marked by a solid character description—age, body type, clothing, hair, hands—of 150 words: "He used a cane, but the big hands he kept folded on it were as steady as stone and speckled with liver spots." Liver spots, a character detail, inform the reader about age.

In Act One, the writer uses Royce as a device for bringing both sleuth and reader up to date on the story's designated scapegoat, his son Bailey—in jail in San Luis Obispo after escaping from prison sixteen years ago. Disease has made Royce weak. He almost had a stroke, he says, when he heard of Bailey's rearrest. Royce has enough strength in Act One to vent his anger at the fickle finger of fate: "Some hot-shoe detective got a bug up his butt and ran Bailey's prints through some fancy-pants new computer system. . . ." Because Bailey Fowler was caught, as Royce says, "by a damn fluke," it's the sleuth's job to rebalance the scales of justice. *Fugitive*, like *The Big Sleep*, is a story of scapegoat replacement. Royce hires the sleuth in Act One. In Act Three, he rescues the sleuth; to rescue the sleuth, he must wound his own daughter; wounded, her foot blown away, the killer-daughter replaces her scapegoat brother behind bars.

Because you know your killer from Weekend 1, you can mute the killer's entrance in your book the same way Grafton mutes Ann Fowler. Wearing her mask of Dutiful Daughter, Ann Fowler drives for Royce; she helps him to a chair; there is no family resemblance. In Act One, Ann Fowler recedes, fading from the scene. In Act Three, she comes out of hiding, teeth bared, snarling like a trapped rat.

• *Gorky Park.*   The third character at the climactic shootout in *Gorky Park* is Irina Asanova. Her costume in Act Three—gold, furs, new boots—has changed from Act One, where she entered in a shabby coat and torn vinyl boots.

In Act One, Irina is tough and abrasive as she repels the sleuth with words: "Believe me, there's nothing I'll do for you. . . . Unless you want me to lose my job, you'll leave." In Act Three, with the corpses piled high, Irina presides over the execution of the killer who brought her to America. With the killer dead, Irina stands over the wounded sleuth like the Queen of Death.

If you were writing a book like *Gorky Park*—where your sleuth falls in love with a death god or death goddess—you would use your Act Three understanding for a focused rewrite of Act One. Irina's rejection of the sleuth in Act One—if he doesn't leave, she'll lose her job—is a counterbalance to the sleuth's rejection of Irina in Act Three: "Go on, run," he says. When she lingers at the crime scene, he gives her another verbal shove: "Do I have to throw stones?"

To rewrite Act One, it helps to know what happens to the characters in Act Three.

2. *Buried Objects.*
Objects that surface in Act Three tell you what objects to bury in Act One.

• *The Money* in *Fugitive.*   The resource base that surfaces in a shoe box in the killer's closet in Act Three is planted in Act One, when the sleuth questions Tap Granger in the local pub. Tap Granger is the partner-in-crime of scapegoat Bailey Fowler. Bailey left their loot—$42,000 gleaned from small-time robberies—with victim Jean Timberlake. According to Tap, the secret died with Jean: "After she died," Tap says, "Bailey told me she was the only one knew for sure where it was, and she never told."

The killer took possession of the money when she killed Jean. At the climax in Act Three, the money in the shoe box has grown: "The statements from Merrill Lynch showed a $42,000 investment in shares of IBM back in 1967. With stock splits in the intervening years, the shares had more than doubled in value." Using the strategy of conceal and reveal, the writer buried the money in Act One so she could dig it up in Act Three.

• *The Little Gun* in *The Big Sleep.* The gun Carmen Sternwood turns on the sleuth at the killer confrontation in Act Three of *The Big Sleep* is the same gun she used to kill Rusty Regan in the back story. The gun in Act Three—Carmen shoots at the sleuth, calling him a "son of a bitch"—is loaded with blanks. When Carmen uses the gun on the sleuth the same way she used it on Rusty, she reveals herself as the killer.

• *The Black Bird* in *The Maltese Falcon.* If an object surfaces in Act Three and there's no place for it in Act One (it's too big to bury; it's too much fun to keep it hidden offstage), then you need to foreshadow it in dialogue, the way Grafton foreshadows the $42,000 in *Fugitive.* That's what Hammett does in *Falcon.* The actual bird statue is held back until Act Two. That means the writer develops an early-warning system, dropping hints that the object is on the way into the story.

In Act Three, the black bird is the focal point of the climax as the greedy bird-hunters assemble in the sleuth's lair to witness Caspar Gutman's ritual scraping of the bird. When his knife scrapes lead, Gutman's world collapses. He thought he had it; he was wrong.

When you load up a symbol with money and murder, it's best to handle it with care, the way Hammett handles the bird. The first mention of the bird is in Chapter 4 in Act One when Joel Cairo, a suspicious Levantine who minces when he walks and wears yellow chamois gloves, hires Sam Spade to find it. The fee is $5,000. Cairo's speech, like his walk, minces along in deliberate hesitation: "I am trying to recover an—ah—ornament that has been—shall we say—mislaid?" Because of Act Three, where Cairo bounds onstage holding a pistol, ready to kill for the bird, the writer can use this mincing dialogue as a mask to disguise the crook and amuse the reader. In Act Three, Cairo is an independent operator, a bird seeker who has joined forces with Gutman temporarily. In Act One, masking his greed, he portrays himself as the representative of the "rightful" owner of the falcon. By refusing to give up the owner's name, Cairo sounds an early warning for the entrance of Caspar Gutman. The Joel Cairo scene is plot point one.

3. *Pivotal Scene.*

Start your rewrite of Act One with plot point one, the pivotal scene. As you recall from the plotting section, plot point one serves two functions: 1) it ends Act One with action or new information or a change of setting; 2) it launches Act Two.

The scene at plot point one functions like a curtain in the theater. The curtain falls; there's a brief pause while the audience catches its breath; the curtain rises again.

The key to rewriting scenes, as we suggested earlier, is the scene profile. A scene profile, like a character profile, begins with a name and then uses specific slots to contain information about the elements of the scene: character, action, dialogue, and setting. Compiling a scene profile takes a short time—ten to fifteen minutes—but the payoff is immense.

The function of the profile is to trigger insights. If you're writing hot, insights pop early in the profile. If you're working the profile and a dialogue line pops into your head, you shift from profile to dialogue and you rewrite. If you're writing cold, you might have to complete the profile just to warm up. A scene profile gives you the discipline to keep working when you'd rather be doing something else this weekend.

• • •

As a model of a profile for plot point one, here's the Joel Cairo scene from *The Maltese Falcon.*

• *Name of the Scene.*   The Black Bird.
• *Position in the Structure.*   Act One, plot point one. This scene bridges Chapters 4 and 5.

• *Character.* The sleuth is onstage when Effie Perine ushers in Joel Cairo, a Levantine hustler dressed like a dandy. (The "Levant" refers to countries in the Eastern Mediterranean—Lebanon, Syria, Cyprus, et cetera). Cairo's black coat is cut tight; his trousers flare over plump hips; he wears fawn spats on his shoes, which are patent leather. His tie clasp is a ruby. His chubby hands drip with diamonds and a ruby that matches the tie clasp. The keynote in Cairo's wardrobe is a pair of yellow gloves.

As Cairo enters, he brings along a fragrance the writer calls "Chypre"—French for the island of Cyprus.

• *Setting.* The time is evening. Objects onstage include office furniture, cigarettes (the sleuth is a smoker), and a flat black pistol that feels small when the sleuth grabs it from Cairo. Dumping out Cairo's wallet, the sleuth finds links to the case: a map of San Francisco, the sleuth's address on hotel stationery, and newspaper clippings noting the deaths of Miles Archer and Floyd Thursby.

Cairo's wallet also contains $365 in U.S. currency and three five-pound notes from Britain. This pittance is important because Cairo offers Spade $5,000—money that he doesn't have on him—to find the bird.

• *Dialogue.* The subject of the dialogue is finding the bird. The key words, repeated several times, are *five thousand dollars.* The dialogue dances around the object of desire as Cairo offers Spade a hundred dollars as a retainer, as Spade doubles the amount to two hundred. The structure of the dialogue is question and answer. The sleuth asks for proof of ownership: "What sort of proof can you give me that your man is the owner?" Cairo, slick as an eel, evades: "Very little, unfortunately."

• *Action.* When Cairo gets the drop on Spade, the sleuth bops him with an elbow while standing on his spat-adorned patent leather pumps: "The elbow struck him beneath the cheekbone, staggering him so that he must have fallen had he not been held by Spade's foot on his foot." The sleuth takes possession of the pistol. Cairo slides into a convenient unconsciousness. Spade searches his stuff.

• *Ritual.* The main ritual is barter. Spade wants money and answers. Cairo wants the legendary bird. The secondary ritual is searching: before he arrives, Cairo searches Spade's apartment;

when he knocks Cairo out, Spade searches Cairo's stuff; when Cairo gets the gun back, he searches Spade's office.

• *Plot Links.* The bird embedded in this scene enters the story in Chapter 16, when the wounded Captain Jacobi drops it at the threshold to Spade's office. The appearance of the bird ends Act Two and launches Act Three of *The Maltese Falcon.*

• • •

The scene profile is your key to rewriting scenes. Because of your preparation—character, plot and subplot, scene building—the parts of the book are in place. Your job now is to analyze without being judgmental, without destroying the creative discoveries of the first draft.

As you carve a path through character and objects heading for scene rewrites, remember that rewriting is a deliberative act. This deliberation, which involves brooding and reflection, places you in an analytical mode. This is different from the first draft, where your creativity went wild. When you rewrite, you step back for a wider view. You measure the book as if you were pacing off a piece of property, counting the plants and trees, because you want a sense of size and shape, of slope and contour, of growth potential, of eventual curb appeal.

WORKING THE NOVEL

Exercises

1. *Narrative Summary.*
To use Act Three as a guide to rewriting Act One, warm up by writing a quick analytical summary of the action. The summary compresses several pages of first draft into a couple of paragraphs.

2. *Character Roster.*
With Act Three squeezed down by narrative, you create a character roster. The character roster leads you to specific objects

(weapons, body parts, wardrobe items, vehicles, et cetera); objects lead you to setting; setting lays the groundwork for rewriting the scenes.

Use this roster to guide your rewrite of Act One. Follow the character roster in the guidelines. Use roles as headings, so you won't leave anyone out. Start with the main characters—killer, victim, sleuth, catalyst—and use the roster for traffic control.

3. *Buried Objects.*

Make a list of objects that surface in Act Three. Start with the climax; move to the sleuth's reward. Use the objects in Act Three to guide your rewrite when you bury them in Act One.

As you rewrite Act One, transform objects around you. If there's a photo on your wall, try a clasp where you describe the photo, changing it to fit a scene from your story: "A girl in a silk chemise. Age around sixteen. Fair hair and a wide brow and deep-set eyes looking into the camera. . . ."

4. *Scene Profiles.*

Before you rewrite each scene, take the time to create a new scene profile. If a dialogue line pops into your head—"What makes you think I killed him?"—write it down and keep filling the page. Don't stop. When your writing triggers an insight, be happy; just keep writing.

5. *Rewrite the Scenes.*

Because dialogue is the shortcut to conflict, it sometimes helps to rewrite the dialogue first. If you write naked dialogue—dialogue lines shorn of quotation marks and attribution like *he said/ she said*—you can dress it up later.

Rewrite plot point one first because it's the big pivot between Acts One and Two. Then cycle back to a rewrite of the crime scene. With the crime scene redone, work through the scenes in Act One, rewriting in a logical sequence.

· WEEKENDS 30–35 ·
REWRITING ACT TWO

Your goal when you rewrite Act Two is to dig deeper into the past, the back story you created on Weekend 5. Each of your major characters has a past. The past contains trauma, that hot dark moment in life that changed everything, that gave the character new direction.

Watching a man freeze to death in Siberia made Irina Asanova yearn for warmth, soft fur, felt boots, America. Irina's Siberian past surfaces in Act Two of *Gorky Park*, as she explains why she and Valerya and Kostia came to Moscow. "Where else can we run to but Moscow?" she asks the sleuth. And then she hammers him, using the death of her friends to bludgeon him about his motives, his intensity, his tenacious grip on the killer quest: "Don't tell me you're going to all this trouble just because a couple of Siberians are dead. We're born dead."

Seeking the key to unlock the heart of John Osborne, Arkady Renko pays an Act Two visit to his father, the Butcher of the Ukraine. The first solid information on Osborne comes from the sleuth's father in Act Two: surrounded by cannibalistic Russians in Leningrad, Osborne executed three German officers and then paid off the military investigators, a clever cover-up for a young American on foreign soil.

William Kirwill, a New York City cop who grew up with crazy Russians, speaks Russian like a native when he enters the book. In Act Two, Kirwill's memories of Jimmy as a Messiah unearth a clue about why Osborne killed him: "He was going to smuggle someone out of Russia and hold a news conference at Kennedy. He was going to be a savior, Renko—at the least, a religious celebrity."

As you rewrite Act Two, you divide the work at midpoint. As we suggested earlier, the midpoint in your story is like a door opening, a threshold crossing that plunges the sleuth into a confusing maze. From midpoint on, the pace of the book quickens. At midpoint, the sleuth gains insight into the case. This insight throws a new light on the connection between the resource base and the killer.

At the midpoint of *"F" Is for Fugitive,* for example, California sleuth Kinsey Millhone makes a discovery about the missing $42,000 first introduced in Act One: no one knows where it is. The scapegoat, Bailey Fowler, left the money with his girlfriend, Jean Timberlake, the victim who got killed on the beach seventeen years ago. After the victim's death, the money vanished. In Act Two, the missing money opens a doorway into the victim's past.

The past surfaces in the form of a file folder, a paper trail of test scores, attendance records, comments from the victim's teachers tracking the victim in her doomed downward spiral. The school nurse missed the signals for teen pregnancy. Reading this file of a confused adolescent on the way down, the sleuth empathizes, taking on the victim's pain: "I could practically feel the heat of noxious hormones seeping through the pages, the drama, the confusion, finally the secrecy."

At midpoint, after verifying that the money was last seen with the victim, the sleuth tracks it through a twisted maze of subplots, of wounded teens and bank jobs, of secret lovers and lost fathers. As the book nears its climax, the sleuth, on the run from the police, has an insight that cracks the case. Pausing for a breather, the sleuth looks down on the victim's shabby apartment: "This was the bluff above Jean Timberlake's old apartment building. Once I reached the wooden stairway, I could climb down to the rear door of her place and hide. To my right, I spotted the glass-and-frame house. . . ."

To escape her shabby world, represented by the shabby apartment that clings like an insect to the hillside, Jean would climb the rickety stairs to an upper world of light and money and the expensive glass house of her secret lover, Dwight Shales, the principal of the high school. Wanting the good life, the victim gave him her body and he got her pregnant. A scandal would kill Dwight's career. He's not a murderer but his secret admirer, Ann Fowler, is. Ann kills Jean, pinning the murder on her brother, a small-time holdup artist, and invests the $42,000 in IBM stock. The money that's lost at midpoint leads the sleuth to the economic insight that opens the doorway to the secret lover who is the living motive for murder. When she connects the resource base to the killer, the sleuth cracks the case. In *Fugitive,* as in most mysteries, the crack widens at midpoint.

Guidelines for Rewriting Act Two

1. *Strengthen Your Midpoint.*

Before you start rewriting scenes for Act Two, strengthen your midpoint with a solid chain of events. Step back from your work and study the events leading up to your midpoint, and the events leading away from it. In *Fugitive*, for example, the writer foreshadows the sleuth's economic insight when Shana Timberlake, the victim's mother, mentions the shabby apartment: "We had an apartment a couple blocks over, but it wasn't much better." In the next scene, the sleuth's client (Royce Fowler, the father of the scapegoat) gets angry about the sleuth's interview with Shana. Anger brings on a coughing fit. The coughing fit brings an ambulance to whisk the client away. The absence of the sick old man brings the sleuth and the killer closer. In a sisterly chat at the family motel, the killer admits she was always jealous of her brother, the scapegoat she's framing for murder.

In the next scene, the phone rings. It's the scapegoat calling, just in time for the sleuth to ask about the missing $42,000. Before she gets a fresh lead, the scapegoat breaks the connection and the sleuth hides the importance of the missing $42,000 from the cops. A visit to the widow of Tap Granger, who died trying to break the scapegoat out of jail, is evidence that the $42,000 is not there: the widow is scraping to stay alive; her husband died trying to earn $2,000, money paid to him by Ann Fowler—a nasty plot to get her scapegoat brother executed in a jailbreak.

This chain of events—victim's mother to scapegoat's dad to scapegoat's sister to scapegoat to the widow of the scapegoat's dead holdup pal—is made possible by the smell of the missing money. Like Christie's cops interviewing a string of witnesses, Grafton's lone sleuth keeps going. At the end of this chain of events is the victim. Access to the victim comes through Dwight Shales, high school principal and secret lover, who rings the doorbell at Tap Granger's shabby house just as the sleuth is leaving. With the arrival of the secret lover, the plot thickens. In a ritual common to most mysteries, the sleuth digs up the past.

2. *Ritual for Control.*

Ritual, a process repeated over and over, sometimes with sacred significance, can hold your Act Two together as it thickens into complication. Ritual is something you might have zipped across in your first draft, so you have a chance to explore it when you rewrite. Grafton develops Act Two of *Fugitive* with different rituals: digging up the past (probing documents to find a reason for the victim's death); crossing thresholds (penetrating the health spa to find the victim's real father); and ascending the economic stairway (retracing the victim's steps up the hillside ladder to find the secret lover who got the victim pregnant in the back story).

When the sleuth saves Irina at the midpoint of *Gorky Park,* he enters a symbolic underworld. The sleuth's ritual, part of the hero's quest, is a descent into a world of death. Irina enters the metro trailed by the minions of the minor death god, Prosecutor Iamskoy. The metro is very deep, "bomb-shelter depth," a dungeon thronged by lifeless lovers locked in death hugs. The metro tunnel is a giant throat that swallows up dead souls: "Where the escalator's descent ended at the low white gullet of the ceiling, Irina stepped off and vanished. . . ." Irina disappears in the depths. The sleuth follows. In a room red as blood, the sleuth finds Irina's scarf, a clue to mark her path. He pushes through a door marked DANGER to find Irina down one more level. KGB poison has taken her down into herself. If she lingers down there too long, she'll die.

To rescue Irina, the sleuth must descend ever deeper. His struggle with the KGB agent is a struggle with an alien being not of this world: ". . . his eyes developed orange cores, brilliant moth eyes as if he were lit from within." The apparition of mythic monster is created by the headlight from a metro engine that almost runs over Irina. The sleuth lifts, twisting her free. The KGB dragons have gone. The KGB poison throbs in her veins, forcing the sleuth to seek help. Irina can't die here. She's the link between Osborne and the three dead bodies in *Gorky Park.* On to the Rebirth scene.

Other rituals central to your rewrite:

• *Treasure Hunt.* Searching the victim's room in *Body,* the police find makeup magic used by the victim to transform herself into Conway Jefferson's Cinderella. Makeup is used in the ritual of masking and disguise. The treasure in *The Maltese Falcon* is a jeweled bird. The treasure in *Gorky Park*—the Victim's Lair scene mentioned above—is fish blood.

• *Threshold Crossing.*   Guided by Dolly Bantry, Miss Marple crosses the threshold into the crime scene of *Body*, a place of death. Aided by Sir Henry Clithering, Miss Marple crosses a police threshold to interview Florence Small, a Girl Guide, a friend of the deceased, and the most important witness in the story.

In *The Maltese Falcon* Sam Spade knocks on the door of apartment 1001 at the Coronet. The door is a threshold. It's opened by Miss Wonderly, the femme fatale death crone killer who now calls herself Miss Leblanc. To have some fun, put masks on your threshold guardians. Her real name is Brigid O'Shaughnessy. Leblanc is French for white, the color of virgins. Brigid rhymes with "frigid." The lady is a cold killer.

• *Execution and Sacrifice.*   Like a white-haired god, Osborne sacrifices three young people to protect his sable empire. Like deadly avenging angels, Irina Asanova executes Andrei Iamskoy as partial payment for her blind eye; and then Arkady Renko executes Osborne in the snow.

Like a death crone, Myra Jane Severance sacrifices her husband to keep her access to the resource base—the Major's fortune, the Major's beach house, ease, safety, the good life.

Like a wronged lover, Carol Lundgren executes Joe Brody to avenge the killing of Geiger, Character G, in *The Big Sleep*.

In *Fugitive*, Ann Fowler sacrifices her mother, cutting out one more heir to the motel. When Dad dies, Ann will sell the motel, adding the money to her IBM hoard.

• *Burial of the Dead.*   Lash Canino earns his reward as a killer substitute when he buries Rusty Regan in an oil-well sump in a wasteland down below Sternwood Manor. Osborne uses the weather to bury his kills in the ice and snow. The killer in *Body* cremates the victim, who resurfaces from the ashes just in time to help strengthen the midpoint.

3. *Enrich Your Rewrite with Figures from Myth and Fairy Tale.*
Irina Asanova is a Siberian Cinderella. As we saw on Weekend
4, she enters the story wearing shabby clothes. In the back story,
Irina connects Osborne to Valerya—another Siberian Cinderella—
who works at the Irkutsk Fur Center. In her first conversation with
the sleuth, Irina is only half joking about selling herself to a director
for a pair of fur-lined boots. Cinderella, born to Siberian cold, hates
having cold feet. When she is reborn in Act Two, Irina emerges from
the sleuth's bed naked under a sheet. For Cinderella, the nakedness
symbolizes a fresh start, a temporary return to the innocence of a
naked Eden. But this is a mystery. In the mystery tale, innocence
dies.

Near the end of Act Two, the sleuth kills their love to get a
confession, tricking Irina with a dummy head in a hatbox: "Yes, yes,"
Irina says. "This is where Valerya lived. Put it back in the box." One
Siberian Cinderella is dead. One still lives. As long as Irina lives, she
wants the boots, the good life, the gold and warmth of Osborne's
America. In Act Three, she sells herself to Osborne again, trading
her body, bartering all she's got to barter. In the Barcelona Hotel in
New York City, she reenters the story wearing gold. An FBI agent
drapes her in fur: "Al took from the closet a full-length black fur
coat and helped Irina into it. It was a sable coat, Arkady realized."

If you didn't tap in to myth and fairy tale in your first draft, try it
now as you rewrite Act Two. Because the Cinderella myth is well
known, comb your plot for any Cinderella figure eager to climb up
from ashes and cinders into a better life. Jean Timberlake, the Cinderella figure in *Fugitive,* dies because she climbs the rickety hillside
stairway to get pregnant by Dwight Shales, the high school principal.
Grafton's Cinderella climbs to escape the ugly apartment. Retracing
the victim's steps, the sleuth finds the going tough, the climb "haz-
ardous." The reason for the climb is on top, the only "classy" neigh-
borhood in Floral Beach, the only game in town for Jean Timberlake.

Because of the strong economic motivation, Cinderella figures
enter your story already on the move up. They are hungry for a
better life; they'll do anything to escape their own particular economic wasteland. If the reader hasn't picked up on the victim as

Christie's Cinderella in *Body,* the author drives the point home with a roomful of detail in "Victim's Lair," a cheap room once occupied by a cheap dancer dying to be a lady. The victim's room, described as "the poorest the hotel possessed," is located at the "extreme end of a mean and dingy little corridor." The room is small, badly furnished, with a crummy view of the blank cliff face.

A mahogany desk is filled with "general rubbish." The victim's lipsticks, part of her escape tool-kit, make an "untidy heap" on the table. To get to the ball, Cinderella uses makeup and wardrobe. The creams and lotions, the nail varnish and eye makeup, are tools for creating a mask, a disguise that allows the victim to cross the threshold into Conway Jefferson's world: "Cinderella turned into a princess overnight!" cries the rich old man, who describes himself as a "fairy godfather instead of a fairy godmother." The mask of makeup and wardrobe works. The old man waves money at her. On her climb to the money, Cinderella dies.

Once you bring a Cinderella figure into your story, you can enrich one fairy tale with another. In *Body,* for example, Christie overlays the rags-to-riches Cinderella motif with three different myths: King Midas, Pygmalion, and the Fisher King.

As Conway Jefferson talks to the police about the money he lavished on the victim, he confesses to having the magic touch— "Everything I touched turned to gold"—which connects him to King Midas. As he tells how he groomed the victim for a better life, the crippled old man evokes Pygmalion, the ancient Greek sculptor who created (with the help of Aphrodite) warm life from cold polished stone: "With education and polishing, [the victim] could have taken her place anywhere." As he speaks of his crippled condition, Conway calls up echoes of the Fisher King from the Grail Quest, wounded but still hanging tough: "My mutilation had not vanquished me."

When you rewrite, heading for plot point two and the climax (Act Three), consider weaving myth and fairy tale into your story. Deepen your characters by linking them to legendary figures like Cinderella, King Midas, the Sick Old Man, and Pygmalion, the sculptor who tapped goddess magic to transform stone to warm flesh.

• • •

WORKING THE NOVEL

Exercises

1. *Frame Act Two.*
Take the time to frame Act Two. Profile both scenes (plot points one and two) before you rewrite. Make sure you know how they connect. Act Two of Christie's *Body,* for example, is framed by two witness interviews. As Act Two opens, the police interview the hotel manager. As Act Two ends, the sleuth interviews Florence Small. If you compare the interviews, jot notes about the differences. The hotel manager interview is sparse, leading nowhere. The Florence Small interview, its atmosphere saddened by the shattered dreams of a teenager hungry for stardom, leads the sleuth to the killers.

2. *Strengthen Your Midpoint.*
After establishing the scene at midpoint, use your scene cards to fasten down a chain of events leading up to that scene and then away from it. If your book is heavy with cover-up, you can build a chain of events leading the sleuth from one obstacle to another, like a series of doors locked with heavy padlocks.

Rewrite the scenes in this chain of events now.

3. *Plot Point Two.*
Rewrite the scene at plot point two. Remember that a scene profile makes rewriting easier. A scene profile gives you an overview; it also helps you select the details you want to develop in the rewrite. Plot point two is important because it serves two functions in the plot: it caps off Act Two with action or an insight; it launches the reader and the sleuth into Act Three.

4. *Develop Significant Rituals.*
When you rewrite, use ritual to deepen the action. If your sleuth climbs stairs, and if those same stairs were climbed by the

victim, turn the climbing into a ritual of ascent. Where was the victim going? Why did she climb up? What's up there? If your sleuth descends, track the descent. The poet Dante went down to check out the Inferno. The sleuth goes down to check out the dungeon of evil in the eyes of the beast: "For the first time he allowed the investigator to see him. A beast looked out through Osborne's eyes. . . ."

5. *Have Fun with Myth and Fairy Tale.*
If you have an old man in your story, what's the resource base? If you have a resource base, who wants a piece? If your old man is sick, you have a time limit. A time limit provides suspense, the ticking-clock device. If you have a sick old man with a ticking clock inside his head, how does he handle his last days? If the sickness is inside his head, maybe he's covering up with a new wardrobe, a new car, a new lady. If the lady is young and pretty and poor, you've got Cinderella. If you've got Cinderella, you can kill her off—the way Christie and Grafton kill their victims—or you can use her the way Martin Cruz Smith uses Irina Asanova, as a femme fatale Death Crone love interest.

· WEEKENDS 36–38 ·
REWRITING ACT THREE

In the first draft, when you were writing to discover Act Three, you went for speed. Your goal was making it to the end no matter what, a wild, breathless sprint for the finish line. In the second draft of Act Three you're going for torque, a slow and powerful gathering together of all the elements of your story to create a center of gravity.

In Act Three, your story moves with relentless resolve toward resolution. You cap off minor characters. You arrange your subplots for the climax. As the climax starts, you want the major characters either on your novel's stage or waiting in the wings because they have a stake in what happens. In Act Three, as you move toward resolution, you can keep the conflict going by letting your characters move at different speeds. Character B wants to rush forward toward resolution while Character A, working a different agenda, dawdles, stalling for time, studying the landscape, testing the wind.

At the climax of *Gorky Park,* for example, the sleuth's agenda differs from Irina's. He wants to survive, to stay alive for the next ten minutes, so he tells Osborne the KGB is here. Irina, blinded by America, scolds him for spoiling her chances: "Why do you say that, Arkasha? You'll ruin everything." What better place for a lover's quarrel than the killer confrontation? Irina's need for warm boots sets her apart from the killing. Like Morgan le Fay at Camelot, another queen of death, Irina will preside over the execution of the killer, sacrificing the king of fur. A femme fatale who has looked death in the face can create conflict with her own agenda.

The key to rewriting Act Three is knowing the climax, the face-off between sleuth and killer where the action peaks, where good clashes with evil, where the killer pays with blood. In your mystery novel, the final confrontation with the killer gives your reader an emotional release. Aristotle, the Greek philosopher who laid down rules for dramatic structure, calls this moment "catharsis," a purging of pent-up audience emotion. When your sleuth takes revenge, she is the instrument of society. If blood is spilled at your climax, it spills with moral certainty: this is the right blood and this spilling is right for this moment; because of the crimes committed, this killer deserves to die.

Because of this moral certainty, the reader is flooded with feelings of justification. Your job in Act Three is to lock in this emotional release, this feeling of satisfaction, for your reader.

Grafton's killer confrontation in *"F" Is for Fugitive,* for example, gives the reader release because of the body count. Ann Fowler, hiding behind the dutiful-daughter disguise, has killed four people— including her own mother—and has sold her brother off as the scapegoat. As the body count mounts, so does the need for vengeance. The scapegoat must be rescued; this killer must pay. When the sleuth arrives at the Fowler family motel for her confrontation with the killer, the four bodies are stacked up inside the reader's mind:

1. Victim One in *Fugitive* is Jean Timberlake. Jean died because she was pregnant with the child of Dwight Shales. Ann Fowler, a secret admirer with a weak chin, loved Dwight, wanted him for herself, killed for her secret desire. At the climax, Ann confesses: "I couldn't have her ruining Dwight's life."

2. Victim Two is Ori Fowler, the killer's mom. Mom died because Dad's about to die. With her brother in jail and both parents dead, the killer can sell the family motel and escape the suffocating small town of Floral Beach.

3. Victim Three is Shana Timberlake, Jean's mom. Shana died because the killer assumed she was having an affair with Dwight Shales. When the sleuth asks why she murdered Shana, the killer confesses, "For sleeping with Dwight."

4. Victim Four in *Fugitive* is Tap Granger, a small-time crook who helped Bailey Fowler steal the $42,000 invested by his sister in IBM stock. Tap Granger dies to shut his mouth about the $42,000. Ann Fowler pays Tap a measly $2,000 to break Bailey out of jail. The jailbreak is a trap. The shotgun supplied by the killer is loaded with rock salt. Tap Granger dies because he's dumb.

The trail of bodies leads the sleuth to the killer. Stacking the bodies up provides justification for taking revenge. The key to revenge is blood sacrifice. If you don't want your killer to die onstage, the way Osborne dies in *Gorky Park,* then you use Grafton's *Fugitive* as a model. Let's explore what happens when Kinsey Millhone confronts Ann Fowler.

Sleuth versus Killer

The setting for the killer confrontation scene in *Fugitive* is the Killer's Lair, Ann Fowler's tawdry suite (bedroom, kitchenette, living room) in the Fowler family motel in Floral Beach. Poking around with her penlight, the sleuth finds a murder weapon—a shell reloader and the rock salt for Tap Granger's jailbreak shotgun—and the motive for murder: IBM dividends dating back to the murder of Jean Timberlake.

Finding the missing $42,000 pulls the sleuth into the killer's mind and across the threshold into danger. The killer waits for the sleuth in bed. In her lap is a shotgun. Her eyes are insane, her face pale as death. Because the sleuth is now a fugitive herself (the cops are after Kinsey), the killer can claim trespass, executing the sleuth as an intruder. Confession gives the reader a glimpse of the beast within—"The slightly receding chin made her look like a rat"—and help arrives just as the killer's confession ends.

The helper is the killer's dad, Royce Fowler, the sick old man who climbs the stairs carrying photos of the dead mother. Back at the midpoint, the writer whisked the old man off to the hospital to clear the stage for Mom's murder. Now he comes back, temporarily reborn and frail with disease, wanting to recall the past before he dies.

Because the old man's "face held such innocence," the sleuth has to talk fast: she must win him over the way Renko wins Osborne. The struggle in this scene is the struggle for the old man. The killer is about to lose her father to disease; the sleuth lost her own father when she was five. Because of the careful groundwork laid earlier, the final confrontation in the killer's bedroom is not only sleuth versus killer and good versus evil. It is also the struggle of the good daughter against the bad daughter for the Lost Father, the father who goes away, the father who lets us down. As the sleuth says, "None of us had survived the wounds our fathers inflicted all those years ago." The phrase *none of us* gathers together the characters who form the core for this mystery: the killer (Ann Fowler), the victims (Jean Timberlake and her dead baby), and the sleuth (Kinsey Millhone). As the Lost Fathers gather like ghosts in the room, sympathy floods the stage. The killer is herself a victim. Blood symbolizes life. Loss of blood symbolizes death. Once blood is spilled, some writers feel no need to execute the killer.

The climax of *Fugitive*, a good one for you to follow in your work, peaks with action as the father reaches for his daughter. He wants to touch her, a sick old man groping for youth and life and family ties. The daughter backs away. The father grabs the barrel of the shotgun. The daughter jerks the weapon away. Father and daughter struggle for control of the murder weapon. The shotgun goes off, blowing most of the killer's foot away. Blood pumps out. The sleuth swings into action: "I was pulling a pillowcase off the bed, wadding it against her mangled foot, trying to stanch the blood spewing everywhere." Witnesses pour into the room. Weeping, the killer curses her father for being lost: "You were never there for me. . . ."

Stepping back, away from the words, you can see the big picture. In Grafton's *Fugitive,* the father hires the sleuth to rescue his son from being a scapegoat. Down deep, the father knows something is wrong. He knows his son is innocent. An innocent himself, he does not suspect his daughter of murder. Following the trail of the scapegoat, the sleuth uncovers two more trails. One is the money trail, the $42,000 last seen with the victim seventeen years ago. One is the trail of Lost Fathers. At the climax of the book, where sleuth faces killer, the two trails converge: the money turns up, transformed into IBM shares; the Lost Father turns up bearing photos of the killer's murdered mom. The photos speed up the timetable: the killer killed her own mother; the bell tolls here, time for this killer to pay.

Stepping away from the words helps us see the larger shape of the plot: *Fugitive* is a story of scapegoat replacement. To save his son, a sick old man gives up his daughter. The instrument used for the sibling transfer is the sleuth.

Guidelines for Rewriting Act Three

1. *Trails that Converge.*

In the plotting section on Weekends 5–9, you developed scene cards. You used those scene cards to track subplots based on character or symbol, making them into threads or trails or tracks followed by the sleuth. Grafton's sleuth follows the missing $42,000 the same way Sam Spade tracks the alleged jeweled bird, the same way Arkady Renko tracks the sables from the garage in Moscow to the Finnish border. In *Fugitive,* the sleuth finds the money in the killer's closet. In *Gorky Park,* the sleuth finds the sables in cages in New Jersey.

You use the climax in your mystery to bring these subplots together, creating friction, heat, and fire. At the moment of intense heat, the reader finds release. *Fugitive* opens and closes with Royce Fowler, a lost father seeking his lost children. Following the trail of Lost Fathers leads the sleuth to a doctor on the hill—he's the father of Jean Timberlake—and to the principal on his hill: the father of Jean Timberlake's dead baby. When the sleuth needs help at the climax of *Fugitive,* the writer brings Royce Fowler back as a change agent. Royce's return works because he's climbed the stairs for a reason—to share photo memories with his daughter. The shotgun blows Royce's innocence away. The sleuth must use the father as a weapon against his own daughter. When the shotgun blows off the killer's foot, the reader finds release. Because she controls her subplots, the writer controls the action at the climax.

Your control over subplots enables you to bring them together when you rewrite Act Three. Grafton needs the lost father, so she brings back Royce Fowler. She does not need another dead mother at the climax, so she kills off Shana Timberlake, leaving her in the hot tub at the health spa. That final image of Shana in the water caps off her subplot and puts the cops on the sleuth's trail.

Back from the Dead

The ritual that drives Act Three of *Gorky Park* is rebirth. Arkady Renko comes back from the dead (his deep knife wound, the KGB truth serum, the constant threat of execution by Pribluda, the inferno of the peat fire) because Irina calls him back to do his job. She calls him out of Russia, calls him across the seas to America, calls him to her bed in the Barcelona Hotel. The sleuth is alive because Irina has power over the killer. The Siberian Cinderella with one eye has bewitched the king of fur. To possess her, Osborne will pay with the stolen sables: "That's the trade; the sables in exchange for Irina and you. Irina because I want her, and you because she won't come without you."

This barter deal, this swap of animal fur for human skin, has power because it opens the sleuth's eyes to his own whoredom, to selling out. Irina loves him; she gives her body to Osborne. Because of the writer's careful separation of subplots—in four hundred pages, the reader does not see Irina with Osborne or Osborne with Kirwill or Kirwill with Irina—bringing them together at last creates a powerful climax.

This careful separation of major characters takes planning. If you were writing *Gorky Park,* you would have one set of scene cards for Irina, one for Osborne, one for Kirwill, and one for Iamskoy. The scene cards would track the characters from their entrance into the story all the way to their exit scene.

Characters Exit the Book

• Andrei Iamskoy, a minor death god, enters the story in Chapter 1, in a "Brush with Authority" scene. He exits at plot point two.

• William Kirwill enters the story in Chapter 4. He replaces the sleuth's helper at midpoint. He makes his exit just before the killer confrontation scene at the climax in Act Three.

• John Osborne enters the story at plot point one, at the bathhouse, wearing a towel. He exits at the killer confrontation in Act Three. The killer's death, a sacrificial act, marks the point where the action peaks.

• Irina Asanova, who enters the story in Chapter 2, presides over Osborne's execution at the climax. The killer is dead. The sleuth is wounded. Upright, on her feet, her mind on those good boots, the death crone exits, leaving the sleuth alone in the snow.

Scene cards take you to the killer confrontation. Scene cards keep your subplots separated until you're ready to bring them together. As the trails of your subplots converge, you're ready to rewrite the climax.

2. *Rewrite Your Climax.*

Your first step in rewriting the climax is to make a list of objects. The second step is to hand over the objects to your characters.

The objects in the *Gorky Park* killer confrontation are snow,

Kirwill's entrails, the dead dogs, Osborne's knife and rifle, a gun for the sleuth, car keys, blood, sables, fur, claws, cages, and Irina's boots.

You hand over the objects to your characters. Osborne has the rifle. The sleuth needs the rifle to survive. He can't take the rifle from Osborne, so he opens a door to his interior, a porthole to the soul, and then he invites Osborne inside: "Arkady let Osborne enter through his eyes. Test my words, Arkady thought; sniff them, chew them."

Because he sees with the sleuth's eyes, the killer executes three agents of the FBI and two agents of the KGB. Blood spills onto the snow. To save himself, the sleuth distracts the killer, throwing open a sable cage. A sable, freed from the cage, leaps free. The sable is more than a sleek animal. It represents money, wealth, empire, a motive for murder. Seeing his precious sables go free enrages the killer. In a moment of inspired writing, the sleuth tosses a sable at the killer. The irony here is a thing of beauty as the Russian investigator, a lowly detective at the bottom of the food chain, lobs an expensive sable at the king of fur.

The killer dodges, the rifle bullet misses its mark. An object in the hands of a character has led to action. To straighten out the action, to make it work really hard, create another list. As we pointed out on Weekend 12, reaction completes the action loop for the reader. List the action; follow it with the reaction, something like this:

Action: Renko arouses the sables.

Reaction: One sable bites Renko.

Action: Irina shouts for help.

Reaction: Renko frees a sable.

Action: Renko throws a sable at Osborne.

Reaction: Osborne fires, misses.

Action: Renko shoots Osborne.

Reaction: Osborne dies.

• • •

Because it tracks the action for you, a list of objects makes the rewriting easier. As you parcel out objects, giving one to each character, you are also planning your rewrite. At the climax of *Fugitive,* one object is the sleuth's penlight. The killer holds a shotgun. The old man, who turns out to be a sleuth's helper, holds photos of Mom.

What happens to the objects in this scene? Using the penlight, the sleuth finds the IBM stuff, the rock salt, the reloader, and the tape the killer used to wage psychological warfare in the motel at night. The beam of the penlight gives the sleuth her first glimpse of the killer in bed with the shotgun that will soon blow her foot away. Finding the killer with the beam of her penlight opens the door to dialogue. The killer's opening line—"Find everything you need?"—shows her with everything under tight control. After two pages of dialogue—a mixture of blame and insane confession—the writer uses the object to change pace, to shift the dynamics of the scene. Kinsey's dialogue line seems innocent enough: "Mind if I turn off the penlight?"

It's dark in here and the sleuth wants more light. Her arms are raised. She's getting tired. She wants to see the killer's face revealed. So she asks permission to turn off the penlight. The killer says okay, then turns on the bedside lamp. The sudden light from the lamp reveals the bestial rat face of the killer. As the killer's finger tightens on the trigger, there's a knock on the door. It's the old man with his object, his plot device—the photos of the dead mom.

• • •

Rewriting the action brings the climactic scene into focus, Weapons take center stage. Faces go pale, signaling the nearness of death, warm blood about to be spilled. With your objects in use to create action, you can rewrite the dialogue. When your characters talk at the climax, they confess, they place blame, they transfer guilt, they say good-bye. Some examples:

- *"F" Is for Fugitive.*   Her foot blown away, her blood spewing the room, killer Ann Fowler takes a moment to blame her lost father: "You were never there for me. . . ."
- *Gorky Park.*   Trying to justify his gutting of William Kirwill, Osborne blames the dead man: "He killed my dogs. That's why I gutted him, because he killed my dogs."
- *The Maltese Falcon.*   When killer Brigid O'Shaughnessy clutches at the sleuth's heart with her claws of twisted love (if he loved her, he wouldn't need the jeweled bird), Sam Spade hits back: "I won't play the sap for you."
- *The Big Sleep.*   Blaming the sleuth for digging up the body of her victim, Carmen Sternwood aims her little gun at him. This is the way a femme fatale like Carmen says good-bye: "Stand there, you son of a bitch."

3. *Rewrite Sleuth's Reward.*

In the first draft you created closure by repeating an image from the opening scene when you wrote the end. In *Body,* the image was the dead body on the hearthrug. The key object was a wardrobe item buried in the description of the corpse. In *Gorky Park,* the image is snow. Watching the snow in New Jersey, the sleuth thinks of home: "It was a Russian snow, thick as cotton. . . ."

Repetition of key images gives the writing closure. Once you have closure, that sense of containment that gives you control over the book, you rewrite the scene for sleuth's reward. Some sleuths get money for their efforts. Most are rewarded with restoring the balance, setting things right with a blood sacrifice. For a sleuth who likes to talk, to explain things, the sleuth's reward scene is the perfect stage for an extended monologue. The monologue not only reveals motive and method, it also shows the sleuth in control. When you rewrite the monologue for your sleuth, you expand the material from Weekend 5, when you developed the back story that brought killer and victim together at the killing place. For this reward scene, you need the proper audience.

For Miss Marple's audience, Christie assembles four old men—Colonel Melchett, Superintendent Harper, Sir Henry Clithering, and Conway Jefferson—who represent the power structure of the

English countryside. A fifth old man, Colonel Arthur Bantry, is excluded. Tainted by the murder, Colonel Bantry has lost stature in the tightly knit community. In Christie World, such a taint keeps the master of Gossington outside the information loop. To find out what the sleuth says tonight, the Colonel will have to ask his wife.

To start things off, Sir Henry takes the role of straight man to the sleuth: "Speaking as Watson, I want to know your methods, Miss Marple." The sleuth smooths her silk evening gown. She's dressed for the occasion. With a ladylike modesty prologue, she launches in: "The facts, as I noted them . . ."

The real reward for the sleuth is setting things right. The monologue is a ritual act, a structure of words used by the sleuth to evoke the moral certainty that throws a halo glow over society's need for revenge.

Sleuths who claim the moral high ground can afford to get tough. In the wrap-up scene for *Body*, Miss Marple can relish the execution of the killer ("I feel quite pleased") because she is good and because the killer is evil.

Arkady Renko, wounded, on his knees in the snow, still has the moral resolve to send Irina off to America: "You *are* home. You're American now, Irina. . . . You're not Russian anymore." Rejected by the sleuth, the Death Crone heads for the car.

In *The Maltese Falcon*, Sam Spade buries Brigid the Death Crone under the weight of a moral monologue. When the police arrive to take Brigid away, Spade sums up the case with an inventory of objects: "She killed Miles. And I've got some exhibits—the boy's guns, one of Cairo's, a black statuette that all the hell was about, and a thousand-dollar bill that I was supposed to be bribed with."

To keep your sleuth on the moral high ground, give the money back.

· · ·

WORKING THE NOVEL

Exercises

1. *Trails that Converge.*
Do some exploratory writing on subplots and how they converge at your climax. It's helpful here to name each subplot, each trail followed by your sleuth. If you have one trail based on an object or symbol (gold, money, jewelry, wardrobe, weapons, et cetera) and another based on a character (Kirwill, Irina, Conway Jefferson, et cetera) or a set of characters (the Lost Fathers in *Fugitive*), you'll be able to keep them separate until you need them for your climax.

2. *Rewrite the Climax.*
Begin with a list of objects. Jot down parts of the setting (closet, rock salt, penlight, IBM shares) and don't forget to include lighting (it's dim and shadowy in this closet). Because it's dark in here, the sleuth needs a penlight. Because the sleuth has a penlight, the writer uses sudden light to reveal the real face of the killer.

Start your rewrite using the objects. Move from object to dialogue ("I want that shotgun now") and action (makes a grab for the shotgun).

3. *Rewrite Sleuth's Reward.*
The key to the sleuth's reward scene is the re-creation of the crime that you constructed on Weekend 5. If you lay the crime out in steps—ten is not too many—you can use the steps as a core for your sleuth's monologue. For writing tips, you might study the monologues in *The Big Sleep* and *The Maltese Falcon*, as well as Miss Marple's monologue in *Body*.

4. *List of Scenes.*
Make a list of scenes stretching from plot point two to the last scene in your book. Jot notes for each scene. Note how each

scene works to push Act Three to the climax, and then from the climax to the end.

5. *Rewrite the Scenes.*
Before you rewrite, take the time to profile each scene. Rewrite each scene in sections: rewrite the dialogue first; then rewrite the action. If you had good luck starting with a list of objects, repeat that process when you rewrite each scene.

Weekends 39–52
Final Draft

The final draft pulls your manuscript into shape. As an important part of the process of writing a mystery, final draft is a series of last judgments. You make judgments on character and style, on rhythm and pace and dialogue, on object and plot and subplot. In the final draft, you polish up your prose. You read and you make judgments and you cut and you rewrite, converting a passage that tells into a passage that shows. In the following example, the writing moves from "telling" to "showing" as the writer moves through the first and second drafts to final draft.

First Draft: "I looked at the corpse. It was a young woman, a girl perhaps. She was too far away to tell exactly. How terribly sad it was to see death come to one so young."

Second Draft: "I looked at the corpse, a young woman, or perhaps a girl. She wore a red dress. Her teeth stuck out. Her arms were bent at the elbow. She wore a raincoat, sadly tattered. There were marks on her throat."

Final Draft: "The corpse lay in the snow, hands across her chest, like Sleeping Beauty waiting for the Handsome Prince. Pale face, all the blood drained out. Pale eyes and white eyebrows, pale hair, very pale lips. The lips were puckered, as if waiting for a kiss. I knelt down beside the body. Bite marks on her throat, dents in the skin, and droplets of dried blood. Her dead eyes stared up at me. I felt a shiver. Her teeth were lined up like little white gravestones. Like the others, she had no name. She was victim number six."

The detail becomes more specific with each draft. As the detail piles up, the thoughts and images inside the writer's head become word pictures on the page. As the word pictures take shape, the writing voice rings with confidence. Instead of telling the reader how the sleuth feels with adverbs (terribly sad, sadly tattered), the writer contains emotion (the sadness of innocence wasted by early death) in the detail: "Her dead eyes stared up at me. I felt a shiver. Her teeth were lined up like little white gravestones."

When you rewrite for your final draft, the work is more fun because your story is plotted. You know where it twists and turns, where it peaks at the climax. The writing you do for final draft knits up the few loose threads that remain. Because of the hard work on character and dialogue, most of the writing is solid. Act Two might need tightening. A few scenes might need repairs. Some key passages might need rewriting.

You locate those passages by reading the manuscript. Reading is step one of the work on final draft. Step two is cutting, pruning, weeding. Step three is rewriting.

Guidelines for the Final Draft

1. *Read the Manuscript.*

Read straight through the book, taking notes as you go. There's a checklist at the end of this reading section. If you've been hungry for feedback, now is the time to ask for it. An efficient way to get feedback at this point is to use your writing friends as readers. They read; you listen and take notes. If you decide to use your friends, you'll get more insights into the writing by planning ahead.

For example, read through the book quickly, making notes, to select half a dozen scenes that need work. Before you rewrite the scenes, cast your friends into character roles. Select a time for the reading. As you listen, envision your writing as theater. Does each scene have a climax? Is the conflict clear? Do the readers stumble over specific passages? Is there too much narrative summary? Does one character hog the dialogue?

Handing over your manuscript is a symbolic act, the writer connecting with the world. Listening to your words coming out of strange mouths provides instant perspective, a fresh look at your work.

Take lots of notes. You're weighing the larger elements of your story, seeking insights into shape and weight and proportion. Is there too much killing? Can you shift some killing offstage, the way Martin Cruz Smith shifts Osborne's gutting of Kirwill near the end of *Gorky Park*? Is there too much blood? Not enough blood? Are there enough bodies? Is the stack of bodies high enough to condemn your killer for punishment? When is the killer revealed to the sleuth? To the reader? Are there too many witness interviews mashed too close together?

The Edit Book

A lot of writers make notes on the pages of the manuscript. When the writing overflows the manuscript, move your note taking to an edit book. An edit book is a separate notebook dedicated to the final draft. If you're reading straight through, you have separate sections for Acts One, Two and Three. You might devote a page in the edit book to the crime scene, to the first encounter, to each re-creation of the crime (a page for each), the most important witness interviews, the longest suspect interrogation, the killer confrontation, and the sleuth's reward. If one of your characters has a long monologue, one that runs over a hundred words, jot down its position in the structure ("Catalyst Monologue, Act Two, between midpoint and plot point two. Check it out for length") and keep reading.

Your notes might be questions you ask yourself: "Where can I move this scene? Where would it work better? Plot point two? Midpoint? To open Act Three?"

Your notes can be reminders to yourself: "Rework the dialogue in the first encounter. They barely know each other. Yet they're bickering like an old married couple. Remember to make a list of objects. Remember to use the objects in the dialogue lines. 'Hand me that towel, Charlotte.' Set the reader up for the next encounter."

When you read with a pencil in hand you get insights into plot and character, scene and style. If you're reading a dialogue and lines come to you, jot them down in your edit book. Five minutes of dialogue now might make the book a prize winner. You can write faster if you don't use quotes. Or attributions like *he said/she said*:

> Hello, Marshal.
>
> Hello, Major.
>
> Hot enough for you?
>
> Yes. I've come to ask you something.
>
> Sounds official, Marshal, when you use that tone.
>
> It's about Lacey Anne.
>
> Come on in. I'll get Ripley to mix you a toddy.
>
> Nothing for me. Thanks.
>
> So. What is it, Marshal?
>
> Did Lacey Anne want to leave the island?
>
> What kid doesn't? Hellfire, I felt trapped here myself when I was her age.
>
> Did she want to leave the island so she could sing with that boy's band?
>
> Every kid has big dreams, Marshal.
>
> Just answer the question, okay?
>
> You want to know was this Julius B. fellow coming to take a meeting. Is that it?
>
> Was he?
>
> Okay. Okay. She called me from town. From that dump on Eddie's side of the marina. . . .

• • •

2. *Read with this Checklist in Hand.*

• *Character Check:*

Are your characters motivated? Does the reader know what each character wants? Are the character agendas clear? When the character enters the story, is there enough physical detail to make a sharp first impression? Which characters are concealed behind masks? Where are they unmasked? Which characters reveal everything with their first entrance, their first speech? Who changes in the story? Where in the structure do the character changes take place? Who stays the same? How have you marked the killer for the reader?

- *Dialogue/Monologue Check:*
For each scene, check to see which character has the power in the dialogue. Who's on the offensive? Who's playing defense? Does the dialogue move in a rhythm of one-two, one-two? Have you connected some dialogue lines to objects in the setting? Which character evokes the past? What is the reason for evoking the past? Where does the dialogue rise to a climax? How long are the monologues? How many monologues are there? Can you compress the monologue?

- *Setting Check:*
How does the reader know the time and place for each scene? The season? The temperature? Where is the light source? Where are the shadows? What image in the beginning of the book comes back to create closure at the end? What objects in one scene connect to objects in another scene?

- *Action Check:*
Does each action have a reaction that closes the loop for the reader? Do the actions and reactions work in a chain, grabbing the reader's attention, building to a climax? Is your action written with strong verbs?

- *Scene Check:*
Does the scene build to a climax? How does the scene hook to the next scene? What character agendas clash to create dramatic conflict? If the scene lacks dramatic conflict, what is your plan? Will you rewrite? Or will you cut?

- *Subplots:*
Have you identified each subplot? Are you tracking the subplots with scene cards and lists? Do you know where each subplot begins and ends? Have you named your subplots (e.g., the

Kirwill subplot, the Police subplot) to help you keep them separate until you decide to bring them together? Which of your subplots converge for your killer confrontation?

3. *Cutting the Manuscript.*

Cutting is hard to do. You've written these words. You've sweated blood to build this book. For almost a year, on every weekend and often during the week, you have toiled in the vineyard of words. You love this rich detail. You don't want to cut.

Cutting clears away what doesn't count, what's not necessary for advancing the plot. Cutting sharpens the dialogue, the description, the action. Cutting is possible in the final draft because you see with new eyes. Material that was important in the first two drafts is no longer necessary. It was important for the creative process. It moved the characters from point A to point B, or from point Q to point R. But now that the book is almost done, you don't need it.

Page count helps you decide to cut. The industry standard for mysteries by first-time writers is 250–300 pages. If the manuscript is too long—if it would make a book of 400-plus pages—then cutting becomes even more important.

When you wrote the first two drafts, you wrote several passages of narrative summary. When you read through the manuscript for final draft, you list the passages in your edit book—Narration 1, Narration 2, Narration 3, et cetera—including notes about subject, purpose, placement in the structure, and length. When you go back through the edit book, Narration 7, for example, might catch your eye. Let's say the subject of Narration 7 is back story on the sleuth. The stated purpose is "to provide information to the reader necessary for understanding the sleuth's emotional commitment to the killer quest." The placement of Narration 7 is central: it ends Act One and it also begins Act Two. The length is thirteen pages.

In mystery fiction, thirteen pages—even for a sizzling scene—is too long. Thinking back, you recall writing this piece late at night, well after midnight, in a blinding hour-long marathon. You recall the insights popping, the wonderful heat of creativity. This was a moment, rare in the writing game, where everything came together. At the time, you felt blessed. Now as you look over your edit book and your updated scene list, you realize that you have converted this lengthy narrative summary into six scenes.

Because you have used the material generated by midnight art, you cut this passage.

Sometimes feedback from friends tells you where to cut. At other times, you cut because the passage doesn't feel right. Some of the most interesting final draft work can result when you cut adverbs.

4. *Cut Those Adverbs.*

An adverb is an adjective with *-ly* tacked on, a suffix attached like a tail. Adjectives modify nouns—the listless corpse—but when you add *-ly* on the end, transforming the adjective into an adverb, the function changes because adverbs modify verbs. In the phrase, "The corpse lolled listlessly on the coverlet," the adverb *"listlessly"* describes the verb, which is *lolled.* Because they are polysyllabic, adverbs possess interesting rhythm. "Listlessly," for example, has three syllables (list/less/ly) that explode with alliteration as the *l*-sound repeats itself. In this example, the repeated *l*-sounds in "LoLLed ListLessLy" weld the adverb to the verb.

Adverbs are handy when we speak. Adverbs help us to stall, to gain time while we craft a reply: "What I meant to imply, actually, was that the corpse was not lolling listlessly, in so many words, but that the mood of the crime scene itself was basically quite listless."

When characters speak, they might use adverbs that mark their particular generation, their niche in this world. Adverbs, used properly, help the writer to develop character. Character G, a walk-on, might appear in a witness interview: "Right, so like, basically, I mean, it was like she majorly blew away the universe totally." Character A, a hard-boiled cop, might reply by saying, "Show me where, bud."

While adverbs might do good work in dialogue, they kill the rest of your writing dead because they hide word pictures. Let's return to the listless corpse. Let's say you're rewriting the crime scene. In the first draft you wrote "listless corpse." In the second draft you changed the sentence, expanding it something like this: "The corpse lolled listlessly." And then, caught up in the sound of those alliterated *l*'s, you rewrote it again: "The luminous corpse lolled listlessly with eyelids of lustrous aluminum alkaloid." While you're having fun with alliteration, the story gets away from you. What's fun for the writer is not always fun for the reader. You might know what you meant, what you intended to convey with the adverb. The reader won't have a clue.

If you chop out the adverb, you'll make a hole. From "the corpse lolled listlessly," you chop out *listlessly,* making a hole. Following the procedure you learned from Character Work (Weekends 1–4) and from Scene Building (Weekends 10–13), you fill the hole with physical detail to create a word picture.

Position: "The listless corpse lay facedown on the coverlet. Her right arm reached out. The fingers of the right hand were frozen in an endless clutching motion."

Wardrobe: "She wore a red dress. The hem of the dress had been ripped."

Lighting: "Her face was in shadow."

Wounds: "The rip in the dress opened into a wide gash that ran along the side of her body, rib cage to thigh. The backs of her legs looked scratched."

Close-up: "Up close, the scratches became claw marks."

When you cut away adverbs, you make room for better writing. Adverbs take up space without doing much work on the page. Cutting out adverbs will help you write a cleaner, sharper final draft that gives your reader images.

5. *Plan Your Rewrite.*

Sometimes you write from the gut. You let go. You follow your instinct. You write with heat and clarity and maximum force. At other times you need a plan. You read. You take notes. You plan out your work by the weekend, the day, the hour. "Saturday A.M. 8–9. Rewrite the first encounter scene. Start with a scene profile. 10 minutes on the profile, 50 minutes on the scene. Hit the dialogue first. Then the action."

The heart of rewriting the final draft is the scene profile. A scene profile takes ten to fifteen minutes. If your book has forty scenes, and if they all need some repairs, your scene profiles will take a total time of ten hours. That is time well spent. A fresh scene profile not only reminds you what the scene is about and where it fits in the story; it also contains the detail that could trigger your mind for a brilliant final draft. Doing a new scene profile takes some discipline. The payoff is tremendous.

To plan out your work for the final draft, revise your list of scenes. Divide the scenes into four groups: Act One; Act Two, first half; Act Two, second half; and Act Three. Grouping the scenes helps you focus on your midpoint. When you're rewriting, it never hurts to take a second look.

In your rewriting plan, consider starting at midpoint and working your way through to the end, to killer confrontation and sleuth's reward. You can start at midpoint now because you know the story. You know how it starts. You know why the killer killed and why the victim had to die. The hard part of the book, as you probably discovered when you wrote drafts one and two, is the stretch between midpoint and plot point two. The book thickens here. Lots of characters crowd the stage. Each character has an agenda that's white hot. If the subplots get tangled, they get tangled here.

Starting your rewrite at midpoint helps you clear out the tangles. In your plan, you lay out the work for the second half of Act Two. Then you follow that with a plan for Act Three. Starting your final draft in the middle gives you flexibility and confidence.

If you're hesitating about rewriting from midpoint, consider this: They shoot movies out of order. They shoot exteriors outside, on location. They shoot interiors inside, on a soundstage. They can shoot out of order because they know the story. Your goal is to produce a stunning manuscript. In mystery writing, the end (where the killer pays) dictates the beginning—the victim is dead, the killer is offstage chuckling, and the sleuth is busy taking inventory.

Before you say no to the rewrite that starts at midpoint, give it a try. Profile a couple of scenes from the center of Act Two. Profile the scene at midpoint and the scene that comes right after midpoint. Writing the final draft from midpoint gets you to the finish line faster. If it doesn't feel right for you, if it doesn't work, feel free to start your final draft in Act One, Scene One, Chapter One.

Have fun with the rewriting. You worked hard getting here.

6. *Keep the Rewrite Simple.*

As we have suggested, good solid physical detail solves most problems in writing. When you describe your corpse, use body parts (*pale blue eyes, albino hair,* et cetera), wardrobe (*gray stockings, gray half slip, gray panties, tawdry dress,* et cetera), and wounds (*bites along the throat, a chunk of flesh torn away exposing the jawbone,* et cetera). When you bring a character into the story, combine body parts (*her arms tucked tight like bird wings*), with wardrobe (*a satin gown with red spaghetti straps*) and motion (*walked toward me with jerky movements*).

If grammar is not your greatest strength, you'd be smart to keep your sentences strong and simple. Avoid those tricky passive-voice verbs (the rifle *was fired,* the door *had been thrown open,* et cetera), and use the power of English by writing in the clean line of subject-verb-object: "The man fired his rifle."

The *subject* is the *man.*

The *verb* is *fired.*

The *object* is *rifle.* This tight unit of *subject* plus *verb* plus *object* creates a consistent center for each sentence.

That same pattern, subject-verb-object, keeps you out of trouble whether you're writing about the weather ("Rain flattened the grass") or writing about politics ("Veep Lays Egg on TV") or writing about a marriage foundering on the rocks ("Wife Stabs Errant Husband with Granny's Heirloom Brooch").

To embellish your writing, you can hang clauses on either end of the subject-verb-object structure. Here's a clause hung on the front: "Without taking any apparent aim, Osborne fired his rifle." Once you have the image (in this case an action image) locked in with subject-verb-object, you add a reaction to complete the information loop. When Osborne fires, the bullet hits an FBI agent: "Wesley's head snapped, half its smooth forehead missing. . . ."

The key to a complete word-picture is *action* followed by *reaction,* a rhythm of one-two:

Action is one: Character A fires his rifle.

Reaction is two: Character W's head snaps.

The word *forehead,* a body part, locks down the description. The word *half* shows the hitting power of the bullet at close range.

When you run across a passage that doesn't sound right, check for adverbs first, verbs second. Cut the adverbs and fill the space, the hole in the passage left by the departed adverb. As you fill the hole, replace your weak verbs *(think, know, believe, understand, imagine, opine,* et cetera) with strong verbs *(cut, slice, hammer, sew, knit, fire, snap, forge, prance,* et cetera). Whether your sleuth is shooting or sewing, strong verbs show action:

thread the needle

bite the thread

slide the needle into the cloth

angle the needle into the tiny buttonhole

Strong verbs surface when your characters dance *(pirouette, stomp, prance, twirl, romp, shuffle, trot,* et cetera) or cut meat *(skin, slice, chop, mince,* et cetera) or play a sport *(tackle, shoot, lob, stroke, dash,* et cetera). One strong verb and some writing discipline can transform a flabby sentence into a passage that glows with hope and promise.

Flabby sentence: Deep inside her mind, in her private sanctuary of self, she had vaguely understood the idea of . . .

Cut the adverb, *vaguely.* Make a hole. Replace the verb *had understood* with *stroked.*

New sentence: Deep inside her mind, in her private sanctuary of self, she stroked the idea like a . . .

7. *Go for Power in Your Prose.*

When you rewrite to create the final draft, you combine the power of intuition—knowing from a hunch, a feeling, a spark along the spinal cord—with the disciplinary power of rules. In writing, there are rules for word order, for spelling, for pronoun reference, for verb tense. Sometimes when you're writing hot, you can use rhythm to break a rule. Let's say your sleuth is thinking, analyzing the case, and your page heats up, and your internal editor orders you to stop at the end of a sentence like a good girl/good boy only you keep going keeping on keeping on because you feel a different rhythm here and for the first time in a long time you feel the magical power of words: "And the face of the killer the white teeth like fangs slashing into meat into white bone and the cries of the victims the awful screams the rivers of blood and I run in my dream down a gray tunnel down a long metal tube lit with lights in little round cages welded to the ceiling and the tunnel leads to a yellow door and the door says Myra Jane in red letters dripping with blood and I throw open the door and . . ."

· · ·

WORKING THE NOVEL

Exercises

1. *Reading.*

To schedule feedback readings with your writing friends, scan the manuscript. Divide the manuscript, separating out the scenes and passages you want your friends to read. Schedule those readings now.

If you don't want feedback from friends, set up a solitary reading schedule for the four sections of your story. Take a full weekend. On Saturday morning, for example, you read Act One. On Saturday afternoon, you read Act Two, first half. On Sunday morning, you read Act Two, second half. On Sunday afternoon, you read Act Three.

Take notes as you read. Mark scenes that need repair. Mark passages that you can cut.

2. *Cutting.*

a. Revise your list of scenes. Do a scene count. If you have fifty to sixty scenes, consider cutting scenes. One reason to cut a scene: it fails to advance the action of the plot.

b. Cut narrative summary. If you have converted the narrative summary into scenes, it should go quietly. If you still need the narrative summary, try to compress it.

c. Cut adverbs. Most adverbs end in *-ly: terrifically, ponderously, enigmatically, logistically, administratively.* Most are polysyllabic. A few are alliterative: *listlessly, flawlessly,* et cetera.

3. *Rewriting.*

When you rewrite a scene, start with a scene profile. Give yourself ten to fifteen minutes. When you rewrite the scene, start with dialogue. To sharpen your dialogue, connect the lines to objects in the setting—"Hand over the shotgun, dear"—and keep your lines short to get that one-two rhythm that sparks dramatic conflict:

- "Hand over the shotgun, dear."
- "When you cough up, dearest."
- "What do you mean, cough up?"
- "The IBM stock, dearest. Have you forgotten?"

When you rewrite a prose passage, remember to remove the adverbs. Then fill the hole left by the departed adverbs with physical detail: body parts, wardrobe items, objects in the setting, wounds, et cetera. Replace weak verbs like *realize, think, feel, understand,* et cetera with strong verbs that show action: *slice, jerk, haul, prance, wedge, fire, snap,* et cetera.

Keep the language simple by using subject-verb-object, a linear trajectory of 1-2-3: "X stroked the idea." X is the *subject. Stroked* is the *verb. Idea* is the *object.* This same pattern of *subject-verb-object* still works when you hang a clause on the front of your sentence to make it more complex: "Deep inside her mind, in her private sanctuary of self, X stroked the idea."

If you change X to a character's name, the sentence takes on character: "Deep inside her mind, in her private sanctuary of self, Myra Jane Severance stroked the idea." To enrich the sentence, add a comparison by using the word *like:* "Deep inside her mind, in her private sanctuary of self, Myra Jane Severance stroked the idea like a pair of felt-lined boots." Because of the 1-2-3 word order and the verb borrowed from athletics (swimming, tennis), the center of the sentence stays solid. "Myra Jane stroked the idea."

To transform the sentence further, change the noun idea to a more concrete noun like *Ming vase:* "Myra Jane stroked the *Ming vase.*" To use the sentence in a scene, change *Ming vase* to *blade,* and then hang a different clause on the front: "Smiling at the sleuth, Myra Jane stroked the blade."

Have fun with your rewriting by transforming those sentences. Final draft is your chance to use the power of language to make your writing a memorable experience for your reader.

Appendix: The Writing Life

Finding a Publisher

When the mystery tale is done, when your instructors and mentors and writing friends have pronounced it ready for the marketplace, you make contact with literary agents. A literary agent acts as your go-between, your link with a particular editor in a particular publishing house. An agent negotiates your contract—advances against sales, royalties, payment schedules, rights (subsidiary, foreign, film), et cetera—and keeps an eye on the marketplace so that he or she can help to guide your writing career.

An agent's job is selling. Your job is writing. Agents read the fine print so you can keep the hand moving on the next manuscript.

There are three ways to make contact with literary agents: 1) a personal link; 2) a writers' conference or convention; or 3) by mail. Let's look at them in order.

Personal Link

You know someone who knows someone who has an agent. This link could be a writing instructor or a fellow writer. You make connections in the writing business the same way you do in other endeavors—by networking.

Writers' Conferences

Agents on the lookout for new clients appear at writers' conferences. Most writers' conferences are held in the summer and there's a great list in the March or April issue of *Writer's Digest* (1507 Dana Avenue, Cincinnati, OH 45207; phone 800 289-0963). If you want to focus on agents who specialize in mystery, there's a good list of mystery writing conventions in *The Mystery Writer's Marketplace and Sourcebook,* also from *Writer's Digest.* The granddaddy of mystery conventions (fans collide with authors) is the *Bouchercon,* named for Anthony Boucher, a critic of the art of mystery writing. (The Bouchercon's big writing prize is the *Anthony.* The big writing prize at the MWA conference is the *Edgar,* named for Edgar Allan Poe, creator of C. Auguste Dupin.)

If your manuscript is ready, you take along copies of your plot synopsis (written on Weekend 9, rewritten when you finished the book) and your first chapter. If you make a connection, the agent will ask to see some work. Some agents read on site. Some ask you to send it by mail.

By Mail

The Mystery Writer's Market Place and Sourcebook, mentioned above, contains an extensive list of literary agents who specialize in mystery and suspense. You can update the information from the "Sourcebook" in *Writer's Market,* published each year by *Writer's Digest* and available in most libraries. *Literary Marketplace* (the industry abbreviation is the *LMP),* available in most libraries, lists editors and agents. *Author Aid Associates* (340 East Fifty-second Street, New York, NY 10022) publishes *Literary Agents of North America,* which lists over four hundred agencies in the U.S. and Canada, has handy subject-matter breakdowns and information on manuscript submissions. Some agents want a query first; some want a partial (two or three chapters and a synopsis); some want synopses only; some want the full manuscript.

If you live in a big city, you might find agents listed under Literary Services in the Yellow Pages. Check your library for Literary Services listings for Manhattan and Los Angeles.

When writing to a literary agent, always send along a *SASE*. That's the industry acronym for

Self-
Addressed
Stamped
Envelope

Editors

Finding a publisher means finding an editor who likes your work. The personal link is best. If you have a friend who can recommend you to an editor, you can bypass the agent for now, writing the editor directly to check the interest level on mystery tales like yours. You'll do better if you're a marketeer, and if you can compress your book into a single sentence that snatches the attention: "This is a story about a killer who kills with a surgical scalpel."

If you're not a marketeer, you connect with an agent first and the agent connects you with an editor.

Since you're a first-time writer, your agent will probably want the full manuscript before contacting an editor. Knowing how tough the writing game is, the editor will want to make sure you can push through to the end. Because of the method in this book, constantly looking ahead to closure, you have pushed through to the end of your novel many times during the writing process.

Working with Editors

Editors move around, from one publishing house to another. They work for peanuts and a love of good writing. Editors are people. They have tastes, likes, dislikes, specialties. At one publishing house, the editor might handle fiction and travel books as well as mystery and suspense. At a larger house, she might carve out a specialty in mystery fiction, with an emphasis on the hard-boiled female private eye.

Editors work hard. Your best bet as a budding writer is to make your editor's job easier by doing a professional job yourself. Have a tight plot driven by great characters. Prepare a professional manuscript. Use your spell-checker to clean up spelling. If you don't know grammar, hire a freelance editor to go over the manuscript before you send it off.

If you were interviewing for a job, you would present yourself as neat and professional so that you could make the best first impression possible. The manuscript you send to the editor makes the impression for you. Make it look good.

A year ago, when you started reading this book, you were an amateur. Now you have a chance to become a professional writer.

The Writing Life

Writing is a lonely business. You're isolated from the world, just you and your notebook, you and your computer. To balance the isolation, you might join a writing group. Most writing groups practice critique, also called "workshopping." In critique groups, Writer X shares her work—sometimes by reading aloud, sometimes with Xerox copies distributed beforehand—and then the writers take turns making comments. If you can take the heat, critique groups are sometimes helpful.

If critique smothers your creativity, try creating a group that does writing practice. Athletes work out; they swim laps; they practice their moves. A tennis player who does not practice, working out problems of angle and spin and strategy, has trouble taking the heavy pressure of a real tennis match. A violin player who does not practice the violin—four to six hours a day, they say—won't be sharp at recital time.

Writers who do writing-practice on a regular basis get better. They dive deeper into their own work, into dream and symbol, into drama and character and plot. The language gets better with practice; when the language gets better, your level of confidence rises. If you haven't tried writing practice—keeping the hand moving while you write under the temporary tyranny of a kitchen timer—get some tips from *Writing Down the Bones,* by Natalie Goldberg.

Selected Bibliography

Babson, Marian. *In the Teeth of Adversity.* New York: Bantam, 1990.

Becker, Ernest. *The Denial of Death.* New York: The Free Press, 1973.

Becker, Ernest. *Escape from Evil.* New York: The Free Press, 1975.

Brinton Perera, Sylvia. *The Scapegoat Complex, Toward a Mythology of Shadow and Guilt.* Toronto: Inner City Books, 1986.

Bruccoli, Matthew J. *Ross Macdonald.* New York: Harcourt Brace Jovanovich, 1984.

Buzan, Tony. *Use Both Sides of Your Brain.* New York: E. P. Dutton, 1983.

Canetti, Elias. *Crowds and Power.* New York: The Noonday Press, 1993.

Cawelti, John G. *Adventure, Mystery, and Romance: Formula Stories as Art and Popular Culture.* Chicago: University of Chicago Press, 1976.

Chandler, Raymond. *The Big Sleep.* New York: Alfred A. Knopf, 1939.

Chandler, Raymond. *Raymond Chandler Speaking.* Gardiner and Walker, eds. Boston: Houghton Mifflin, 1977.

Chandler, Raymond. *The Simple Art of Murder.* New York: Ballantine, 1972.

Christie, Agatha. *Agatha Christie: An Autobiography.* New York: Ballantine, 1978.

Christie, Agatha. *The Body in the Library.* New York: G. P. Putnam's Sons, 1942.

Collingwood, Donna. *Mystery Writer's Marketplace and Sourcebook.* Cincinnati: Writer's Digest Books, 1993.

Cornwell, Patricia D. *All That Remains.* New York: Avon, 1992.

Cornwell, Patricia D. *Postmortem.* New York: Avon, 1990.

Field, Syd. *Screenplay.* New York: Dell, 1979.

Field, Syd. *The Screenwriter's Workbook.* New York: Dell, 1988.

Gardner, John. *The Art of Fiction.* New York: Vintage, 1985.

Gill, Gillian. *Agatha Christie: The Woman and Her Mysteries.* New York: The Free Press, 1990.

Goldberg, Natalie. *Writing Down the Bones: Freeing the Writer Within.* Boston: Shambhala, 1986.

Goodman, Felicitas D. *Ecstasy, Ritual, and Alternate Reality.* Bloomington: Indiana University Press, 1988.

Grafton, Sue. *"F" Is for Fugitive.* New York: Bantam, 1990.

Grun, Bernard. *The Timetables of History.* New York: Simon & Schuster, 1991.

Hammett, Dashiell. *The Maltese Falcon.* New York: Vintage Books Edition, 1972.

Harris, Thomas. *The Silence of the Lambs.* New York: St. Martin's, 1988.

Haycraft, Howard, ed. *The Art of the Mystery Story.* New York: Carroll & Graf, 1992.

Herbert, Rosemary. *The Fatal Art of Entertainment: Interviews with Mystery Writers.* New York: G. K. Hall, 1994.

Hocart, A. M. *The Life-Giving Myth and Other Essays.* London: Methuen, 1952.

Keating, H.R.F., ed. *Agatha Christie: First Lady of Crime.* New York: Holt, Rinehart and Winston, 1977. (Colin Watson: "The Message of Mayhem Parva.")

Layman, Richard. *Shadow Man: The Life of Dashiell Hammett.* New York: Harcourt Brace Jovanovich, 1981.

Lindsey, David. *Mercy.* New York: Doubleday, 1990.

Madden, David, ed. *Tough Guy Writers of the Thirties.* Carbondale and Edwardsville: Southern Illinois University Press, 1968.

Marling, William. *Dashiell Hammett.* Boston: Twayne, 1983.

Morgan, Janet. *Agatha Christie: A Biography.* New York: Alfred A. Knopf, 1984.

Most, Glenn W., and William W. Stowe. *The Poetics of Murder: Detective Fiction & Literary Theory.* San Diego: Harcourt Brace Jovanovich, 1983.

Muller, Marcia. *Edwin of the Iron Shoes.* New York: Mysterious Press, 1977.

Parker, Robert. *Paper Doll.* New York: G. P. Putnam's Sons, 1993.

Ray, Robert J. *The Weekend Novelist.* New York: Dell, 1994.

Rico, Gabriele. *Writing the Natural Way: Using Right-Brain Techniques to Release Your Expressive Powers.* New York: Jeremy Tarcher, 1983.

Sanders, Dennis, and Len Lovallo. *The Agatha Christie Companion: The Complete Guide to Agatha Christie's Life and Work.* New York: Delacorte Press, 1984.

Simenon, Georges. *Maigret's Memoirs,* trans. Jean Stewart. New York: Avon, 1989.

Simpson, Dorothy. *Dead on Arrival.* New York: Bantam, 1986.

Smith, Martin Cruz. *Gorky Park.* New York: Random House, 1981.

Steinbrunner, Chris, and Otto Penzler, editors-in-chief. *The Encyclopedia of Mystery and Detection.* New York: McGraw-Hill, 1976.

Walker, Barbara. *The Woman's Encyclopedia of Myths and Secrets.* San Francisco: Harper San Francisco, 1983.

Wingate, Anne. *The Scene of the Crime: A Writer's Guide to Crime-Scene Investigations.* Cincinnati: Writer's Digest Books, 1992.